Palgrave Studies in the History of Economic Thought

Palgrave Studies in the History of Economic Thought publishes contributions by leading scholars, illuminating key events, theories and individuals that have had a lasting impact on the development of modern-day economics. The topics covered include the development of economies, institutions and theories.

More information about this series at
http://www.palgrave.com/gp/series/14585

Katia Caldari · Marco Dardi ·
Steven G. Medema
Editors

Marshall and the Marshallian Heritage

Essays in Honour of Tiziano Raffaelli

palgrave
macmillan

Editors
Katia Caldari
Dipartimento di Scienze Economiche
e Aziendali
Università di Padova
Padua, Italy

Marco Dardi
Dipartimento di Scienze per
l'Economia e l'Impresa
Università di Firenze
Florence, Italy

Steven G. Medema
Department of Economics
Duke University
Durham, NC, USA

ISSN 2662-6578 ISSN 2662-6586 (electronic)
Palgrave Studies in the History of Economic Thought
ISBN 978-3-030-53034-1 ISBN 978-3-030-53032-7 (eBook)
https://doi.org/10.1007/978-3-030-53032-7

Cover credit: Manuela Raffaelli

This Palgrave Macmillan imprint is published by the registered company Springer Nature Switzerland AG
The registered company address is: Gewerbestrasse 11, 6330 Cham, Switzerland

Introduction

"It's all in Marshall." So said Pigou, time and again, as we are told. The modern economist and even several of Marshall's immediate successors at Cambridge would beg to differ, of course. But for the historian of economics the interesting question is not whether there are or are not important lacunae in Marshall's system; instead, it is to understand what that system is and how it came to be—the latter being inextricably connected to the former.

The last three decades have witnessed a transformation in our understanding of Alfred Marshall's contributions to economics as historians have increasingly focused on this latter question. Against interpretations that placed Marshall in the neoclassical framework and highlighted the limits and problematics of his approach, this more recent line of research has shed important new light on the evolution of Marshall's thinking and, in the process, allowed us to disentangle the apparent inconsistencies within Marshall's analysis, to discover its often hidden roots and motivations, to highlight its frequently neglected aspects, and to better understand and appreciate its complexity. Tiziano Raffaelli played a fundamental role in this transformation of Marshall historiography and in stimulating a renewed interest in exploring the contributions and legacy of this great Cambridge economist. The set of original essays here collected testify to and confirm the importance of this new approach, as well as the ongoing significance of Raffaelli's insights. In doing so, they also further enhance our understanding of Marshall and his influence.

The Philosopher as Environmentalist and Historian

Tiziano was born in Vecchiano, a suburb of Pisa, in 1950, into a family of deep-seated political traditions related to the Italian Communist Party (PCI). He studied in Pisa attending *Liceo Classico* and the faculty of philosophy from which he received his degree in 1975. A scholarship from the Domus Galilaeana, a prestigious Pisan foundation for the history of science, enabled him to continue his studies for a few formative years which were spent partly at the London School of Economics and partly at the Department of Philosophy of Pisa University. Here he began his academic career as researcher in 1981. As a pupil of the Marxist philosopher Nicola Badaloni, he specialized in epistemology and the philosophy of science, a field that he had entered through Popper's *Logic of Scientific Discovery*, the subject of his degree thesis, and within which he concentrated on the methodological problems of the social sciences. In his first long essay on the subject, *Filosofia sociale e metodo della scienza economica* [*Social philosophy and the method of economic science*], published in 1980, he argued that methodological debates in the history of economic thought should be regarded not as a neutral arena in which the technical pros and cons of scientific procedures are assessed, but as the port of entry for all the ethical and political premises that implicitly or explicitly play a major role in the formation of economic theories.

Given Tiziano's Marxian lineage, such a position was perhaps inevitable. Yet his familiarity with Popper, especially the early (Viennese) Popper, exerted a characteristic twist on it and pushed him in less predictable directions. In a later revocation of the reasons for his juvenile fascination with Popper (Raffaelli 1994a), of all the themes touched upon by the philosopher Tiziano picked up the dismissal of all claims to systemic truth in science, and made it into a sort of anti-systemic system based on the rejection of holistic interpretations of scientific theories in favor of a piecemeal, local, fallibilist approach to truth. He appreciated the fact that, if transferred from the epistemological ground to a political one, this attitude worked as a safeguard against all kinds of absolutism, both left-wing and right-wing. Here one may see an anticipation, and perhaps the source, of Tiziano's main intellectual interests of his mature years: Hume and Smith, with their refusal of the "spirit of system," the evolutionary trial-and-error process underlying Marshall's economics, the style of thinking shunning foundational rituals that was shared by his greatly beloved Keynes and Cattaneo.

In this early phase, however, an academic career was a secondary concern. Taking a long leave of absence from the University, Tiziano devoted most of his energies to participating in the activities of the PCI, of which he was for a while a local leader. Alien to all forms of uncritical fideism, open-minded and non-partisan, with a particular love for country life innate in his family background, he ended up finding his political niche in a sector, that of environmental policies, which was regarded with a certain suspicion, if not open hostility still in the 1970s, by orthodox militants of the party. At the end of the 1970s, he was one of the founders of Legambiente, perhaps the largest Italian environmental association stemming from, but independent of, the political left. And acting first as councilor in charge of finances on the municipal *giunta* of Vecchiano, his native town, and later as head of the Department for the Environment of the Province of Pisa, he made a substantial contribution to the setting up of the natural park of Migliarino San Rossore and Massaciuccoli, a wide coastal area with unique natural and anthropic features, over the administration of which he was to preside from 1983 to 1987. This experience had great impact on his life, both positive and negative.

During his presidential term at the Parco, Tiziano advocated a scheme of environmental restoration projected by the architect and urbanist Pierluigi Cervellati that contemplated re-flooding limited areas of the territory in order to partially recover the original characteristics of wetlands that had been canceled by successive land reclamations for agricultural purposes over the centuries. Like all projects of environmental restoration, this too met opposition from local lobbies attached to political groups and the local press, which used all available means, including personal defamatory smear, in their fight against the project. To this, Tiziano opposed his characteristic habit of reasonable, non-aggressive dialogue extended to friend and foe alike, but also, behind it, a firmness nearing quiet but invincible obstinacy on matters of principle. Inevitably tension mounted till it reached the breaking point in 1987, with his sudden resolve to turn down the possibility of a second term at the presidency of the Parco, and at the same time to quit all active political involvement and return full-time to academia. Always unassuming, Tiziano did not like to comment on the specific reasons for this even with friends and relatives. In later writings on environmental issues, of which he always remained an attentive student, there are passages that seem to indicate an ongoing critical reflection on his past experience at the Parco, like the following lines taken from a 1993 book review: "The environmentalist movement (...) has often, out of necessity, taken the role of the prince's counselor, sometimes forgetting that only that which establishes roots in the culture of a people is going to last. Let it be clear that I am not asking for, nor carrying out, self-criticism; neither do I feel any yearning for a left that is concerned only with recording consensus by promoting spontaneous processes, no matter whether these are right or wrong" (Raffaelli 1993, 897).

The second phase of Tiziano's life, as a dedicated scholar and University teacher, began at that time. Having remained dormant in the years of political engagement, his academic career now began to develop along the usual lines: a period as lecturer in the history of political doctrines in Pisa; then in 1998 as Associate Professor of the history of economic thought at the Faculty of Economics of the University of Cagliari; and lastly, in 2004, the Chair in the same discipline in Pisa, attached to the degree in Philosophy. The crucial episode in this phase, the one which was to affect his research itinerary in a decisive way, was his encounter with Giacomo Becattini in the late 1980s. The meeting between the two was a real *coup de foudre* from the very beginning, perhaps also because of common traits of political experience: an early uneasy militancy in the communist party, a shared passion for environmentalism and the territory. The background of their relationship and the way it developed are narrated in detail in Dardi's chapter in this volume. Here it is enough to say that Tiziano was immediately recruited by Becattini to a research project that at the time involved a historical part on Alfred Marshall and an economic part on industrial districts in the interpretation of Italian economic development. Tiziano was engaged in both, but certainly it was in the former, the Marshall part, that he achieved his most brilliant results and attained international standing in the discipline.

This part of Tiziano's life story is well known to those acquainted with recent Marshall scholarship. It began at Becattini's suggestion with the editing and interpretation of five esoteric philosophical manuscripts going back to the years (the late 1860s) that preceded Marshall's decision to turn himself into a professional economist. Gradually, his close reading of these manuscripts yielded a clue that opened a completely new view of the economic works of Marshall's maturity. At the center, there was the discovery that the scheme of the working of the individual mind found in the manuscripts could be transferred with no break of continuity to the study of social organization and, in particular, of the many ways in which a modern industrial society deals with the flow of new knowledge and its solidification into a stock of social, institutional, and technological mechanisms. One of the philosophical manuscripts, the by-now widely known "Ye Machine", which contains the curious blueprint of a thinking automaton capable of learning from experience, provides a perfect anticipation of Marshall's future theory of social and economic evolution, with life forces and automatic routines continuously interacting, and with automatisms being an emanation of the life forces themselves in their effort to ensure better conditions for the maintenance and empowerment of their functional capacities. No longer the biology vs. mechanics dualism, this perspective shows biology as thriving on and at the same time being constrained by mechanics. It is a typically post-Darwinian scheme that recurs almost obsessively throughout Marshall's work; yet, curiously, it passed unnoticed by interpreters, or was noticed as only inessential extravaganza unrelated to the main economic theme. It is a classical case for manuals of the history of science: someone sees something that many had looked at without seeing.

Tiziano's new view of Marshallian economics has produced a considerable flow of literature over the last twenty and more years. His annotated edition of the manuscripts (Raffaelli 1994b) joined to his 2003 volume on *Marshall's Evolutionary Economics* (Raffaelli 2003) have provided the necessary reference for all the participants in this process of historiographic revision. Those who had the pleasure of collaborating with him in research projects remember the atmosphere of scholarly harmony that surrounded him, with his affability and sociability fostering feelings of non-rivalry and friendly cooperation in all. Beyond acting as a generator of seminal ideas, he was also an excellent organizer of the process of their diffusion. The two Elgar collective Marshall volumes, the *Companion* (2006) and the *Impact of Alfred Marshall's Ideas* (2010), owe their realization to his initiative and his determination in managing a large number of contributors and solving delicate interpersonal situations. He was the soul of the *Marshall Studies Bulletin*, the specialist newsletter born in 1991 on Becattini's initiative with the blessing of John Whitaker—another long-term friendship based on close affinity of style and mindset. The *Bulletin* continued as an online publication after 1996 practically without any funds and relying entirely on volunteer work. Tiziano believed in this journal as an arena for debate and for making archival sources available to all scholars. If the publication began to slow down (it finally came to a halt with the 2012 issue), this was partly due to his declining health, the first symptoms of the progressive auto-immune disease that appeared in the early 2000s and would plague his last years. But he had also to struggle against the dearth of contributions resulting from the bibliometric criteria introduced in the evaluation of research—a major obstacle that the *Bulletin* with its non-existent resources was unable to overcome.

It would be unfair to stop here in a review of Tiziano's work without mentioning his many contributions in areas other than Marshallian economics. Not only a Marshall specialist, he wrote (among other subjects) about Keynes, Keynes as a pupil of Marshall (see, e.g., Barrotta and Raffaelli 1998, Chapter 3; Raffaelli 2000), the Cambridge tradition in industrial economics (Raffaelli 2004), American institutionalism (Barrotta and Raffaelli 1998, Chapter 4), and on Italian economists of various ages with a special predilection for Cattaneo (Raffaelli 2014). In recent years, he particularly felt an urgency not to remain stuck with Marshall forever, but to move on to new subjects. Had he had the time to develop it, his next project would have been that of bringing his long meditation on the texts of Adam Smith to the attention of an international readership by reorganizing and rewriting in English a number of essays and lecture notes scattered in various Italian publications over a period of many years. One of these texts, actually a reader's guide to the *Wealth of Nations* for his philosophy students (Raffaelli 2001), came to the notice of a reviewer of the *Adam Smith Review* in 2008 and was the occasion for a rejoinder (Raffaelli 2008) in which Tiziano offered a glimpse of his interpretation of the classical problem of the relationship between the *Wealth* and Smith's other great works, primarily the *Moral Sentiments*. As in the case of Marshall, his interpretation was original, fully thought out, and succeeded in bringing fresh insight into an issue that has been investigated by hosts of interpreters in recent decades. It deserved to enter the international debate, and Tiziano had just begun to work to that effect (see the posthumous Raffaelli 2018) when, sadly, his time came to an end. He died on the 14th of January 2016 of sudden heart failure while intent on correcting the proofs of his latest paper.

The Essays

While it would be impossible to capture the full span of Tiziano's influence in a volume such as this, the essays presented here are broadly reflective of the effects of his work on Marshall and his place in the history of economic thinking. But as we noted earlier in this introduction, these essays also represent important contributions to Marshall scholarship—the appropriate way to honor a friend, collaborator, and model of the scholarly virtues.

The chapters found in the first part of the volume aim at revisiting Marshall's economics using the tools made available by this new approach to Marshall historiography. In doing so, they highlight certain aspects of the Marshallian contribution on which this approach sheds new light and underline its modernity with respect to current literatures in areas such as industrial organization, innovation, and economic development and progress.

Marco Dardi sets Raffaelli's work in context by tracing the roots of his Marshallian research program in the Italian cultural and political milieu of the late twentieth century. It turns out that Raffaelli's research was a late sprout from a project initiated in the early 1960s by his mentor Giacomo Becattini, who developed it through the years in close confrontation with what he perceived as the "spirit of the age" both in the academe and the country. The chapter reconstructs the shifting perspectives, and accordingly the shifting images of Marshall, that resulted from this highly context-sensitive historiography.

Independently of the Marshallian research conducted by the Italians, Brian Loasby had started a program of his own since the 1970s in which Marshall stood out as a theorist of the nexus organization/knowledge set in a line of thought going from Smith to Coase and offering an alternative to standard neoclassical theory. This was an important source of inspiration for Raffaelli in his reconstruction of Marshall as a cognitive evolutionist. In his chapter, Loasby goes into a personal recollection of how, and by means of which intellectual influences, he was gradually led to an approach to the history of organization that was quite unique in his time, an epoch still dominated by general equilibrium theory as the supreme benchmark of economic theory.

The evolutionary thread is further drawn out in Cosimo Perrotta's reappraisal of Raffaelli's analysis of Adam Smith and Alfred Marshall, focusing on their views of historical process and probing the similarities and differences that characterize their respective approaches. In particular, as Perrotta shows us, Smith and Marshall share an evolutionary perspective—a subject probed deeply by Raffaelli—grounded in the concepts of the division of labor and specialization. It is through this evolutionary viewpoint that the two economists interpret the historical process of society and identify the most important obstacles to (for Smith) and spurs toward (for Marshall) a progressive society.

It hardly needs stating that Tiziano's contributions to Marshall scholarship have stimulated new ways of understanding some of the well-covered aspects of Marshall's analysis. Neil Hart's essay revisits the issue of external economies—a concept devised by Marshall and subsequently applied to a wide variety of situations, but which some have claimed he introduced to reconcile increasing returns and competitive equilibrium. Hart argues that, in light of the new view originated by Raffaelli, the "reconciliation" thesis is a total misinterpretation due to an inability to get free from conventional views of competitive equilibrium and to appreciate the way Marshall applies the equilibrium concept together with external economies to the explanation of patterns of development in an evolutionary setting. From the idea of "localized" external economies Hart, like Dardi and Loasby although from a different angle, extends the discussion also to Marshall's influence on contemporary literature on industrial districts and local systems in general.

Marshall is well known for attempting to build a bridge from the *analysis* of equilibrium processes under varying conditions to the *evaluation* of those outcomes. While his development of the tool of consumer surplus is his most well-known contribution here, Marshall's welfare thinking went well beyond this. Katia Caldari and Tamotsu Nishizawa revisit Marshall's manuscripts written for his unpublished book on economic progress to draw out his views on the concept of wellbeing. As the most important outcome of progress, human wellbeing is for Marshall to be understood in its economic, ethical, and political facets. Wellbeing is therefore strictly connected with industrial and labor efficiency, productivity, human capability, and creativity, but also with a general moral improvement which is necessary to properly use the fruits of economic growth. However—and Marshall particularly emphasized this aspect in his old age and in the notes written for his unfinished volume—wellbeing also requires a certain degree of state intervention that, especially through taxation and public spending, may foster a true economic progress.

The methods of the history of science loom large in Tiziano's work, and Harro Mass utilizes Susan Faye Canon's concept of "Humboldtian science" to clarify some aspects of Jevons' and Marshall's methodological approaches. In order to understand world phenomena, the German polymath von Humboldt developed an approach which included empirical inquiries, collection of data, the use of diagrams and mathematics.

Taking Humboldt's procedure as benchmark, Maas investigates in detail Jevons' and Marshall's use of diagrams, graphs, and mathematics. Whereas Jevons' approach can be defined as Humboldtian for the importance given to data collection, measurement and mathematics, it is far from Humboldtian in its failure to point us toward a comprehensive understanding of the world phenomena. Marshall's approach, in contrast, should be considered Humboldtian not so much for his well-known use of curves, graphs, and mathematics as for the way in which phenomena are considered and examined as part of a complex whole. Far from being a simple exercise in style, the use of the term "Humboldtian" allows Maas to focus his attention on the working method rather than on the underlying philosophy and economic thought of the two economists.

The Jevons—Marshall juxtaposition also features prominently in Keith Tribe's essay. Here, Tribe proposes a new angle from which to reconsider Marshall's "curious treatment" of Jevons's *Theory*, his silence on Sidgwick's *Principles of Political Economy*, and his campaign for separating Economics and Politics from the Cambridge Moral Sciences Tripos. This comes in the form of a detailed story that starts from Stuart Mill's *Utilitarianism* and continues along two lines—Jevons's reaction to it on the one side, the Cambridge reaction through Grote and Sidgwick on the other. Tribe argues for a sort of convergence between the two lines, united by the "formal utilitarian rationalism" found in Jevons and Sidgwick, from which it is plausible to assume that Marshall wanted to distance himself.

The essays found in the second part of the volume focus on some of Marshall's influences on the economic analysis and approach that developed after his death and on the training of some economists. Here, too, Raffaelli's contribution proves to be an extremely valuable resource. The first two essays in this section focus on connections between Marshall and his most famous pupil, Keynes—a subject which has received a goodly amount of treatment in the historical literature but which, too, has come to be examined anew, including by Raffaelli (2000) himself, through the lens of Raffaelli's work on Marshall. The first of these, by Paolo Paesani and Annalisa Rosselli, takes up Marshall's writings on speculation, linking them to the late nineteenth-century scientific literature on the subject. Marshall's view, as Paesani and Rosselli nicely document, was a very affirmative one, emphasizing the beneficial role that speculators (professional ones in particular) play in the resource allocation process. Though Marshall was cognizant of many of the potential problems with speculative activity, his overall confidence that the benefits would outweigh the costs in the long run set him apart from Keynes, whose concerns about the disruptive effects of speculative activities made him much more pessimistic about their social utility.

The essay by Carlo Cristiano and Maria Cristina Marcuzzo juxtaposes the views of Marshall and Keynes on the situation in the United States and, in particular, the growth of large-scale industry there. In contrast to a number of their prominent American counterparts, both Marshall and Keynes had a healthy appreciation for the trusts that came to prominence in the United States during the late nineteenth and early twentieth centuries–a viewpoint reflected in, among other places, Marshall's *Industry and Trade* and Keynes's criticisms of certain facets of Roosevelt's New Deal. As Cristiano and Marcuzzo admit, the extent of Marshall's influence on Keynes's views here is unclear, but there can be little doubt that the commonalities between teacher and pupil shine through in their respective views on industrial theory and policy.

One area of Marshall scholarship that began to flourish only recently is the study of how Marshall's ideas have influenced economic thinking beyond the shores of Great Britain, a topic that was the subject of a volume on *The Impact of Alfred Marshall's Ideas* (2010), edited by Raffaelli et al., that functions as something of a sequel to the aforementioned *Companion to Alfred Marshall*. The final two chapters in the present volume extend that line of research by taking up specific threads of Marshall's reception in the United States—one by an English-trained economist whom one would expect to resist Marshall but did not, and another by a University of Chicago-trained economist who might be expected to embrace Marshall but instead became one of his most vocal critics.

For most economists at Chicago, Marshall was simply an input, the supplier of an approach to economic analysis. For Ronald Coase, however, Marshall was much more than this—a subject of fascination and, at times, almost a reverence and obsession, as the essay by Steven Medema demonstrates. As both a student and a professor at the London School of Economics, where indifference and even antipathy toward Marshall were widespread, Coase would not have ranked high on the list of those expected to become Marshall's first (though ultimately unsuccessful) biographer, let alone one who drew on Marshall's methodological approach to castigate both modern economics generally and certain of his ("Marshallian") Chicago colleagues in particular. Medema probes Coase's biographical work on Marshall and his discussions of Marshall's economics for clues as to the sources of Coase's affinity, suggesting explanations that are at once personal and professional.

Roger Backhouse takes up the criticism of Marshall developed over time by Paul Samuelson, who received his introduction to Marshallian analysis at the hands of Jacob Viner while taking Ph.D. courses as an undergraduate at Chicago. Samuelson was among those who contributed to the "end of the Age of Marshall," both through his own efforts to set economics on an alternative footing and through his severe critiques of Marshall's attitude toward mathematics, his conception of biology, and his overall theoretical approach. Though Samuelson famously wrote that "the ambiguities of Alfred Marshall paralyzed the best brains in the Anglo-Saxon branch of our profession for three decades," Backhouse demonstrates that, behind this harsh criticism, Samuelson's writings reflect a (more or less concealed) admiration for Alfred Marshall, whom he definitively considered "a great economist."

Samuelson's swipes, of course, cannot negate the enormity and breadth of influence that Marshall had on subsequent economic thinking, and the fact that this influence spans the spectrum from Keynesian economics to Chicago speaks to the broad applicability of the Marshallian toolkit. Like Marshall, our friend Tiziano built impressively on that which came before. And, as with Marshall, our understandings will be forever affected by his work.

Katia Caldari
Marco Dardi
Steven G. Medema

References

Barrotta, Pierluigi and Tiziano Raffaelli (1998). *Epistemologia ed economia*. Torino: UTET.

Raffaelli, Tiziano (1980). *Filosofia sociale e metodo della scienza economica*. Bari: De Donato.

______. (1993). Città territorio ambiente, quella grande sconfitta. *Il Ponte* 49 (7): 894–98.

______. (1994a). K.R. Popper, la ricerca non ha fine. *Il Ponte* 50 (10): 86–95.

______. (1994b). Alfred Marshall's early philosophical writings. *Research in the History of Economic Thought and Methodology*, Archival Supplement 4: 53–159.

______. (2000). Keynes's apprenticeship with Marshall. *History of Economic Ideas* 8 (2): 121–52.

______. (2001). *La ricchezza delle nazioni. Introduzione alla lettura*. Roma: Carocci.

______. (2003). *Marshall's Evolutionary Economics*. London and New York: Routledge.

______. (2004). La tradizione marshalliana di economia industriale. In: N. Bellanca, M. Dardi, and T. Raffaelli editors, *Economia senza gabbie: Studi in onore di Giacomo Becattini*. Bologna: Il Mulino, 349–78.

______. (2008). Tiziano Raffaelli's response to review by Maria Pia Paganelli. *The Adam Smith Review* 4: 290–93.

______. (2014). The role of intelligence, institutions, and Place in Carlo Cattaneo's economics. *History of Political Economy* 46 (2): 265–80.

______. (2018). The race for wealth: Smith's effective therapy to put anxiety to task. *The Adam Smith Review* 10: 254–71.

Raffaelli, Tiziano, Giacomo Becattini, and Marco Dardi, eds. (2006). *The Elgar Companion to Alfred Marshall*. Cheltenham: Elgar.

Raffaelli, Tiziano, Giacomo Becattini, Katia Caldari, and Marco Dardi, eds. (2010). *The Impact of Alfred Marshall's Ideas*. Cheltenham: Elgar.

Contents

List of Contributors

Roger E. Backhouse University of Birmingham, UK, and Erasmus University Rotterdam, The Netherlands.

Katia Caldari Dipartimento di Scienze Economiche e Aziendali, Università di Padova, Padua, Italy.

Carlo Cristiano Department of Law, University of Pisa, Italy.

Marco Dardi Dipartimento di Scienze per l'Economia e l'Impresa, Università di Firenze, Florence, Italy.

Neil Hart School of Economics and Industrial Relations Research Centre, University of New South Wales, Australia, and Institute of Business Research, University of Economics, Ho Chi Minh City, Vietnam.

Brian J. Loasby Emeritus Professor of Economics, University of Stirling, UK.

Harro Maas Centre Walras-Pareto for the history of economic and Political Thought, Institute for Political Studies, University of Lausanne, Switzerland.

Maria Cristina Marcuzzo Honorary Professor, University of Rome Sapienza and Accademia dei Lincei, Rome, Italy.

Steven G. Medema Department of Economics, Duke University, Durham, NC, USA.

Tamotsu Nishizawa Faculty of Economics, Teikyo University, Tokyo, Japan.

Paolo Paesani Department of Economics and Finance, University of Rome Tor Vergata, Rome, Italy.

Cosimo Perrotta Formerly Professor of the History of Economic Thought at the University of Salento, Lecce, Italy.

Annalisa Rosselli Department of Economics and Finance, University of Rome Tor Vergata, Rome, Italy.

Keith Tribe Senior Research Fellow, Department of History and Archaeology, University of Tartu, Estonia.

List of Figures

Jevons and Marshall as Humboldtian Scientists

List of Tables

Revisiting Marshall's Economics

Alfred Marshall in the Lower Valdarno

Marco Dardi

1 Introduction

"I was one of those consulted about [the project of the *Elgar Companion to Alfred Marshall*] … For that [editorial] team the first name on my list was Raffaelli, and believing that managing this project would need a good deal of extensive discussion, and recalling the observation (whose originator I cannot recall) that 'Alfred Marshall is alive and well and living on the banks of the Arno', it was easy to add two other names" (Loasby 2016, p. 20). This long quotation bears witness to the fact that around the year 2000 the international community of Marshall scholars was aware of the existence of an Italian research team of three people operating in Tuscany and of the leading role in it played by Tiziano Raffaelli. The other two names mentioned by Loasby refer to the late Giacomo Becattini (1927–2017) and to the present writer. The habitual residences of its members place the team "on the banks of the Arno" between Florence and Pisa, an area commonly known as the Lower Valdarno.

M. Dardi (✉)
Dipartimento di Scienze per l'Economia e l'Impresa, Università di Firenze, Florence, Italy
e-mail: marco.dardi@unifi.it

K. Caldari et al. (eds.), *Marshall and the Marshallian Heritage*, Palgrave Studies in the History of Economic Thought,
https://doi.org/10.1007/978-3-030-53032-7_1

The present reconstruction of the story of the team is aimed at illustrating the context, phases and motivations of a research programme that was less coherent and homogeneous than may appear from the outside. In the story, which for me began in 1970 and, for Becattini, dated back to at least ten years earlier, Tiziano made a relatively late entry around 1987. His entry, however, marked a substantial discontinuity quite soon. While the intellectual leadership of the first and longer phase belonged unquestionably to Becattini and Tiziano's ideas determined a change in direction that in my case was slowly absorbed and internalized, this was not so with Becattini, who hailed it with sympathy but continued along a line of his own. In the initial acknowledgements of the Italian version of Becattini (2000), his thanks to the other two members of the team were accompanied by the remark "[they] have followed paths of historical research to a large extent parallel to mine"—meaning no overlaps, although no great distance either. Since the atmosphere in the team was of close-knit friendship, our divergences remained a matter of private discussion and were never displayed in public if not implicitly. Looked at in retrospect, this internal dialectics seems to be mainly the effect of the generational gap between us, a gap that reflected differences in intellectual and political contexts between the post-war Italy in which Becattini received his early formation and the years around 1970 in which Tiziano and I trained as young researchers. A part of the explanation is also due to changes in the general trend of economic theory during the last quarter of the century, changes to which the two of us, again I think for generational reasons, were more responsive than Becattini. It is because of this "spirit of the times" feeling that, being the last survivor of the team, I resolved to lay bare the internal differences among us in the hope that this is of some interest, at least from the point of view of the history of historiography.

Given the chronology, Becattini inevitably will have the lion's share in this reconstruction, which starts (Sect. 2) from the origins of the Marshall project in the loads of questions that crowded his mind around 1960 and the reasons that pointed to Marshall as being the most likely help in trying to answer them. In Sect. 3 the next stage of the research: an image of Marshall as a protagonist of the demise of the classical model of capitalism in the Victorian era was reconstructed and defended in the face of the classical resurgence that characterized the Italian academic and political scene in the 1970s. As the end of the century approached, however, this political contextual pressure gradually lost strength, and Sect. 4 documents the taking over of two different concerns. On the one hand, there was Becattini's progressive absorption in a line of applied research that was based on the concept of industrial district, with the Marshall research becoming instrumental to it; on the other, Tiziano entered the team with a new agenda centred on Marshall's cognitive evolutionism and the way in which this could be shown to bear upon all his economics. As explained in Sect. 5, from this point on and scarcely visible from the outside but perfectly clear to the three insiders, the Lower Valdarno became host to two historical characters who shared the name Alfred Marshall and other external features but—so to speak—had different souls. This difficulty did not prevent our collaboration in the *Elgar Companion to Alfred Marshall* and other projects. In fact, I think it taught us to regard historical research with a sense of greater detachment and humility, or, at least, this is as much as I feel inclined to argue in the brief conclusive reflections of Sect. 6.

2 Origins of a Research Programme

Formally speaking, a historical research project on Marshall was launched by Becattini in 1970 in the form of an application to the Italian National Research Council asking for financial support for a small team of researchers, among whom this writer and a few others who dropped out at rather early stages. But that was not the beginning, nor was it by chance that, of all economists, Marshall was chosen as the target. A few years earlier Becattini had dealt at length with Marshall in a book (Becattini 1962) dedicated to an inquiry, midway between economic theory and the history of economic thought, into the evolution of the theory of value from the classical Ricardo-Marxian position to the theories of imperfect and monopolistic competition that were still an active research area at the time. The questions that prompted this investigation were those of a young would-be academic eager to participate in what he perceived to be the renovation process of the Italian economic culture, a process that was pervaded with politics in a country still in the recovery phase from fascism and the war. Re-examining these questions in their context helps to understand where Becattini's interest in Marshall came from and why he developed his later research in the way that he did. In fact, the 1962 book shows us more than that: a wellspring of fundamental problems to which Becattini was to return periodically throughout his lifetime, it holds the key to the general evolution of his ideas and the role played by the interpretation of Marshall in it.[1]

Becattini's main concern[2] at the time was the approach to economic science that he indicated with the term "objectivism", meaning by this the assumption that whatever economists are interested in can be studied in the same way as objects of the natural sciences, i.e. as an entity with a structure and laws of behaviour of its own to be discovered by means of the same methods used in the natural sciences. Objectivism in this sense chimed for him with "mechanicism", "naturalism", "determinism", all terms that imply an underestimation or the utter exclusion of free human intentionality from the factors that determine economic phenomena and, at the same time, a rejection of the idea—reduced to the state of illusion—that these phenomena reflect to a significant extent the purposes that drive human agents to action. The question is whether or not a theory based on such an abstraction is sufficient to cope with actual social issues or, instead, misses some essential factor without which any grip on reality is barred. Here, Becattini borrowed his terminology from a philosophical debate on Marx's approach to scientific explanation that had been going on in Italy since the early 1950s[3]: for an abstraction to be adequate for the purposes of social science it needs to be "determinate" or "real", which in this particular case can be taken to mean that it must reflect the actual absence of the entity the theory is abstracting from in the situation to

[1]While I can speak as a direct witness for most of Becattini's activities after 1970, for the earlier period I must rely on written evidence and on what I remember of our conversations across the years. Important documentary sources come from Becattini's personal papers which I have been surveying and cataloguing over the last two years with a view to creating a publicly accessible Giacomo Becattini Archive at the Social Science Library of the University of Florence. I take this occasion to thank Professor Fabio Sforzi with whom I am sharing the task, without involving him, of course, in the personal opinions I shall express in the rest of the chapter.

[2]This paragraph and the next are based on the Becattini (1962) volume and the almost contemporaneous (1961) article "Scienza economica e trasformazioni sociali. A proposito di un recente volume di Paolo Sylos Labini" [economic science and social transformations: apropos of a recent volume by Paolo Sylos Labini], reprinted in Becattini (1979a, pp. 3–40).

[3]The debate originated from the book *Logic as a Positive Science* (1950) by the Marxist philosopher Galvano Della Volpe, at the time an influent thinker of the Italian Marxist left. Most likely Becattini became acquainted with it through writings by Giulio Pietranera and Lucio Colletti. The latter, a pupil and, later, a critic of Della Volpe, set forth his own retrospective view of the debate in Colletti (1974).

which the same theory is supposed to refer. Thus, assuming as we must that human intentionality can never be entirely suppressed, objectivism can be a determinate or real abstraction on condition that it is applied to historical situations in which there are forces operating in such a way as to nullify or distort the intended effects of human action.[4]

For Becattini the locus classicus of determinate abstraction in economics was the capitalist society as described by Marx, and by Ricardo as interpreted by Marx, namely a society in which workers and capitalists are alienated alike, both being stripped of effective human purpose and reduced to the role of mere means to ends that are not of their choice: workers, because the proletarian condition bars access to the possibility of conceiving, not to say of realizing, purposes of their own beyond mere subsistence; capitalists, because the necessity of reproducing capital acts on them as an impersonal coercion from which they are unable to cut themselves off. In Becattini's perception, however, this picture represented an early model of capitalism that in present times had been superseded. In mature capitalism, intentionality rules ubiquitous: the very fact that, thanks to the spread of the Marxian message, workers have developed class conscience transforms them, and capitalists for reaction, into agents having the power, limited though this may be, to conceive independent intentions and to transform them into fact. This later model of capitalism was evidence of the crisis of the classical, Ricardo-Marxian one: no longer a pure accumulative mechanism, it had outgrown its original features and tended to evolve into still indeterminate directions. For the Becattini of 1962, then, objectivism was no longer a determinate abstraction, and the task of economic theory was to look for abstractions of a different kind, ones able to account for the part played by the subjective element in determining economic outcomes. In this task, he saw the source of theoretical innovations begun a long time ago in the post-classical age and still under way in the 1960s. At that time, economic subjectivism was still a shapeless perspective for him.

[4]This search for historical determinateness in the use of scientific abstraction is strictly related to other recurrent themes in Becattini's methodological perspective, such as the idea that the "freedom to hypothesize" is the scourge of contemporary economic theory, his rejection of methodologies based on successive approximations, and more in general his dislike of the dissociation between theory and analytic technique (see Becattini 1962, p. 146). That such convictions could conflict also with aspects of Marshall's methodology—just think of the link between *ceteris paribus* and successive approximations—will be discussed below in Sect. 5.

A few biographical details will help to set these concerns in context. Family origins and traditions rendered Becattini a natural member of the Italian Communist Party (PCI), in which he was operative for a few years in his early youth and where he began his readings of the works of Marx and of Antonio Gramsci. Possibly the problematic Marxism of Gramsci, whose *Prison Notebooks* began to be published in the late 1940s, inoculated him against the dogmatic, Soviet-style official doctrine of the party. As a student at the economic faculty of the University of Florence, however, he met a professor of political economy, later to become his mentor, Alberto Bertolino, whose ideological background was based on the Italian neo-idealist philosophy of Croce and Gentile, and whose political ideas leaned towards the "liberal socialism" movement originated by Carlo Rosselli in the 1920s and represented in post-war Italy by the short-lived *Partito d'Azione*. Certainly not a Marxist, and a thinker not likely to make concessions to objectivist views of society, given his idealistic slant. Although nowadays scarcely remembered as an economist, Bertolino was by all accounts a charismatic figure. At his school, Becattini became acquainted with an approach to the social sciences that viewed economic phenomena as the outwards signs of an essentially unitary spiritual life, as external projections of a system of ideas and values that individuals make their own, independently of their particular social condition, in as far as they feel that they belong to a certain place and historical time. It is hard to say to what extent Becattini's progressive estrangement from PCI militancy during the course of the 1950s—but not from communism as an ideal of social justice—was due to the dramatic news coming from behind the Iron Curtain, or to impatience with the rigid doctrinarian discipline of the party, or to this contact with a completely different ideological perspective, one in which personal intellectual freedom was valued over and above class structure and loyalty.[5] The official split with the party came in 1958, but the separation was never definitive, at least not on the sentimental plane. Certainly, on the intellectual plane Becattini finally

[5] Although, it must be said, in the case of Italy the gulf between idealism and Marxism was not impassable. I have already mentioned the importance for Becattini of his early readings of Gramsci, a Marxist author who retained visible traces of the idealistic formation he had received during the course of his studies at the University of Torino. Becattini himself spoke of Gramsci's work as having provided him with a sort of "bridge" between Marx and Bertolino (Becattini 1979a, pp. vi–vii).

felt free to explore the possibilities of subjectivism suggested by "bourgeois" economic theories, but he never managed to emancipate himself completely from the Marxian complex. In particular, Marx's condemnation of bourgeois economics as apologetics or "vulgar economy" continued to hold a grip on the ex-activist for the rest of his life.

According to Becattini, the alleged subjectivism of pure economics, be it the Austrian school or Walrasian general equilibrium, could not provide a basis for introducing a satisfactory notion of intentionality into economic theory. The reduction of intentionality to one-dimensional maximization and the exclusive focus on states of mutual consistency of individual maxima concealed for him a return to objectivism in new clothes, a new form of the old, no longer determinate, abstraction. A few years later, in the early 1970s, he was to find a precise expression for his dissatisfaction in Spiro Latsis' concept of "situational determinism", which seemed to him to capture perfectly the kind of objectivism disguised in the modern subjectivist theories of value (Becattini 1979a, pp. 10 fn and 269; 1979b, p. 13). If subjectivism dwells anywhere, it must be with authors who show some awareness of the "crisis" of contemporary capitalism, of the ongoing changes in its moral bases, and the consequent necessity for economists to understand the economic effects of the emergence of new motivational systems. In the late 1950s, he indicated Marshall, Keynes, the imperfect/monopolistic competition literature and the New Welfare economics as possible champions of this point of view. In 1962 he reduced the selection to Marshall alone.

Why Marshall of all these people? Curiously enough, the choice seems to descend more from the communist matrix than from Bertolino, for whom Marshall was not a special favourite. First, there was the fact that Marshall was one of the few "bourgeois" economists for whom some PCI economists showed respect, sparing him the label of "vulgar economist".[6] But even more decisive was the ideological cut clearly visible in the whole of Marshallian economics. The signal that Marshall's economics did not abstract from subjective intentionality as understood by Becattini was the idea that labour is not only a means to ends that are alien to it, but is also an end in itself, given its importance in shaping almost all aspects of the

[6] Becattini found confirmation of this in articles published in the PCI journal *Critica Economica* edited by the Marxist economist Antonio Pesenti from 1946 to 1956, and in lecture notes of the correspondence courses in political economy organized by the Istituto Gramsci, the party's cultural foundation.

life of a human being, the physical as well as the mental and moral ones. For Marshall, labour at all levels, from the merely executive worker to the entrepreneur who makes plans and organizes other people's labour, defines a form of life, provides the labourer with knowledge, habits and education, and constitutes a foundation of his self-esteem. Production and enterprise thus come to reflect the intentionality not of mere arbitrageurs between differently profitable activities, but of agents who strive to realize their projects of life as best as they can, given their original circumstances. Consequently, in Marshall's capitalism it is possible to discern a projection of creative minds and an environment in which creativity is cultivated and motivated.

If this is Marshall's ideological background, an economic theory consistent with it should be able to integrate all the above-mentioned aspects into its logical structure. If final choices concern not only consumption, but also the field of employment of one's own skills and, in the case of entrepreneurs, capitals, what should a theory of value look like in order to account for the interaction of these different types of decisions? This is the test, called a test of "substantial" or "ideological" as opposed to "formal" consistency, to which Becattini submitted Marshall's theory in the central chapter of his 1962 book.[7] Surprisingly enough, after close examination of the theoretical structure of the *Principles of Economics*, this first encounter with Marshall was concluded with a "fail". According to Becattini, Marshall failed because his theory did not deal in a consistent way with the space of choice of the producer, intended as either worker or entrepreneur, and the space of choice of the consumer. Both spaces were partitioned into "industries", but this generic term was taken to mean an "existentially homogeneous sector" in the former case—industry being the field of activity in which the worker/entrepreneur decides to realize his own project of life—and groups of basic needs in the latter, in which industry stands for the set of firms that provide the means to satisfy each group.

Becattini's idea of focusing the critique on difficulties with the concept of industry was clearly inspired by Sraffa's articles of 1925/1926, but his ambition was even more radical. While Sraffa's target was the impossibility of defining the industry in the Marshallian set up consistently with variable returns, hence with a "symmetric" theory of value, Becattini aimed

[7] Becattini (1962, Chapter 4). An English translation of that text appeared in the last issue of the *Marshall Studies Bulletin* (Becattini 2012).

to prove that the impossibility extended to the very definition of industry as a term of reference valid for all the agents involved in transactions on both sides of the market. The inconsistency in the latter case was between the demands of the theory of value—equilibrium prices having the task of coordinating both consumers' and producers' choices—and a social philosophy in which the choices of all these agents refer to different "existential" spaces that do not generally match the economic categories. If considered according to today's standards of theoretical rigour, the arguments displayed by Becattini in the 1962 volume do not appear to be as logically compelling as he assumed. This was perhaps inevitable, given that he insisted on the "ideological" consistency of the theory, which is a somewhat fuzzier notion than mere "logical" consistency.[8] As we shall see, while the problems of the definition of industry reappear at a crucial knot in the evolution of Becattini's ideas, in his later encounters with Marshall the critical argument developed in the 1962 book never resurfaced, and his assessment of Marshall's theoretical performance was to become on the whole much more positive.

3 Marshall in the Post-classical Transition

I have dwelt on these preliminaries because they show us the origin of the narration of post-classical British political economy developed by Becattini over the years from 1970 to 1990. The latter are the years in which his research took on an explicitly historical character, its core being Marshall's personal and intellectual biography within the context of the Victorian age. The political subtheme, however, remained the same as ten years earlier: an attempt at identifying a way to escape from classical objectivism, avoiding the traps of "vulgar economy" and opening the way to a critical understanding of the historical mutations of capitalism. However, the project then had to be carried out in the light of the new situation created by the extraordinary relevance that Sraffa's theoretical scheme of *Production of commodities* was assuming within the Italian academic and political debate.

[8] In a long review of the book Rosario La Rosa, then a young researcher at the University of Catania, pointed out the existence of logical gaps in the argument that damaged Becattini's case (La Rosa 1965). In private correspondence with La Rosa, Becattini acknowledged the relevance of the remark and expressed his intention of writing a rejoinder, which, however, never materialized.

Later on, something must be said about Becattini's other activities during the decade that separated the 1962 volume from the 1970 project. For now it suffices to mention the following. Sergio Steve, a professor of Public Finance at the University of Rome, a good friend of Piero Sraffa's and one of Becattini's academic mentors, advised him to send Sraffa a copy of the volume. In a courteous letter of acknowledgement Sraffa, without commenting on the main theses of the book, praised the chapter on the Marshallian system as being "particularly original and convincing".[9] Further correspondence and direct contacts on the occasion of trips to Cambridge followed. It was probably Sraffa who convinced Becattini that serious research on Marshall could not be pursued without an immersion within the mass of archival materials lying in boxes in the Marshall Library and still mostly unexplored (a systematic probing began only in the late 1960s, at the hands of Krishna Bharadwaj and Rita Mc Williams Tullberg). Furthermore, Sraffa's edition of Ricardo's works and correspondence constituted an example of scholarly excellence that could not fail to impress Becattini. At the beginning of 1970 the project was set in motion, and the summer months were spent on a first survey of the Marshall papers. There were two goals: the editing of an Italian translation of Alfred and Mary Paley Marshall's *Economics of Industry* for a new Italian series of "Classics in Political Economy" and the selecting of an as yet unspecified collection of Marshallian manuscripts for publication.[10] I am unable to reconstruct at this distance in time the

[9] Letter from Sraffa to Becattini dated 25 November 1962, Becattini's papers. One may find it odd that Sraffa had nothing to say about the main claim of the book, namely that objectivist theories of value of the Ricardo-Marx type have lost their historical relevance in the face of contemporary capitalism. This is all the more surprising if one considers that the book contained an explicit reference to Sraffa (1960), with the remark that the circularity of the Sraffian scheme could be seen as Ricardian objectivist philosophy cast in an analytic scheme in which "the position of man … is that of an intermediate commodity" (Becattini 1962, pp. 49–50). If ever there was a direct confrontation between Becattini and Sraffa on this theme during their Cambridge meetings, no trace remains either in print or in unpublished documents. As we shall see below, it was only after Sraffa's death that Becattini, in papers of the 1980s, would reaffirm his thesis on the historical irrelevance of the theoretical scheme set forth in *Production of Commodities*.

[10] By mere chance, during the years in which they were both searching through the same archives, the paths of Becattini and John Whitaker never crossed, and they continued not to cross until the late 1980s although they knew of each other's work. Becattini's original plans for a collection of unpublished economic manuscripts were upset when the two-volume *Early Economic Writings of Alfred Marshall* edited by Whitaker for Macmillan came out in 1975. This was one of the many occasions that Becattini missed (others will be

reason for the *Economics of Industry* of all Marshall's works. In the text of a letter of 1971 to an Italian correspondent (Alberto Campolongo, a habitual translator of texts in political economy for Italian publishers) I have found an emphatic statement to the effect that this book is "much more important, for the history of neoclassical economics, than all the other works by Marshall except the *Principles*". However, there is no explanation as to why, and later works by Becattini himself do not seem to support the claim.

By fits and starts over the course of the 1970s, interspersed among the other activities that we shall examine in Sect. 4, Becattini embarked upon a series of tours of British archives and libraries, interviews with still living direct or indirect witnesses, contacts with specialists in various aspects of British history of the period, etc. All this work resulted in an impressive collection of historical materials concerning Marshall and his affiliates in Bristol, Oxford and Cambridge, Alfred and Mary's family background and biography, and the social, economic and intellectual Victorian context in which they lived. It would take years before the first tangible product of this huge investment would see the light, in the form of an essay of about one hundred pages entitled "An invitation to re-reading Marshall", published in Italian in 1975 as the introduction to the translation of the *Economics of Industry* (Becattini 1975a). This essay, together with many later shorter papers on Marshall and related subjects that give the impression of being the emerging tenth of an iceberg of knowledge, gained for Becattini the reputation of being an authority on Victorian social thought. Despite his publishing almost exclusively in Italian, this grew rapidly into an international reputation, thanks to the network of relations established during the course of his investigations.

The continuity between the 1962 volume and the 1975 essay is apparent. With respect to 1962 there is a widening of the primary sources, which now include unpublished or previously unknown texts, as well as a shift of the object of the research to the biographical and intellectual itinerary that ranges from Marshall's formative years to the *Economics of Industry*, with a brief coda on the *Principles*. Thanks to his mastery of the historical context, Becattini is now able to insert Marshall's personal story within the frame of what he describes as the process of emancipation of British culture from the Ricardian model of early capitalism.

mentioned in footnote 15) because of a systematically overcrowded agenda that resulted in his realizations always lagging behind his plans.

This model is depicted as a "cultural anachronism" in the face of the waking up of romanticism and idealism in Great Britain. The attempts of the ruling class to secure a consensual social order based on negotiation and the conscious participation of all the classes make it appear an anachronism also from a political point of view. Becattini lays special emphasis on John Stuart Mill's *Principles of Political Economy*, a work that tried to strike a compromise between Ricardo's focus on distribution as a wheel in the process of capital accumulation and a new point of view according to which distribution depends entirely on social institutions, may change with the latter and, in a society constituted like the present one, is implemented by the mechanism of exchange. In Mill's resetting the crucial step is the last one, implying as it does the removal of the labour relationship between worker and capitalist from the "deep" level of the structural laws of capitalism to the "surface" level of market phenomena (Becattini 1975a, pp. xxxi–xxxvi).

Marshall enters the story at this point. His aim was to advance Mill's line by bringing into it greater analytical powers and a fresher vision of economic theory. Although Jevons's "revolutionary" manifesto, the *Theory of Political Economy*, was still being discussed in the 1870s, Becattini is careful to point out that the labour-value versus utility-value dispute did not seem to be of any particular concern to Marshall. What fascinated the young scholar from the start was, instead, the problem of communism, about which he read a great deal of socialist literature, especially Lassalle and Marx, and traces of which can be discerned in much of his early work, in spite of his dismissal of the theory of surplus value and his apparent lack of sensitivity with regard to the theme of labour alienation (Becattini 1975a, pp. xliv ff.). Having discarded Jevons's way of evading the Ricardian model, Marshall's own way passed through a better-equipped updating of Mill's attempt at revising the relationship between the deep-rooted laws of capital accumulation and the surface laws of exchange in the explanation of distribution. The proposal developed in the 1870s took on the shape of an anticipation of the period analysis of the *Principles*: a model of exchange equilibrium branching out into a collection of connected models, each one based on a different specification of the adjustment mechanisms left free to operate. While superficial explanations involve a minimum of mechanisms, the more these are allowed into the model, the deeper the explanation reaches in linking prices and distributive variables to capital accumulation.[11]

Crude and imperfect though they were, these were Marshall's first steps in an ambitious theoretical itinerary that with time would lead him to the *Principles*. With respect to this itinerary, *Economics of Industry* emerges from Becattini's scrutiny as a step aside and, contrary to the high preliminary assessment of its importance that he gave in 1971 (see above in this section), not even a well-thought-out one. Premature in its attempt at theoretical synthesis, the book marked a regression in comparison with other more original and promising writings of the period. Furthermore, Becattini sees it as the expression of an "ideological U-turn" from the pro-social sentiments of Marshall's early years to an overly simplistic view of capitalism as the optimal solution to the problems of human development—possibly an hyper-reaction to the socialist and Marxian challenge, or a result of the strong impression made on him by his first-hand contact with American capitalism during the tour in the USA of 1875, and in any case a view that he would later regret. On the whole there is enough for judging the book as being the nearest Marshall ever came to "vulgar economy" (Becattini 1975a, pp. lxxxvii–xciii) and for justifying his later rejection of it, with its withdrawal and the destruction of all the copies he could put his hands on. Not everything in the book is to be discarded, however, and Becattini does not fail to point out a few small gems hidden in the details, one of which is worth mentioning here for the importance it will have in the development of his future research. This is the argument, found both in the *Economics of Industry* and in the chapters "Pure Theory of Domestic Values" privately printed by Sidgwick in 1879, according to which the concentration of production within a few large units is not necessary in order to exploit the advantages of production on a large scale, because the same advantages can be obtained from a large number of small productive units, provided that these are assembled in the same district. Little more than a hint, it is noted however by Becattini as a brilliant anticipation of future developments in industrial economics and is used as a defence against Sraffa's later critique of Marshall's variable returns (Becattini 1975a, pp. xcviii–ci).

[11] Becattini's sources in this reconstruction include unpublished manuscripts and the partially published *Theory of Foreign Trade*, all written in the 1870s. These texts are now available in Whitaker's (1975) edition of Marshall's early economic writings.

To bring the story one step forward, this narrator must now exit from behind the scenery and come on stage. Being a very late product of the 1970 research project, my book on the "young Marshall" (Dardi 1984) was intended originally as a development of Becattini (1975a), by covering the entire itinerary from the early economic manuscripts to the *Principles* and by entering more in detail into the analytical issues and difficulties that Marshall had met along the way. My starting point was the debate on the wages-fund in the late 1860s, with Mill's "recantation" of the same in response to an attack from William Thornton. The terminal point was placed in the theory of value and distribution as stated by Marshall in the *Principles* Book V and VI. Entirely in line with Becattini's approach, I too decided that the tone of the story from beginning to end was set by the problem of industrial relations, rather than by the theory of value. The central plot can be summarized as the progressive demise of the need for a unitary theory of value/distribution in favour of what in the *Principles* turned out to be a collection of analytical schemes with a common pattern suitable for treating problems of adjustment to partial equilibria, each one with a special field of application of its own. Applications go from adjustment in fast standardized markets dominated by professional dealers at one extreme to slow movements of factor prices in the very long period at the other. Passing from the former to the latter through a gradation of intermediate situations, the sharply defined economic rationality of professional dealers gradually recedes, leaving increasing room for the operation of other classes of agents whose motivations, knowledge and capacities are of a more uncertain kind. Correspondingly, the scheme loses in definiteness and becomes more and more blurred as we move towards the long period extreme. The latter is actually described not in terms of convergence to some equilibrium position, but as an open-ended process in which distribution, factor endowments, techniques and the quality of the labour force move jointly in a loosely defined connection: the broad-brush sketch of the possible future evolution of capitalism that can be found in the final chapters of the *Principles*.

Being in close touch with Becattini during the entire preparation phase of my volume, a strong agreement between the two of us on this view of Marshall's final achievement was established and lasted until at least the early 1990s. This can be seen from the many papers on Mill, Fawcett, Marshall and the Marshallian school that Becattini published in this period. He was fond of the idea of getting free from the constriction of having to refer to an "essentialistic" theory of value—meaning a unitary theory relying on some abstract entity such as "labour" or "utility" (Becattini 1984, pp. 26–27). The gamut of mechanisms of adjustment to partial equilibria described above was for him the occasion to return to the notion of "determinate" or "real" abstraction that had intrigued him so much in his early years (see Sect. 2 above): the stereotyped behaviour of professional dealers, he argued, can be analysed abstracting from subjective factors and the abstraction is "real" because this is what professional markets actually do, while the subjective element, uncertain and historically variable, emerges more and more obtrusively as the analysis extends to a wider range of markets. Thus even Marshall was accorded his own determinate or real abstraction although the layout of his theory remained fastened to subjectivism and historicism (Becattini 1983a, pp. 51–59). Lastly, Becattini liked the idea of the progressive blurring of equilibrium values, exactly identified in the very short run and more and more uncertain as the analysis moves on to longer periods. Although for Marshall, as well as Ricardo, observed "market prices" always gravitate towards longer period "normal values", in the indefiniteness of the attractor Becattini saw a reversal of the philosophy of the Ricardian gravitation: for Marshall, the important thing was the tendency of the phenomenon, not its limit which may well be a nebula instead of a point (Becattini 1986, pp. 45–47).

These last remarks are revealing of who Becattini's interlocutors were at the time, and what the political target of the historical reconstruction we proposed was: still left-wing objectivism, but in the Italian situation of the 1970s this meant a variety of neo-Marxian positions that took their inspiration from Sraffa, from his *Production of Commodities* and his interpretation of Ricardo. Sraffa's wage-interest frontier for given levels of production seemed at the time to offer the possibility of reaffirming the old Marxian thesis of the inevitability of class conflict without becoming encumbered with the theory of labour-value and all its complications. Since the frontier was graphical and one-dimensional, everybody could understand it. In Italy in the 1970s, conquering the status of the "independent variable" of the frontier became the catchphrase on both sides of the social divide. The objection that all this may be an optical illusion due to the assumption of given production levels—a step that Marx would never have taken—was the first and most obvious for a person like Becattini who had begun his study of economics on Marx's texts.[12] Besides, the fact of reducing distribution to a couple of uniform rates—one for wages and one for interest—according to Becattini[13] led to an additional, and certainly not "real" abstraction: not only the abstraction from the feedback of prices and distribution on production decisions, but also from the very process of levelling different rates to a common value. In as far as it requires workers and firms to move from one sector to the other, the levelling process is dependent on existing subjective attitudes and reacts on them at the same time, thus affecting the final outcome. Here is an abstraction, then, that "dissolves the specifically human element of the problem all at one stroke" (Becattini 1983b, p. 54; on this point see also below, Sect. 5). A few years later, returning to Sraffa's work as a whole, Becattini even suggested that, in the famous articles of 1925 and 1926, one could discern a determination to keep out of the field of political economy all those theoretical constructs that might constitute "dangerous means by which impressions, perceptions, opinions and all this kind of subjective stuff might be introduced into the inner nucleus of the theory of value" (Becattini 1986, p. 51).

In 1987 Tiziano Raffaelli joined the Valdarno team emerging from philosophy and from a trying stint in the public administration (see the introduction to this volume). Initially, his collaboration fit in entirely with the main line of research conducted up to then: always Marshall and the post-classical transition, a theme the segment of which he explored was related to the controversies on wages and trade unions leading up to the rejection of the wages-fund theory (Raffaelli 1987). Work on Marshall's

[12] It is fitting here to recall the interpretation of the same historical situation by another historian of economic thought apparently at odds with Becattini. In Macchioro (1981) we find the thesis that Marxists, by accepting Sraffa's extrication of class conflict from the labour theory of value, assented also to moving the conflict from the objective, structural plane in which Marx had embedded it to the subjective and voluntaristic plane of the trade unions' willingness to struggle for more favourable positions on the wage-interest frontier. Be it labelled as subjectivism, with Macchioro, or objectivism, with Becattini, it is however clear that for both authors the reduction of the central social issue to movements inside an one-dimensional space amounted to a fundamental delusion.

[13] This is based on Becattini (1983b). It must be noted that in this article the implicit target behind Sraffa was the influential neo-Ricardian economist Pierangelo Garegnani, with whom Becattini had been in close contact during the years in which the former was teaching at the University of Florence, from 1969 to 1974. There had been no lack of occasions for controversy between the two of them.

philosophical papers began a bit later. In December 1990 the team made its international debut with the conference in celebration of the centenary of Marshall's *Principles* held in Florence at the Faculty of Economics. A debut it was, because although Becattini had already an international reputation, up to then we had been writing mostly in Italian and with reference to a mostly Italian debate. By this time, Tiziano was able to present the first results of his research on the philosophical papers, but their implications for the interpretation of Marshall's economics were still unclear. Thus, the Marshall that the team presented at the conference was still the champion of a view of post-classical capitalism that provided an alternative to those proposed by old and new types of Marxism and by the various trends of neoclassical theory. The conference was a success[14] and this obviously flattered us, but I think I can say that it marked the end of a phase focused on a semi-political debate that by that time had fewer and fewer ties with the questions currently discussed in economic theory. In my view, it was not by chance that Becattini's paper at the conference was about Marshall and communism (Becattini 1991). I like to think of it as the last act of a long political season begun many years earlier with Becattini's resolve to leave the PCI and continued with his search for new foundations for thinking critically about capitalism, always against the background of a sort of interior dialogue with Marx, Sraffa and some of the latter's Italian followers.

4 Bifurcation: Industrial Districts and Cognitive Evolutionism

When I say that in the 1990s a new phase opened in the works of the team, I have two circumstances in mind. One is the gradual development of the economic implications of the Marshallian philosophy of mind hidden in the early philosophical manuscripts and brought to light and explained by Raffaelli. The other, the feeling that the original Marshall project, now more than twenty years old, had exhausted its drive while Becattini himself was increasingly engrossed in a different project, one that concerned post-war Italian economic development examined afresh

[14] According to the non-partisan opinion of John Whitaker, see Whitaker (1991). The conference volume was edited as a two-volume special issue of the journal *Quaderni di Storia dell'Economia Politica*, vol. 1, issues 2–3 of 1991, and vol. 2, issue 1 of 1992.

through that newly-built conceptual instrument that he dubbed "Industrial District" (ID). For the sake of continuity, I shall start from the latter.

In Sect. 3, I hinted at the amount of time and energy spent in accumulating a mass of research materials on Victorian social thought that Becattini was able to utilize only to a very limited extent. Many projects conceived in the 1970s and 1980s ended in nothing.[15] This was certainly not out of laziness but because in those same years he was busy along two parallel[16] research lines, the history of economic thought having to contend with the industrial development of Tuscany for Becattini's time and attention. The roots of the research on Tuscany go back, again, to the late 1950s and to the Italian debates concerning the institution of regional governments to decentralize public administration and the implications of this structural reform for economic policy, at a time in which the central government was considering for the first time the possibility of resorting to some form of national planning in order to co-ordinate the Italian economy. Initially involved in research on particular local industries commissioned by public agencies, Becattini quite soon realized the importance of providing regional administrators with all the knowledge necessary for contributing in a conscious, bottom-up fashion, to the identification of the targets of national planning (Becattini 1963). The appointment to the direction of a newly formed Research Institute for the Economic Planning of Tuscany (IRPET), from 1968 to 1973, allowed him to become intimately acquainted with the characteristics of the economy of this region, studied in the phase of transition from its mainly agricultural pre-war ordering to a new and peculiar pattern of "light" industrialization. In opposition to the common belief, both to

[15]The list of aborted projects includes an ambitious collective volume on political economy and society in Victorian Britain for the Torinese publishing house Einaudi; a coffee-table book on Alfred & Mary Marshall's Sicilian holiday during the 1881–1882 winter, to be distributed by the Banco di Sicilia on occasion of the centenary year; the constitution of an international Marshall Society; and a biography of Marshall, plans and rough drafts of which go back to the late 1980s. Correspondence between Becattini and Peter Groenewegen reveals that the last project bounced back and forth between the two of them for a long while, until in the end Becattini had to surrender, regretfully, to Peter's superior efficiency in self-organization.

[16]This is slightly inaccurate, because parallel means having no intersection while in this case, as we shall see, the two research lines eventually did meet. But this happened no earlier than the late 1970s, after almost twenty years of separate development.

the right and to the left of the political spectrum, that considered this kind of industrial structure to be inadequate for the development of a modern industrial country, in it Becattini saw an original and promising model, and occupied himself in a lengthy struggle in order to advocate its maintenance and promotion.

As Becattini himself acknowledged, the crucial concept in this phase was that of "social culture", which he found formulated by his mentor Bertolino in a seminal study on the non-economic roots of economic underdevelopment (Bertolino 1957). According to Bertolino, a society that maintains a standard of living below its economic potential shows by this very fact a "repugnance to conform to economic rationality" that calls for an explanation in historical and sociological terms. The core of his explanation was identified in intellectual and psychological dispositions common to all social strata and revealed in the "organic system" of the existing institutions and in the moral and political philosophy by means of which that system is commonly justified and defended by those who live in it. This was Bertolino's social culture: "knowledge and … faith, both fused in an elementary doctrine, present in the various acts of each person irrespective of his position in society" (ibid., p. 632): a theoretical construction that bears clear marks of social organicism and of the idealistic imprinting of Bertolino's thought.

In accepting this concept and by extending its application to an explanation of the reverse phenomenon, i.e. economic development, Becattini revealed all the distance that, already in the early 1960s, had accrued between himself and a Marxist approach centred on the class structure of capitalism. The feeling of belonging to a cultural community may prevail over the objective criteria that split or unite individuals according to their position in the process of capital accumulation, and he believed that this was the case with the post-war Tuscan economy that he was studying at the time. A local culture that takes pride in the industrial activities traditionally located in its territory and appreciates work well-done, including entrepreneurial work: this is the prerequisite which, together with contingent historical factors, explains the emergence of the Tuscan "light" industry, a fabric of systems of small firms localized in places characterized by absent or low-level social strife, high mobility of positions, availability of latent entrepreneurial capacities. Perhaps the theme "industry as a field of existential choice" that we met in Becattini (1962) had its origin precisely here, in the observation of social cultures that express themselves, among other things, by nurturing special forms of industrial development. In retrospective, it is indeed surprising that in spite of this common theme, his inquiry into Marshall's theory of value and his fieldwork on the Tuscan economy failed to intersect from the beginning.

1975 is the year in which a long stint of research along these two lines came to fruition simultaneously with two major publications, the already mentioned Marshall essay Becattini (1975a) and the research report Becattini (1975b) on the Tuscan economy (officially, the latter appeared as "edited" by him but, in fact, he wrote it entirely). The two were still apparently unconnected to each other, although at least two important links were already there. One was the argument we saw in Sect. 3 concerning groups of small firms assembled in the same place and able to generate large-scale economies with the same efficiency they would have were their total production concentrated in one large establishment. A second link was the discovery, in the unpublished chapters of Marshall's *Theory of Foreign Trade* of 1875–1877, of the theme of the "economic nations" within the political nation, a theme that indicated Marshall's alertness to the sociological processes by which industrial ties tend to metamorphose into feelings of belonging, transforming well-organized industries or trade unions into "industrial republics" in which employers and/or employees are bound together by a sort of "patriotic spirit". In his 1975 Marshallian essay Becattini pointed out that this merge of sociology and industrial analysis threw a new light on the notion of "industry" as the unit of reference for the theory of value of the *Principles* (Becattini 1975a, pp. lxii–lxv)—the notion, as we know from Sect. 2, that he found so critically flawed in his early examination of Marshall's theory of value in Becattini (1962).

Still four years of gestation and finally, in Becattini (1979b), the spark went off: connect belonging to efficiency via social culture—with social recognition being the strongest incentive for all types of labour, and spontaneous external cooperation among small firms as a substitute for internal organization—and here is the ID, a local society expressing itself through a local industrial system that is able to foster and mobilize all the human resources required to secure a competitive edge. This was a new concept that, unsurprisingly from what we have just seen, Becattini introduced as a possible solution to the problem from which he had started in 1962: finding an economic category that may work both as a unit of reference for the decisions of economic agents and a unit of analysis for the economist who studies them. The ID is able to perform such a task.

A share in the genesis of the concept is due to Marshall and his external economies, but a certainly no-smaller share to Bertolino's social culture and to a familiarity with the Tuscan industrial landscape.

The main lines of Becattini's research on Marshall were not substantially affected by the entry of the new concept at least until 1990. Naturally, attention to the aspects of Marshall's economic theory that were more directly relevant for the ID was heightened, but these did not go beyond the aspects already mentioned above, i.e. external economies and the hints at a sociology of belonging. A decisive role in the process of rounding off the concept of ID and in tilting Becattini's research priorities in favour of the latter was played by his participation for many years (from 1979 to 1997) in a collective project for the reconstruction of the history of Prato, the Tuscan town famous for harbouring a textile industry of medieval origin. In this multidisciplinary research programme, funded by the Prato Municipality and supervised by the French historian Fernand Braudel, Becattini was assigned the task of directing the team (historians, sociologists, economic geographers, etc.) in charge of studying the economy of Prato during post-World War II period, a period of intense development of local industry along lines that seemed to mimic the typical features of a living ID. Although he was in his mature years, this is to be counted as a second formative period for him. First of all, for the exposure to a continuous and meticulous confrontation between a concept still in the making and a specific historical case that seemed to flesh it out. Secondly, for the experience of working at close quarters with social scientists who possessed sensibilities and methodological habits different from those of an economist.

The results are clearly visible if one compares the first formulation of the ID in the 1979b article with the later Becattini (1989): differently from the former, the latter provides a thorough and accurate specification of the elements—social culture and industrial organization—that make up an ID, as well as of the logic of their interaction and mutual reinforcement. Another novelty is conspicuous in the 1989 article. The ID is now and will continue to be so from now on, renamed the "Marshallian" ID (MID), a terminological choice that may have engendered some confusion by suggesting the idea that the ID as a theoretical concept was originally formulated by Marshall himself. In fact, in Marshall's works one can find frequent descriptions of IDs as being particular places in the variegated industrial landscape in turn-of-the-century Britain, but no hints of an intention to transform the plainly denotative term ID into a theoretical concept (more on this point below). Thus, the "M" added to ID is not meant to indicate the origin of a concept which is entirely the creation of Becattini out of a synthesis of motives that, as we have seen, came from Marshall as well as from Bertolino and the Tuscan economy.[17] Rather, it signals an aim to invest Marshall with the role of ideal torch-bearer of a school of thought the core issue of which is the bond between society and industry, the school to which ID studies unquestionably belong. Hence the M of MID—a brand, not a certificate of origin.

This is also the beginning of a change of direction in Becattini's interest for Marshall. If his Marshall up to the 1990 conference was the economist who dealt with the evolution of capitalism from the grim mechanistic system of Ricardo and Marx to the looser, composite and open-ended structure sketched in the *Principles*, the Marshall of the new phase is nailed to one and only one aspect of this evolution over all the others, namely the destiny of local societies in their dealings with increasingly demanding systems of industrial organization. This was not necessarily the first or the main aim of Marshall's economic work, but the almost exclusive focus of Becattini on the MID from 1990 on made it appear so. As we shall see, this will eventually lead to a partially new characterization of the historical figure of Marshall. But before we enter into that, we should turn to what was going on at the same time with the other members of the team.

We left Tiziano at the 1990 Florentine conference presenting a first survey of Marshall's early philosophical manuscripts, the story of which is worth a brief digression. The existence of the four papers had been known to both Whitaker and Becattini since the early 1970s. They were mentioned in both Whitaker (1975, pp. 7–8) and Becattini (1975a, pp. xl–xliv); however, in neither case did the clue connecting these early musings in the philosophy of mind to Marshall's economic work crop up. Intuition told Becattini that these papers should not be disregarded, and I can recall his repeatedly trying to convince me to have a go at them. My ignorance of the terms of the philosophic disputes in which Marshall

[17] Although it cannot be excluded that Becattini himself intentionally contributed to feeding this ambiguity. In Becattini (1979b) the passage "now that, *hiding behind Marshall's gown*, I have introduced *my* proposal" (emphasis added) leaves no doubt as to the origin. Yet in later reprints of this article, and also in its English translation in Becattini (2004), the whole sentence was cut out without notice.

let himself be involved, however, joined to the rather unappealing aspect of the long piece entitled "Ye Machine", clearly the main item in the collection, were enough to discourage me. In the meantime, in 1978 two of the manuscripts appeared (to no great effect) in a book by Reba Soffer on the history of social ideas in England (Soffer 1978). A few years later the Florentine philosopher Cristiano Camporesi, prompted by Becattini, discussed them in a volume on British philosophy of science in the nineteenth century (Camporesi 1985), but did not venture into the economist territory. We thus arrive at Tiziano's taking charge of the task and his thickly annotated edition of the manuscripts and rich commentary, which were made available immediately after the conference.[18]

In addition to deciphering and clarifying the texts, Tiziano's unquestionably most important contribution was the long series of papers leading up to the Raffaelli (2003b) volume in which, step after step, he revealed the extent to which the cognitive model found in the manuscripts penetrated practically all the parts of Marshall's mature work, from the more strictly economic ones to those relating to ethical and cultural aspects of social life. Tiziano's global reinterpretation brought to light a not so evident but quite strong conceptual unity that all previous Marshall scholars (and I am including Becattini and myself in this group) had missed. Industry and markets, together with all kinds of formal and informal institutions, social customs and what he called the "character" of people—Marshall set out to investigate all these objects by looking at them from a single perspective according to which these constitute the different facets of a boundedly intelligent evolutionary process through which intelligence and all the phenomena that it manages to a limited extent to control co-evolve. If this was Marshall's research programme, then the study of how boundedly intelligent beings develop their intelligence through interaction with the surrounding environment—which was exactly the central theme of the manuscripts—was its natural groundwork.

Briefly, a sketch of the core ideas highlighted by Tiziano. Up to a point Marshall explains the mind as a complex mechanism able to respond automatically—i.e. according to given patterns—to already experienced external impulses, and creatively—i.e. by using patterns so as to construct non-automatic responses—to unprecedented impulses that are difficult to

[18] The first edition was as a discussion paper of the Florentine Department of Economics in 1991, prior to being published as an archival supplement to Warren Samuels' journal in 1994 (Raffaelli 1994a).

deal with by means of patterns alone. Creative responses that succeed in repeated trials become new patterns embodied in the mechanism. This explanation comes to a halt when we consider that *sui generis* ability which Marshall defines as "self-conscience", affirming that it cannot be accounted for in terms of any mechanism, no matter how rich in patterns. This ability is responsible for the development of abstract ideas, primarily the idea of the self, then followed by all the ideas that bridge the gap between the mere ability to respond (creatively or not) to the environment and the elaborations of thought in the various branches of science and art. Mental development is thus a process in which patterns and human consciousness grow by means of creative, conscious and successful uses of patterns in the interaction with the external world.

Passing on from the individual to the social level, with intelligent beings interacting in an environment of equally intelligent beings, the collective equivalent of the automatic mental mechanism—it is Marshall himself who invites the analogy (Raffaelli 1994b)—can be identified with the stock of all the rules, customs, routines, algorithms, machines, etc. existing at any moment in a given society. The growth of the stock is a function of its current status and of the flow of environmental impulses that exceed its capacity to respond automatically. This latter flow is therefore, in turn, a function of the gaps existing in the stock and of the variety of its individual components, given that each of these is a potential source of impulses for the others, the more so the more diversified these are. As can be seen, this scheme has all the typical features of a process of cognitive evolution.

Is the cognitive, evolutionary economist revealed by Tiziano the same Marshall whom we in the Valdarno team used to study before 1990? I would answer that the latter Marshall is included in the former, but does not represent its core. If the pre-1990 Marshall was identified by the aim of ferrying economic science from the Ricardo-Marx system to a configuration suitable for a model of post-classic, socially cohesive capitalism, the aim of Tiziano's Marshall is that of checking whether capitalism satisfies the conditions for such a transition to occur, conditions that are located in the ability of the system to engender the necessary individual and collective intellectual capacities. The gist of Marshall's problem now lies in the ways in which society generates incentives to innovation and responds to them with a growth in the stock of available patterns and level of self-conscience. It is ultimately a problem of economic and social organization that puts Marshall on a less directly political (I am thinking of Becattini) line of thought, one that is closer to Smith, Babbage and Darwin (see Raffaelli 2003b, p. 52; see also the chapter by Loasby in this volume) than to Marx and Ricardo. Note also that Tiziano insists on linking his Marshall to the explosion of cognitivism and neural science within the social sciences that occurred during the last decades of the twentieth century, with plenty of references in particular to Herbert Simon and Marvin Minsky. This means that the topicality of Marshall that he aims to reconstruct consists no longer in opposing various types of Marxism or neo-Marxism, but in an ability to converse with the latest end-of-century theoretical innovations.

Lastly, is Tiziano's Marshall the same Marshall on whom Becattini was focusing in his post-1990 MID research programme? Here again I would say that the latter is included in the former, and this time much closer to its core than in the previous case, but there is still a slight distance between the two. Indeed, the first and most evident field of application of the cognitive approach discovered by Tiziano is precisely the theory of the organization of industry, in which Marshall explicitly used the analogy with the architecture of the mind. From here, through a discussion of the performance of systems of small firms in comparison with large business, one is naturally led to identifying the ID as a type of industrial system for which Marshall's conceptual framework is most appropriate, and Tiziano followed Becattini enthusiastically along this line of research (Raffaelli 2003a, b, pp. 72 ff.). Yet a difference remained. Becattini's ID is a local social culture that expresses itself through an industrial structure cut to size and successful, where "expressing itself" means that collective sentiment views that particular structure as the image of its own identity. Marshall's cognitive approach does not sort such strongly characterized cases from an open and changeable typology of local systems, all capable of organizing the growth of their capacities through a reciprocal adaptation of culture and industry in a possibly infinite number of forms. Brian Loasby, who is an admirer of both Becattini's ID and Tiziano's cognitive Marshall, is very clear on this point: "Industrial districts were particularly clear manifestations of a universal economic phenomenon, and so it is important … not [to] exaggerate their distinctiveness as a form of industrial organization […] What is readily observed and sharply defined in an industrial district may be harder to see and less distinctive in other forms of industrial organization, but it is there none the less" (Loasby 1998, pp. 70, 83).[19]

In conclusion, we can take 1990 as a symbolic date that marks the beginning of a new phase in the works of the Valdarno team, a phase in which internal subtle differences will deepen, leading its members in divergent directions, but will not dissolve it.

5 Two Marshalls in Lower Valdarno

From the very beginning Tiziano had remarked that, by re-reading Marshall in the light of his early cognitive evolutionism, apparently peripheral parts of his economic work—notably those relating to the organization of markets and industry—gained in coherence and relevance with respect to the central themes of value and distribution (see, e.g., Raffaelli 1994b, pp. 501–502). By developing this hint, however, he raised the problem of what exactly the connections were between the newly discovered evolutionary approach to industrial organization and the period analysis of Books V and VI of the *Principles*, which is entirely based on an extensive use of partial equilibria. At this juncture, I may permit myself a second appearance in the story.

My 1984 book had dealt with partial equilibria in the concluding part, but remained entirely within the pre-1990 perspective, in which the equilibria were framed as the outcome of Marshall's search for a way out of the strictures of classical value theory. It took some time for me to understand the reach of Tiziano's new view and to find a connection with the old themes. In the process I received decisive help from a senior colleague at the University of Florence, Antonio Gay (1940–2018). Not particularly interested in the history of economic thought, but a member of the

[19] On this point, see also the chapter by Neil Hart in this volume. Perhaps an unintentional indication of the distance between Becattini and Tiziano *re* ID can be perceived also in the arguments that they used in discussing the ID as an environment favourable to industrial innovation. While Tiziano relied on the Marshallian cognitive scheme in terms of the pattern/creativity duality (e.g. in 2003b, Chapter 4; note also the view of IDs developed by Loasby 1998), Becattini preferred to resort to different conceptual frameworks such as those developed by E. de Bono or I. Nonaka and H. Takeuchi (see Chapters 3 and 4 in Becattini 2004).

Florence school of Bertolino,[20] Gay taught me to consider partial equilibrium as a method for endowing the dynamics of an economy with a sort of scaffolding that enables us to analyse economic change in terms of the tendency of the economy to converge to higher-level components by moving inside lower-level ones, the former always being nested inside the latter. Independently of the mathematical formalization that we attempted in a joint paper (Dardi and Gay 1991), the idea was that, in a space of states of the economy, a Marshallian partial equilibrium can be defined as a locus in which particular conditions of "normality"—"everything as expected" for a particular class of economic agents—hold. Change, i.e. movement in space, is driven by agents in a "creative" mood, namely agents who are considering new ways to reap economic benefits that are latent in the current state. Such a state cannot be an equilibrium for them; however, since in general not everyone will be in a creative mood at the same time, the same state will be an equilibrium—a partial one—for other classes of agents, so that movement will occur *within* that equilibrium. When the creative drive exhausts its force, as it necessarily will, the economy will enter a higher-level equilibrium, i.e. a locus of states regarded as normal by both the previous innovators and those who have remained in equilibrium all the time. Think of an economy as a complex system always subject to more or less local, endogenous or exogenous disturbances creating partial disequilibria, and this simple scheme will provide tools for reasoning about its transformations in terms of the overlapping of adjustments of this kind.

The analogy between this way of decomposing economic change and the cognitive evolutionism highlighted by Tiziano is striking. "Normal", the qualification of equilibrium states that Marshall stressed in the *Principles* as being more appropriate than "competitive", evokes situations that can be dealt with by means of ordinary routines or patterns. Outside normal equilibrium, the latter turn out to be inadequate and new lines of action must be devised. In so doing, however, all the usable patterns will

[20] Gay was a pupil of Bertolino in the early 1960s. Differently from Becattini, he pursued an independent line of research entirely contained within the field of mathematical economics. Yet breeding did tell in the end, since with an innovative use of non-standard hypotheses he found ways to import massive doses of Bertolino's idealistic view of society into his mathematical models.

be brought to bear in an effort to create new ones.[21] As in the case of the individual mind, the collective mind reacts to a crisis in its apparatus of automatic response by using the same apparatus in a non-standard way, in order to upgrade it to the needs of the new situation and thus close the gap. This shows that the model of the evolution of the mind can be used also as a model of the process by which the economy adjusts to novelties: a process that, in the light of this model, can be equated to a sort of collective learning.

After some initial hesitation (see 2003b, pp. 42–44), Tiziano welcomed this extension of his interpretation with what appeared to me to be increasing conviction: this is clear, for example, in Raffaelli (2008). I would like to quote from the text of a speech that he gave on the occasion of the presentation of the *Elgar Companion* volume at the Italian Cultural Institute in London in October 2007[22]: "The right perspective on Marshall's analytical economics was Marco's specific contribution. He immediately saw the similarities between the early model I had resurrected and Marshall's analytical tools, when read in a heterodox way, as he was doing of his own". A possible objection to this reading could be that, by focusing on partial equilibrium, it ends by giving too much emphasis to the "mechanical" Marshall, leaving the Marshall of the biological metaphors in relative obscurity. But I think an answer to this can be found in Raffaelli (2007), a paper that contains a superb "roundabout" discussion of Marshall's methodology. The distinction between a mechanical type of discourse and a biological one does not mean that there are two alternative methodologies that exclude each other and one of which is superior to the other: rather, Tiziano argued that these are two complementary parts of the same methodology, both necessary and "interconnected to form a coherent system" (Raffaelli 2007, p. 138). In this composite methodological system Tiziano saw an expression of Marshall's rejection of reductionism both at the epistemological and the

[21] The point was forcefully made by Marshall in a passage in *Industry and Trade* rightly emphasized by Tiziano (Raffaelli 2003b, pp. 56–57), according to which there could be no successful change if those who decide to put it into effect could not rely on part of the existing patterns remaining unchanged. See also Loasby's chapter in this volume, on partial equilibrium as a necessary component of Marshall's approach to the explanation of economic change.

[22] This must be taken at my word, because to my knowledge this text has never been published. I am quoting from the file (dated 26 September 2007) he sent me a few days before the meeting, which I have kept ever since then.

ontological levels, consistently with his theory of cognition as a system that co-evolves with its environment by means of a combination of automatic and creative uses of its mental endowment. Right or wrong, there emerged the notion that Marshall's entire work, methodology, theory and applications, conform to an idea of economic knowledge, as well as of any other kind of knowledge, as consisting of an incomplete set of heterogeneous patterns that are always open to revision and updating.

Did Becattini appreciate the new Marshall all of one piece that emerged from Tiziano's revision? In a sense he did, his public praise of Tiziano's and my work was always generous and without reservations. Yet there is no doubt that he was pursuing his ID, or MID project with almost exclusive determination, and was not excessively concerned that the image of Marshall he was moulding to this purpose exactly matched ours. A synthesis of the final result of his own personal re-reading of Marshall in the course of the 1990s can be found in Becattini (2000), the text of his farewell speech at the University of Florence that he delivered in January 2000. From the very title, "Marshallian Anomalies", the difference of tone is immediately apparent. "Anomalies" in Becattini's use of the term means deviations from mainstream—both in Marshall's and, partly at least, in our own time—economic theory. But if Marshallian anomalies exist, and excluding that Marshall is all-anomalous, then a non-anomalous Marshall must also exist, namely one who is aligned to, indeed an originator of, the theoretic mainstream. Thus, the character jumps out of this reconstruction split into two selves in conflict with each other: the "normal" economist who received wisdom numbers among the founding fathers of neoclassicism, and the anomalous one who entertains ideas alien if not opposed to it. The anomalies indicated by Becattini are six in number, but all of them have more or less directly to do with the feedback of economic action on the conscience and knowledge of the subjects who act, this being the link through which the way economic activities are organized affects the character of economic agents, which in turn affects that organization in endless spiral. The anomalous Marshall is traced in Books IV and VI of the *Principles* and in *Industry and Trade*,[23] as well

[23] It must be noted at this point that, because of the central role of industry in both Becattini's and Tiziano's interpretations of Marshall, a text such as *Industry and Trade*, with its rich reasoned survey of varieties of industrial systems in connection with national and local ethos, had supplanted the *Principles* as the main reference work for both of them (see Raffaelli 2009).

as whenever he speaks of IDs and "economic nations" (see Sect. 4). The normal one is, of course, the author of Book V of the *Principles*, the repository of equilibrium analysis. The fact that "fourth-book" Marshall is judged to be anomalous with respect to "fifth-book" Marshall means that Becattini sees no possible agreement between the two, as if the study of equilibria no matter how partial precluded consideration of the interaction between industrial organization and character. At this point, the favour with which he had regarded partial equilibria, at least for a while in the 1980s (Sect. 3 above), has completely disappeared.

In re-reading now what we wrote during the years around 2000, I find it striking that Becattini saw irreconcilability and internal conflict where Tiziano and I saw coherence and methodological pliability. That makes me return to Becattini's historicist background in comparison with the type of historicism that can be discerned in Marshall's idea of economics as "the reasoned history of man". In this very formula, Marshall admitted that the same rationally understandable processes can be seen at work in different historical circumstances, set in motion by different specimens of humanity. One of the tasks of economics is to devise methods for bringing the intrinsic logic of these processes to light, and there is no doubt that he conceived the analytical grid of Book V within this perspective. If Becattini saw the display of this analytic apparatus as the betrayal of a research programme based on the indissoluble connection between industry and character, this must reflect a more absolute and radical idea of historicism than the one that transpires from Marshall's works. A clear indication of this can be found in the already mentioned Becattini (1983b), a critique, as we saw in Sect. 4, of Sraffa and the neo-Ricardian position that, curiously enough, can be applied exactly in the same terms to Marshall's partial equilibria. Indeed, be it the "gravitation" of market prices towards the natural or normal levels of Ricardo, or the use of partial equilibria to explain the way an economy adjusts to local disturbances, Becattini's critical argument hit in the same way: every change in the economic world is a message that passes through human conscience and representations; consequently, the subjective attitudes of economic agents will generally change, and since there is no exact science dealing with how these attitudes react to different stimuli, it will in general be impossible to determine the limit-state of a sequence of economic adjustments by means of purely theoretical reasoning of any kind (Becattini 1983b, p. 52). This kind of historicism, then, rejects all the methods that resort to some form of *ceteris paribus*—partial equilibrium being one of these—in order to break up complexity, on the grounds that in studying economic phenomena it is epistemically safer to give full force to the notion that a fundamental unity underlies all the aspects of social life: "Every cut clumsily made in this totality creates a situation of conceptual confusion" (ibid., p. 50).[24]

Probably nobody noticed, but at the CNRS-IDEFI-LATAPSES conference on Marshall in Sophia-Antipolis, December 2000, the Valdarno team was present in full force with two different Marshalls: my theorist of how the economy adjusts through partial equilibria (Dardi 2003), and Becattini's dissatisfied neoclassical theorist that nurtured a number of potentially subversive anomalies (his paper for the conference, Becattini [2003], contained an abridged account of the anomalies of Becattini [2000]). At the conference, both Tiziano and Becattini referred to my paper, the former acknowledging that there was a point in it (Raffaelli 2003a, p. 259) and the latter praising it with a flattering "fascinating", but denying that my argument could apply to the work of the mature Marshall (Becattini 2003, pp. 27–28). In subsequent years, however, these diverging views did not prevent us from collaborating in the editing of two collective volumes on Marshall for Edward Elgar, and Tiziano and me from participating in the Elgar ***Handbook of Industrial Districts*** edited by Becattini, together with Bellandi and De Propris. In the Elgar *Companion*, there was a chapter of mine on partial equilibria and no trace of Becattini's split between "fourth-book" and "fifth-book" Marshall, because he himself had decided not to raise the issue and discretely stepped back. As Tiziano said during the above-mentioned speech of presentation of the *Companion* in London: "In the end, the trio who edited the Elgar Companion proved to be complementary, though not always in agreement".

6 Conclusions

In a sense, the story I have recounted here is quite ordinary: in a research group, individual differences are either mediated or, if they persist and

[24] See above, footnote 4, on Becattini's deeply rooted methodological convictions since the times of Becattini (1962). The organicist historicism that resurfaces in this Becattini (1983b) is certainly more suggestive of Bertolino than of Marshall's mildly rationalistic (in the sense explained above in the text) approach to history.

come short of breaking the group apart, are sidestepped more or less elegantly. The latter is what we did, unable to mediate between positions that were ultimately found to rely on different philosophies of history. From my account it has perhaps transpired that the philosophies in question were in fact the ones towards which each of us, given his experience and cultural background, was consciously or unconsciously inclined. I realize now what I did not realize at the time, namely that none of us actually managed to construct a rigorously philological image of Marshall in spite of the considerable amount of historical and philological research effort that we poured into the enterprise. The fact is that we all wanted our own Marshall to be able to fulfil some particular achievement on our account. Before recruiting him in promoting his ID-based industrial economics, Becattini wanted Marshall to be able to counter Marxists and Sraffian neo-Marxists in interpreting the possible evolution of contemporary capitalism. Tiziano and I wanted him to have a say of his own in the flood of cognitive and neural research sweeping through all the fields of economic theory before our eyes. In moments of low spirits, I used to think that Becattini's perspective was out of date, with his fixation on Marx, communism and the like, while our perspective seemed to me the more promising one and to be in line with the spirit of the age. Now I can see that we all were playing the same game, namely projecting our desires onto the historical Marshall. However, the desires were different, and this too was to be accounted for as a historical fact.[25] If the experience of historiography as we practised it in the Valdarno team has a lesson to teach, to me it is that absolute objectivity in the history of ideas is a false goal, that what one can at best achieve with it is to live one's own time as if seen through somebody else's eyes—possibly somebody with eyesight so powerful that at least some clarity may be gained from it.

[25] This practice of projecting different desires on the same historical character was not an exclusive of our team, however. As the opening of Medema's chapter in this volume suggests, something similar may also have been going on among Chicago "Marshallians" in Coase's times.

References

Becattini G. 1962, *Il concetto d'industria e la teoria del valore*, Torino: Boringhieri.

Becattini G. 1963, "Prospettive dell'inserimento della regione toscana nella programmazione economica nazionale", in URPT, *La Toscana nella programmazione economica*, Firenze: Tipografia Nazionale, 25–59.

Becattini G. 1975a, "Invito a una rilettura di Marshall", introduction to Alfred and Mary Paley Marshall, *Economia della produzione* [Italian translation of *Economics of Industry*, 2nd edition], Milano: ISEDI, ix–cxiv.

Becattini G. 1975b, *Lo sviluppo economico della Toscana, con particolare riguardo all'industrializzazione leggera*, edited by G. Becattini, Firenze: IRPET-Guaraldi.

Becattini G. 1979a, *Scienza economica e trasformazioni sociali*, Firenze: La Nuova Italia.

Becattini G. 1979b, "Dal «settore» industriale al «distretto» industriale. Alcune considerazioni sull'unità d'indagine dell'economia industriale", *Rivista di economia e politica industriale*, 5:1, 7–21 [English translation in Becattini 2004, chapter 1].

Becattini G. 1983a, "Introduzione", in John Stuart Mill, *Principi di economia politica* [Italian translation of *Principles of Political Economy*], Torino: UTET, vol. 1, 9–63.

Becattini G. 1983b, "Sul concetto di «saggio uniforme del profitto»", in Aa. Vv. *Economia politica e filosofia*, Milano: Franco Angeli, 41–56.

Becattini G. 1984, "Da Marshall a Keynes: Rapporti personali e influenze intellettuali nella formazione della scuola economica di Cambridge", in *Alfred Marshall e John M. Keynes: Rottura o continuità?* edited by M. Ridolfi, Rimini: Maggioli, 9–29.

Becattini G. 1986, "L'interpretazione sraffiana di Marshall", in *Tra teoria economica e grande cultura europea: Piero Sraffa*, edited by R. Bellofiore, Milano: Franco Angeli, 39–57.

Becattini G. 1989, "Riflessioni sul distretto industriale marshalliano come concetto socio-economico", *Stato e Mercato*, 25, 111–128 [English translation in Becattini 2004, chapter 2].

Becattini G. 1991, "Market and Communism in the Thought of Alfred Marshall", *Quaderni di storia dell'economia politica*, 9:2–3, vol. 1, 161–188.

Becattini G. 2000, "Marshallian Anomalies", *Marshall Studies Bulletin*, 7, online at https://www.disei.unifi.it/cmpro-v-p-119.html.

Becattini G. 2003, "The Return of the 'White Elephant'", in *The Economics of Alfred Marshall: Revisiting Marshall's Legacy*, edited by R. Arena and M. Quéré, Houndmills and New York: Palgrave Macmillan, 13–31.

Becattini G. 2004, *Industrial Districts. A New Approach to Industrial Change*, Cheltenham, UK, and Northampton, MA, USA: Edward Elgar.

Becattini G. 2012, "The Marshallian System", *Marshall Studies Bulletin*, 13, online at https://www.disei.unifi.it/cmpro-v-p-97.html.

Bertolino A. 1957, "Aree depresse e cultura sociale", *Economia Internazionale*, 10: 4, 625–646.

Camporesi C. 1985, *Scepsi scientifica. Fenomenismo e agnosticismo nella filosofia Britannica dell'Ottocento*, Roma: Editrice Ianua.

Colletti L. 1974, "A Political and Philosophical Interview", *New Left Review*, 86, 3–28.

Dardi M. 1984, *Il giovane Marshall: Accumulazione e mercato*, Bologna: Il Mulino.

Dardi M. 2003, "Alfred Marshall's Partial Equilibrium: Dynamics in Disguise", in *The Economics of Alfred Marshall: Revisiting Marshall's Legacy*, edited by R. Arena and M. Quéré, Houndmills and New York: Palgrave Macmillan, 84–112.

Dardi M. and Gay A. 1991, "Dinamica e storicità nei *Principi* di Marshall", *Economia Politica*, 8:2, 227–247.

La Rosa R. 1965, "A proposito di una possibile relazione tra problematica del concetto d'industria e teoria del valore", *Annali della Facoltà di Economia e Commercio dell'Università di Catania*, 11, 198–225.

Loasby B.J. 1998, "Industrial Districts as Knowledge Communities", in *Industry, Space and Competition. The Contribution of Economists of the Past*, edited by M. Bellet and C. L'Harmet, Cheltenham, UK, and Northampton, MA, USA: Edward Elgar, 70–85.

Loasby B.J. 2016, "Knowledge in Economic Theory and Economic Systems", *History of Economic Ideas*, 24: 1, 15–23.

Macchioro A. 1981, "Oggettivismo e soggettivismo negli anni '70", *Società e storia*, 11, 161–176.

Raffaelli T. 1987, "Questione operaia e teoria del salario in Inghilterra (1865–74)", *Quaderni di storia dell'economia politica*, 5:1–2, 183–233.

Raffaelli T. 1994a, "Alfred Marshall's Early Philosophical Writings", *Research in the History of Economic Thought and Methodology*, Archival Supplement 4, 53–159.

Raffaelli T. 1994b, "Il ruolo degli studi psicologici di Marshall nella sua analisi dell'organizzazione dell'industria e degli affari", *Giornale degli economisti e Annali di economia*, 53:10–12, 499–523.

Raffaelli T. 2003a, "Requirements and Patterns of Marshallian Evolution: Their Impact on the Notion of Industrial District", in *The Economics of Alfred Marshall: Revisiting Marshall's Legacy*, edited by R. Arena and M. Quéré, Houndmills and New York: Palgrave Macmillan, 254–268.

Raffaelli T. 2003b, *Marshall's Evolutionary Economics*, London and New York: Routledge.

Raffaelli T. 2007, "Marshall's Metaphors on Method", *Journal of the History of Economic Thought*, 29:2, 135–151.

Raffaelli T. 2008, "The General Pattern of Marshallian Evolution", *Evolutionary and Institutional Economic Review*, 4:2, 239–350.

Raffaelli T. 2009, "*Industry and Trade* Reconsidered", *History of Economic Ideas*, 17:3, 59–74.

Soffer R.N. 1978, *Ethics and Society in England: The Revolution in the Social Sciences 1870–1914*, Berkeley, Los Angeles and London: University of California Press.

Sraffa P. 1960, *Production of Commodities by Means of Commodities. Prelude to a Critique of Economic Theory*, Cambridge: Cambridge University Press.

Whitaker J.K. 1975, "The Evolution of Alfred Marshall's Economic Thought and Writings over the Years 1867–90", introduction to *The Early Economic Writings of Alfred Marshall, 1867–1890*, edited by J.K. Whitaker, London and Basingstoke: Macmillan, vol. 1, 3–113.

Whitaker J. 1991, "Reflections on the Centenary Year", *Marshall Studies Bulletin*, 1, online at https://www.disei.unifi.it/cmpro-v-p-97.html.

The Organisation of Knowledge and Knowledge as Organisation

Brian J. Loasby

1 A Personal Perspective

'Do not be deterred from reading Marshall's *Principles* about halfway through the year. He wrote about an economic system which has passed away; but he was a much greater man than his successors, and the ideas presented by great men have a habit of lasting a long time'. That was a prominent element in the introductory advice attached to the reading list which was provided by Charles Carter, the Director of Studies in Economics at Emmanuel College, Cambridge, to first-year undergraduates in that college in 1949, when I arrived after national service in the Royal Army Educational Corps.

I can claim to be one of the very few university professors (perhaps indeed the only one) who had actually received any training as a teacher, on a standard three months course at the Army School of Education, where each intake was under the care of a Company Sergeant-Major from the Brigade of Guards, with a Regimental Sergeant-Major in overall charge, together with a full set of bugle calls, and optional play-readings

B. J. Loasby (✉)
University of Stirling, Stirling, UK
e-mail: b.j.loasby@stir.ac.uk

K. Caldari et al. (eds.), *Marshall and the Marshallian Heritage*, Palgrave Studies in the History of Economic Thought, https://doi.org/10.1007/978-3-030-53032-7_2

with the son of Earl Wavell—a notable set of distinctions which we recognised at the time and which I am happy to recall. This was followed by eight months practice as a teacher, attached to the 5th Regiment of the Royal Horse Artillery, a unit in which proficiency depended on relevant technical skills; this was reflected both in the Sergeants' Mess and in the classes that I took within the regiment when compared with soldiers from other groups.

That experience may have influenced my response to the teaching which was provided at Cambridge, where the principal means of instruction was a programme of lectures arranged by the Economics Faculty. Although it soon became clear that there were substantial differences of views within the Faculty, many of which were presented as necessary (but often contradictory) truths, there were no opportunities to question the lecturer. Nor was there any provision for contacts with lecturers who were based in colleges other than one's own, so that at the time of my final examination hardly any of the teaching staff had any idea who I was. The chief exceptions to this isolation were the two final-year options which I took, on the British Economy 1875–1900 and US Economic History, in which class sizes were small and the lecturers were keen to engage in discussing the issues and their implications. The treatment of the former topic was particularly instructive in revealing that all the major problems which were apparent in the British economy in the 1950s were already discernable before 1900.

Face-to-face teaching was provided by each college for its own students, and normally by members of that college, in weekly meetings with pairs of students, who were each expected to write an essay a week on a topic which was provided by the supervisor. It was therefore normal to complete a degree course in economics without having ever spoken to most of the professional economists in the university, although it was sometimes possible to learn something (about Cambridge economics rather than the British economy) from their manner as well as their expositions. For me, what I learned was often different from what I was being taught.

It would be safe to assume that not all the directors of studies in Cambridge offered advice similar to that which I received from Charles Carter. I took his advice, although I cannot claim to have understood all of Marshall's arguments—some of which were being dismissed in books and in lectures as apologetics or sheer confusion. What I believe was much more unusual is that by the beginning of the second year, prompted by Carter, I had also read Marshall's *Industry and Trade* (published in 1919), which seemed to be ignored in all formal teaching. Although the contents of that book are of uneven value, three chapters which are devoted to analysing the distinctive features of the French, German and American economies in the early twentieth century might reasonably be considered as expositions of national systems of innovation, each of which rested on distinctive ways of formulating problems and searching for solutions; these systems are summarised in the chapter headings as 'individuality and refinement in production' for France, 'science in the service of industry' for Germany, and 'multiform standardization' for the United States. I was able to recognise the relevance of this approach to my final-year options. Throughout my career, I have been suspicious of the notion of 'the one best way', either of running a particular kind of business or of seeking to develop a particular field of study.

As a result of John Whitaker's work, and its extension by Tiziano, Marshall's presentation of these distinctive systems of innovation may now be seen to have much more fundamental relevance, as an application of his theory of the human mind. Like his account in the *Principles* of the virtues of industrial districts, this is a theory of the generation of knowledge—or strictly, of knowledge claims which can be supported by evidence—within particular intellectual, social and industrial communities. Such a theory is not easily accommodated by a formal notion of general equilibrium. It may, however, be traced back to Marshall's concept of 'Ye Machine', which was developed, before he turned to economics, from Charles Babbage's notion of a calculating engine which could be adapted to the analysis of a particular set of problems. Tiziano wrote insightfully and elegantly about Marshall's route to economics and its lasting effects, not least in Marshall's emphasis on evolutionary processes and, therefore, necessarily, on partial rather than general equilibrium (Raffaelli 2003).

Much later I realised that in *Industry and Trade* Marshall had also anticipated Coase's recognition of the importance of transaction costs in shaping the organisation of economic activities. He argued that because higher-volume traders could anticipate larger benefits from market efficiency they had the stronger incentives to bear the costs of organising systems for handling these transactions; therefore, markets for goods and services would normally be organised by suppliers and labour markets by buyers.

Towards the end of a meeting of Marshallians in Sophia Antipolis in 2000, John Whitaker suggested that Marshall's objectives in developing both the understanding of economic reasoning and its application to real-world economic systems would have been better served by shifting his focus from increasingly defensive revisions of the *Principles* to incorporating substantial applications of his evidence-based ideas of how a competitive economic system worked. How long John had held that view I do not know, but it seems likely that Charles Carter would have agreed. So would I.

Carter was my supervisor for the first two years, before moving to a Chair at Queen's, Belfast. His departure was, I believe, a crucial benefit for me, because he seemed to close down rather than open up discussions, which I am sure was not his intention: even in distant retrospect I cannot explain this effect. In my final year, my supervisor was an American graduate student from another college, who did an excellent job of improving my understanding and essay-writing—and so, I have ever since believed, made possible an academic career, of which I then had no expectation, by way of an unexpected first-class degree. It was only later that I came to recognise that Carter, whose first-class degree had been ensured by his performance in statistics (Williams 2004, p. 40), had never believed that mathematical reasoning was a sufficient response to uncertainty, either in economic theorising or in running a business. Like Marshall, he thought that the proper objective of economists was to explain how economic systems actually worked, and that in order to do this it was essential to understand the practical operations of firms which relied on human potential and respected human limitations.

Carter's later career reflected that belief. After moving to Manchester he collaborated with Bruce Williams in some detailed studies of management processes within firms which were willing to co-operate, and he explained the value of such studies—for the firms as well as the investigators—in the *Westminster Bank Review* (Carter 1962, pp. 2–11). One of their discoveries was that whether an unsatisfactory outcome of a project prompted further action depended on the prior specification of a measurable objective with which that outcome could be compared. Problems are not self-evident, but are defined by differences between what is perceived and the reference standard which is applied (often automatically) by the perceiver, that, of course, implies that focussing on inappropriate reference standards may lead to work on irrelevant problems as well as the neglect of what really matters. This may happen in firms, whole industries, and academic communities, as well as in everyday life.

Carter's perspective on economics was clearly signalled by two significant choices that he made. When appointed Vice-Chancellor of the new University of Lancaster, which admitted its first students in 1964, he chose Philip Andrews as the first Professor of Economics. He must have been well aware that Andrews had been dismissed as a serious economist in both Cambridge and Oxford; John Hicks, who gave some helpful advice to George Richardson in developing his early career, had warned him that contact with Andrews would be unhelpful. When Andrews died in 1971, Carter appointed his long-time collaborator Elizabeth Brunner as his successor. Some years later she invited me to be an external examiner for an Italian graduate student; this was followed by an invitation in 1987 from Giacomo Becattini to deliver lectures in Florence, Pisa and Bologna, which introduced me to the Italian economists who were to justify the later claim that 'Alfred Marshall is alive and well, and living on the banks of the Arno'—and which is presumably the justification for my inclusion in this commemoration.

Carter subsequently selected George Shackle (whose ideas he had introduced to his supervisees in Cambridge, and thus made another contribution to my conception of the proper content and methods of economic studies) to write a textbook on the theory of the firm, under the title *Expectation, Enterprise and Profit* (Shackle 1970). We may notice that Shackle's final chapter begins with the statement 'Equilibrium means in economics the best momentary adjustment to existing circumstances', followed almost immediately by the assertion that '[t]o forget that the business of living, and ... the business of producing and exchanging goods, essentially and inescapably requires the continuous and endless gaining of knowledge, is to divorce our theories from half their subject-matter' (p. 148). The book concludes by denying the sufficiency—although not the usefulness—of equilibrium theory. 'The paradox of business, in its modern evolution, is the conflict between our assumption that we know enough for our logic to bite on, and our *essential*, prime dependence on achieving *novelty*, the novelty which by its nature and meaning in some degree discredits what has passed for knowledge' (p. 148). In any comprehensive account of the Marshallian heritage, Shackle deserves substantial attention.

However, the trigger for the Marshallian revival was an unimagined consequence of Ronald Tress's ambitions for the Economics Department at the University of Bristol. He was concerned that no-one on his staff was sufficiently expert in modern micro-theory and sought a bright young economist to provide this expertise. By 1960 he had found a 27-year old who had progressed from the University of Manchester to Johns Hopkins and Cambridge: his name was John Whitaker. I arrived in Bristol a year later, for the specific role of Tutor in the newly created Centre for Management Education, which was intended to provide courses for people who were moving from departmental to general management (and who presumably needed only to be instructed in the economic way of thinking). This was a very modest experiment when compared with the idea of a business school, which was already being promoted by a group of businessmen—and was therefore easy to close down when the flow of applicants failed to expand as required.

I took no part in undergraduate teaching and spent most of my time in a separate building which was devoted to this project, and although I got to know the members of the Economics Department who taught on these courses, neither I nor the course designers perceived any potential connection between the study and practice of management and modern micro-theory. I knew of the reason for John Whitaker's appointment and therefore assumed that we would have no academic interest in common; I have no recollection of any meeting with him during my time in Bristol.

There can be no question that it was Whitaker's arrival in Bristol, which was intended by Tress to update the teaching of modern micro-theory in his Department, that initiated the Marshallian revival. In this initiation, I had no role whatsoever. It was only at the end of the Marshall-focussed conference at Sophia Antipolis in 2000 already mentioned, when he and I were the only participants who were staying overnight, that I asked him what had prompted this improbable interest. His answer was that he had found himself in a building which bore Marshall's name and had wondered what Marshall had been doing there. I had never thought to ask that question, being interested in the content and continued relevance of Marshall's work rather than its provenance. The publication in 1961 of Guillebaud's variorum edition of the *Principles* (Marshall 1961) had apparently concluded the final act of Marshallian studies, and the extraordinary enterprise of tracing and publishing almost everything that Keynes had ever written seemed to have exhausted the historical interest of economists (and now threatened to exhaust the funds of the Royal Economic Society). Keynes had made some use of the uncatalogued collection of Marshall's papers in composing his memoir; why should anyone else bother with it? John Whitaker did.

This is a classical example of the importance of problem-finding, which I had already learnt from some of the businessmen whom I had interviewed as a Research Fellow in Birmingham, at the same time that Carter and Williams were establishing its importance in business by their studies in Manchester noted earlier, but about which I then knew nothing. In my own interviews, I found that those who had already moved to a new location or who were engaged in planning such a move were keen to point out that moving had forced them to ask basic questions about their present business, which could easily be ignored, or even unperceived, while their attention was focussed on its daily operation. A few noted that most of the improvements which were associated with their new premises could have been introduced on their old site—but added that this would not have happened without the stimulus of relocation; one even suggested that every firm should move during the tenure of each managing director.

My interest in what determines the perception of a problem which seems to deserve attention in any organisation (and, of course, by any individual)—a perception which can, of course, be mistaken—may have influenced my subsequent appointment to the Bristol Management Centre. It seemed to match the perspective of the Director, David Clarke, who came from the Administrative Staff College in Henley, and it prompted substantial references in his teaching to Chester Barnard's (1938) *Functions of the Executive*, Burns and Stalker's (1961) *Management of Innovation*, and Cyert and March's (1963) *A Behavioral Theory of the Firm*.

None of these would have been of much interest in most economics departments at that time, and the first two were clearly not written by economists or intended to be read by them. However, all three seemed consistent with my own investigations of what happened in running a business (and as I subsequently discovered, with Carter's own investigations of business behaviour). It was much later that I discovered that Herbert Simon had been impressed by the relevance of Barnard's work and had discussed it with him, and I have never sought to compare Barnard's and Marshall's explorations and explanations of the working of firms. (It might still be instructive to do so, but I will leave that to others.) It was also much later that I acquired an active interest in the role of problem-finding in the development of economic theory as well as in the development of economic systems.

2 Marshall's Theory of Economics

Whitaker discovered that Marshall's presence in Bristol from 1877 to 1881, in the twin roles as Principal of the new University College and Professor of Economics, was directly attributable to the slow progress of the campaign to remove the prohibition of marriage for College Fellows in Cambridge. However, it is not obvious why Whitaker's discovery that Marshall went to Bristol to solve a strictly personal problem, and subsequently moved to Oxford and then back to Cambridge as natural stages in developing his career, should lead him to undertake a major exploration of Marshall's path from mathematics to the *Principles*. Indeed, it is far from obvious why any Cambridge-trained economist in the 1960s should have seen any career advantage, or even much intellectual interest, in considering how Marshall's view of economics was influenced by that path.

It is, of course, an essential feature of modern Marshallian studies that the path matters, both in the development of economic systems and in the development of any field of study. Although Cambridge was not a world leader in mathematics when Marshall was a student, that was a prestigious option, and his Tripos result was, in retrospect, ideal. Whereas the First Wrangler at Cambridge was expected to be a leader in mathematics, the Second Wrangler had substantial freedom to choose his own field of enquiry. Like many of his contemporaries, Marshall was concerned with improving the condition of the people, and by the mid-1860s there seemed to be substantial reason to believe that significant improvements could be achieved by the development and application of locally appropriate knowledge, not least in industry.

Marshall's emerging preference for a detailed study of the working of economic systems may well have been encouraged by a major event in his own field. Having been thoroughly trained in Euclidean geometry as an axiomatic system which delivered the only possible complete and coherent system of geometry, Marshall was confronted with the emergence of non-Euclidean geometry, also axiomatic, in which Clifford, his friend when they were both Fellows of St. John's in 1868–1871, was particularly interested. A closed system may provide a sense of security, but inhibits the discovery—or the creation—of novelty. Marshall's focus, as analyst and as an individual, was 'with human beings who are impelled, for good and evil, to change and progress' (Marshall 1961, p. xv); the possibility of doing so rested on his belief that '[e]conomic evolution is gradual' (Marshall 1961, p. xiii). Thus although 'the problem of normal value belongs to economic Dynamics' (Marshall 1961, p. 366, fn. 2), it can be tackled because, although change is continuous, every particular episode of change is limited in both scope and duration. Indeed, no change is possible unless those who wish to undertake it can rely on an environment which is in many respects stable. We can now see how this close complementarity between automaticity and innovation matches Marshall's early ideas about how the human brain works.

For Marshall, economics is a study of processes in time, not of models in which time is a parameter; and such a study must go 'step by step: breaking up a complex question, studying one bit at a time, and at last combining ... partial solutions into a more or less complete solution of the whole riddle' (Marshall 1961, p. 366)—although this solution may cease to be adequate when circumstances change. A concept of equilibrium as a stable set of relations on which a set of agents can rely (at least in current circumstances) may help economists to handle both change within a framework and changes of framework; but any such equilibrium must necessarily be partial—limited in both scope and time; and different versions of equilibrium are likely to be needed in order to explain developments in different environments and time periods.

What deserves to be emphasised is that the selection of a concept of equilibrium which is appropriate to the problem to be addressed is not simply a methodological issue for those seeking to create better schemes of analysis. Breaking up problems and combining, and modifying, partial solutions is also how an economic system works—not surprisingly, since it is operated by humans and therefore must respect both human capabilities and human limitations. As we shall see later, this was recognised by Adam Smith, whose earliest surviving work presented the *History of Astronomy* as the creation of new systems in order to accommodate new perceptions, as a powerful illustration of both the limitations and the potential of the human mind (which had been emphasised by David Hume) long before he turned his attention to identifying the processes of thought which created new methods of production.

Marshall (1961, p. 241) adopted from Herbert Spencer the central principle of development by progressive differentiation and new patterns of integration, and applied this principle directly to the development of industry. For Marshall, industrial economics was not, as Coase ([1972] 1988, p. 60) complained it had since become, merely applied price theory; it was the core of the subject. Both co-ordination and growth within an economy depend on the ways in which activities are distributed within and between firms and on the ways in which firms are connected and differentiated. This is what Coase (1991) has called 'the institutional structure of production'. Our understanding of economic systems similarly depends on the ways in which our studies of these systems are themselves connected and differentiated, as both Smith and Marshall recognised.

However, Marshall's (1961, p. 138) suggestion that organisation might be recognised as a fourth factor of production, because 'Organization aids knowledge', was not likely to be adopted by those later economists who were concerned with efficient allocation and believed that this required a focus on constructing an equilibrium for a system in which both production functions and individual preferences were well defined. However, the construction of relevant knowledge is itself an organisational problem; it is a matter of classification, differentiation and selective connections, in the first (and last) instance within individual brains, as Marshall had illustrated in his model of 'Ye Machine', and as Hayek explained in *The Sensory Order* (which will receive attention later). Both recognised, as Smith had done, that human knowledge is necessarily dispersed and incomplete, and that its effective application requires selective connections between appropriate subsystems of knowledge, within individual brains and within groups, each of which constitutes what Herbert Simon called a quasi-decomposable system. Marshall's economics and modern economies are both quasi-decomposable systems.

As Marshall realised, organisation takes many forms, and these forms need to change over time as the relationships both within and between categories of knowledge change. In Marshall's definition, increasing returns operate through organisational change; they emerge over time and cannot legitimately be included in a single production set. Allyn Young (1928) elaborated this idea with unMarshallian panache.

Firms reproduce within their structures and practices the equivalent of the two circuits within the brain of Marshall's 'machine'. The embodiment of apparently secure knowledge in operating and managerial routines which require little conscious attention allows a focus on specific problems and possible opportunities, some of which are generated by the application of these routines. Understanding the business, anticipating changes, making judgements, taking opportunities and providing leadership are all part of the businessman's job (Marshall 1961, pp. 297–298); and the search for solutions is guided by decision premises and procedures which provide some bounds to uncertainty, which, as Shackle

(1969, p. 224) pointed out, are 'essential to the possibility of decision'. However, in Marshall's time as in ours these bounds may be wrongly defined by some businessmen and the premises and procedures which are currently in use may therefore lead them astray—as Marshall clearly acknowledged. This fundamental human limitation applies to economics and to every field of knowledge.

Barnard's book was prompted by his recognition that very few firms have a long life: their efficient orientation to their current environment becomes a major obstacle to adaptation—and even to any recognition of the need for adaptation when circumstances change. It was therefore desirable that routines, premises and procedures should vary somewhat within each industry—in contrast to the supposedly ideal world of perfect competition, in which the optimal technology for every situation is already known. It is perhaps the supreme irony that Barnard's own company proved incapable of reacting effectively to fundamental changes in the technological, social and political environment, as explained in detail in *The Fall of the Bell System* (Temin and Galambos 1987).

Marshall took a particular interest in two forms of organisation which have been almost completely ignored by those economists who are fascinated by the notion of a general equilibrium: the co-operative movement, in both production and retailing, and industrial districts. Both forms had advantages of physical and cognitive proximity which could encourage a continuing search for something better within a particular field by developing, accessing and applying the particular knowledge of many people within a relatively stable environment—although both have since proved much less effective in adapting to external change.

In my home town, there was a natural connection between the two, because it was dominated by shoemaking and clothing, with engineering as a support to both. Both were sewing-machine industries; and the new technology which was developed during the second half of the nineteenth century was accessible at relatively low cost—especially in shoemaking; because the principal supplier of machinery chose to lease rather than sell their products. Therefore, most firms were founded by salesmen or, in shoemaking, by those with particular practical experience in making the best use of animal hides. The turnover of businesses was fairly high throughout the period of growth, and after the early years, when bankruptcy was liable to be attributed to incompetence or dishonesty, the reports of business failure were generally accepted as a normal consequence of technical and organisational progress. A few firms were organised as co-operatives—including a clothing firm which became the largest manufacturing business in the town. There was also a co-operative retail society which was by far the largest retailer, with a substantial range of products in a large store in the town centre and food stores in residential areas. For both commercial and social reasons, there was a substantial dividend on purchases; this provided useful information about customers, although not, as with current commercial schemes, details about their buying practices, and it was intended to encourage not only regular custom but also saving, especially for house purchase. That was also supported by buying a substantial area of land on which many houses were built for owner-occupation, which was predominately funded by building societies.

When presented with an unexpected opportunity to stay on as a postgraduate I was determined to avoid economic theory, which did not seem to me particularly helpful in understanding how real economies worked (a decision which had also been made, for similar reasons, by a graduate from the previous year), and looked for a historical theme. I quickly settled on a case study of my own industrial district, relying primarily on printed records and interviews with the current managers. I made no attempt to apply, or even to refute, the theory of imperfect competition, and I could see no advantage in applying the concept of general equilibrium, because the organisation of this industry made no provision for all the contingencies which would need to be incorporated in a general equilibrium; and that was not a remediable defect. There are no guarantees about the future. Shoemaking in Britain is now virtually extinct—as are many other lines of business which once flourished.

In the mid-twentieth century, Marshall's work was heavily—and sometimes disparagingly—criticised for two fundamental, and apparently related, defects. The first was its reliance on partial equilibrium, which, as the adjective implied, was necessarily incomplete. The second was that partial equilibrium was easily associated with the notion of imperfect competition, which necessarily produced welfare losses, and according to the diagrams which were used to display the logic of imperfection these were typically substantial. However, both kinds of criticism made casual assumptions about human knowledge and also about human psychology.

3 Andrew Skinner

In drawing attention to both the foundational importance and the peculiar character of human knowledge, the leading role in the second half of the twentieth century was undertaken by Andrew Skinner, who took full advantage of his role as joint General Editor of the Glasgow Edition of the works of Adam Smith, which was launched in 1976 by the publication of new editions of *An Inquiry into the Nature and Causes of the Wealth of Nations* (Smith [1776] 1976a), to mark its bicentenary, and *The Theory of Moral Sentiments* (Smith [1759] 1976b). The latter had been the first of Smith's publications, developed from a lecture course which Smith had undertaken to replace that given by Thomas Craigie, who was retiring because of ill-health (as explained in the Introduction to the Glasgow Edition). The characteristics of human psychology and the origins and significance of institutions as a direct consequence of that psychology are widely underestimated both in the understanding of economic systems and in understanding the behaviour of economists. Skinner recognised that they are at the core of Smith's work.

Skinner emphasised the significance of Smith's theory of human knowledge, which gave proper respect to the twin principles which had been established by his friend and mentor David Hume: first, the truth of any supposedly universal proposition can never be demonstrated by evidence, because its consilience with unknown evidence from the past and inaccessible evidence from the future must always rest on unverifiable assertions; and second, new ideas can never be produced by purely logical reasoning from what is currently accepted as established knowledge. The combination of these principles undermines the status of rational choice theory as a core principle in economics and therefore undermines the status of general equilibrium as a state of affairs which can be achieved either by planning or by human interaction within a market structure. Either method would require a complete list of goods, each defined not only by its characteristics but also by its location (how precise?), date (and time of day?), and the state of the world on each date, which must include all possible events and innovations.

Smith recognised that Hume's principles invalidated the claim that Newton's theory, which seemed so remarkably congruent with all relevant observations, was necessarily correct, and he scrupulously and explicitly avoided such a claim in his presentation in *The History of Astronomy*, observing that he had 'insensibly been drawn in, to make use of language expressing the principles of this one, as if they were the real chains which Nature makes use of to bind together her several operations' (Smith 1980, p. 105). Schumpeter cited this work as the supreme example of the quality of Smith's mind. It is the most significant of the papers which Smith selected for preservation and publication after his death. The reference to the predicted return of Halley's Comet in 1758, as support for Newton's system (but not proof), indicates that the text was untouched after that date.

Smith's theory of knowledge emphasised the importance of focussed motivation, and was based on the strictly non-rational elements of surprise, wonder and admiration; the latter included the aesthetic appeal of 'systems as machines'—a concept which was explored by Alfred Marshall just over a century later—and the crucial role of imagination in the construction of new combinations, which is not a conspicuous feature of a general equilibrium model, although it may help in the creation of such a model. That knowledge is always provisional and future knowledge is always unpredictable has been recognised by scientists who have reflected on the nature of their enterprise. A relatively brief but powerful exposition was provided by John Ziman (1978); as his title, *Reliable Knowledge*, suggests, his focus is on the ways in which scientists try to ensure that their results are safe to use. A much more detailed version was produced later, somewhat provocatively called *Real Science* (Ziman 2000).

The emotional factors which are the explicit focus of *The Theory of Moral Sentiments* are essential elements in Smith's overall scheme for understanding the human situation and the human potential for good or ill—in comparison with which the scope of general equilibrium as a theoretical system is very limited. 'The same love of system, the same regard to the beauty of order, of art and contrivance, frequently serves to recommend those institutions which tend to promote the public welfare. … We take pleasure in beholding the perfection of so beautiful and grand a system' (Smith [1759] 1976a, p. 185); and this is 'a deception which rouses and keeps in continual motion the industry of mankind' (Smith [1759] 1976a, p. 183). These factors are prominent in Smith's (1983) *Lectures on Rhetoric*, where effective communication exploits our admiration for order. However, the 'beauty of order, of art and contrivance' may also lead us wildly astray, for example, by persuading the learned to accept Descartes' cosmology (Smith 1983, p. 146) and inducing the poor man's son to be guided by illusions of future comfort and status (Smith [1759]

1976a, p. 181). In economics this appeal of coherence and completeness has surely been a major inducement to represent the whole economic system in a model which incorporates every possible good, date, location and contingency.

In his *History of Astronomy*, Smith (1980, p. 77) observed 'how easily the learned give up the evidence of their senses in order to preserve the coherence of the ideas of their imagination', a phenomenon which we may observe in the history of economics, most obviously in the exaltation of general over partial equilibrium, which has significantly impeded our understanding of the working of economic systems—and also our understanding of Adam Smith, as Andrew Skinner well knew.

In *The Wealth of Nations* Smith explained how the creation of knowledge is promoted by a closer focus of attention on particular operations. This is achieved by a finer division of labour—even, as Smith insisted, among people whose abilities are very similar, because these abilities may be turned in somewhat different directions, and so deliver a wider range of knowledge. Smith's recognition of the human limitations which were emphasised by Hume is crucial, because they allow the division of labour to deliver benefits at two levels: people specialise on different activities and within each activity they may conceive and explore different options. If there is 'one best way' of performing any activity, no-one can be sure what it is—although quite often they believe that they have found it. Increasing affluence makes possible new divisions, which in turn may promote further increases in affluence.

This Smithian process is the justification for Marshall's law of increasing return—which is clearly not a property of a production function, to which it was wilfully degraded by model-builders without his vision, but a property of a cognitive process. For both Smith and Marshall the purpose of economic organisation is to promote the recognition, development and application of differentiated knowledge—where this differentiation was often a product of this organisation, notably the emergence of industrial districts, which facilitated variation and the diffusion of successful variants. By contrast the agent homogeneity which is assumed in models of perfect competition 'might reasonably be regarded as a denial of Adam Smith's central principle erected into a system of political economy' (Richardson 1975, p. 353).

The combination of coherence and change which was described by Smith required a particular kind of social system, which in turn depended on particular psychological attributes. 'Man, who can subsist only in society, was fitted by nature to that situation for which he was made' (Smith [1759] 1976a, p. 85). In an exploration of Smith's treatment of the relationship between moral philosophy and civil society, Skinner provides an admirable summary of Smith's view.

> [I]t is in *The Theory of Moral Sentiments* rather than *The Wealth of Nations* that Smith fully explained the psychological drives which support man's desire to better his condition, an argument that is linked in turn to the pursuit of wealth, the desire for status, and the admiration of our fellows.
>
> Equally important is Smith's analysis of self-interest and the need for constraint, where he established the point that men are led as if by an invisible hand to generate barriers against their unsocial passions by natural as distinct from artificial means. It will be noted that man's capacity to erect barriers against his self-interested passions, which is so essential for the orderly conduct of *economic* affairs, depends critically on his capacity for *moral* judgement. (Skinner 1996, p. 70)

Moral judgement, of course, has no role in the economics of rational choice, being replaced by preference functions which are beyond question—though we should note that welfare economics must exclude interpersonal preferences, which Smith's analysis clearly does not. (Nor does Alfred Marshall's.) We might note that moral judgement may be significant in decisions which are made under uncertainty, and since, as Frank Knight (1921, p. 268) observed, without uncertainty 'it is doubtful whether intelligence itself would exist', we may expect to find that interactions between intelligence and moral judgement are sometimes important. Adam Smith and Andrew Skinner would surely agree.

4 Hayek

The remarkable parallels and complementarities between Smith's theory of economic development and the evolutionary theory of the growth of knowledge through the development of domain-relevant connections which was subsequently developed by Marshall are now reasonably well known. Less widely recognised are the similarities between Smith's views and Hayek's evolving perspective on the necessary limitations of individual human knowledge, and the implications of these constraints for the organisation of both academic and economic systems.

Shackle went to the London School of Economics to work with Hayek, but was induced by accounts of Keynes's forthcoming book to change both his topic and his supervisor. However, we might wonder how Shackle might have reacted to indications of Hayek's continuing concern with the working of the human brain, which was not fully revealed until the publication of *The Sensory Order* (Hayek 1952) almost twenty years later. Hayek had served in the Austrian army in Italy in the final stage of the 1914–1918 War and had observed the contrast between the good order which was maintained by the artillery regiment in which he served (which did not surprise me when I eventually read about it) and the disorderly behaviour of some other troops when all were instructed to proceed to Vienna for discharge. As noted earlier, problems are defined by differences, and Hayek turned to psychology for a resolution of this particular difference. In his preface to *The Sensory Order*, he writes that his study of psychology led to an impasse: 'though I felt that I had found the answer to an important problem, I could not explain what the problem was' (Hayek 1952, p. v). It took him thirty years to construct his explanation; it was worth the wait, though one cannot help wondering about the cost to economists (including myself) of this long-delayed exposition.

Hayek was well aware that the concept of equilibrium, which seemed central to economic analysis, was intimately connected with that of the knowledge which was possessed by economic agents, or to which they could readily gain access, as of course were both Marshall and Keynes—but not Sraffa or Joan Robinson. In a paper entitled 'Economics and Knowledge', he asked 'to what extent formal economic analysis conveys any knowledge about what happens in the real world' (Hayek 1937, p. 33) and 'how much knowledge and what sort of knowledge the different individuals must possess in order that we may be able to speak of equilibrium' (Hayek 1937, p. 48). This led him to 'a problem of the *Division of Knowledge* which is quite analogous to, and at least as important as, the problem of the division of labour. It seems to be the really central problem of economics as a social science' (Hayek 1937, p. 49).

What now seems remarkable is Hayek's failure, at this time, to recognise the significance of Adam Smith's proposition, based on the conception of human knowledge as unrefuted conjectures, that the division of labour was the most effective means of organising the continuing creation of knowledge—even (significantly) if those choosing different specialisms had very similar cognitive potential, and the implication, of which Marshall was well aware, that the knowledge which is created by this process cannot be predicted in detail and cannot therefore be included in a model of general equilibrium.

Hayek may, however, be forgiven for being ignorant, at that time, of Smith's conception of human knowledge, both of individuals and within a particular community, as a cluster of unrefuted conjectures, each of which has been created by those who were especially concerned with a particular field of knowledge in order to create or restore order within that field, and which may subsequently need to be replaced when those individuals or that community cannot accommodate new evidence within that cluster. Almost all economists were probably equally ignorant, because the relevance of this conception, even to Smith's own subsequent work, had not yet been recognised. A comparison between Smith's and Hayek's conceptions of the problems and possibilities of human knowledge, and the ways of improving its quality, might be valuable, and this could be extended to include Marshall's approach to knowledge, as explored and illuminated by Raffaelli. It will however probably be sufficient here to outline Hayek's exploration of the process, the power and the limitations of human sense-making which he eventually presented in *The Sensory Order*, more than thirty years after his initial stimulus to understand diverse responses in a shared environment.

Hayek begins by noting that 'in order to give a satisfactory account of the regularities existing in the physical world the physical sciences have been forced to define the objects of which this world exists increasingly in terms of the observed relationships between these objects, and at the same time more and more to disregard the way in which these objects appear to us' (Hayek 1952, pp. 2–3). Therefore, 'events which to our senses may appear to be of the same kind may have to be treated as different in the physical order, while events which physically may be of the same or at least a similar kind may appear as altogether different to our senses' (Hayek 1952, p. 4). It is the sensory order with which Hayek is concerned; but it is worth noting that human beings may benefit from relying on different forms of order for different purposes.

'[T]he transmission of impulses from neuron to neuron within the central nervous system is ... conceived as the apparatus of classification' (Hayek 1952, p. 52). Now '[i]f sensory perception must be regarded as an act of classification, what we perceive can never be unique properties of individual objects but always only properties which the objects have in common with other objects. Perception is thus always an interpretation' (Hayek 1952, p. 142). Therefore, '[t]he qualities which we attribute to the experienced objects are strictly speaking not properties of that object at all, but a set of relations by which our nervous system classifies them. Or, to put it differently, *all* we know about the world is of the nature of theories and all 'experience' can do is to change those theories' (Hayek 1952, p. 143). Moreover, 'since all we can ever learn from experience are generalizations about certain kinds of events, and since no number of particular instances can ever prove such a generalization, knowledge based entirely on experience may yet be entirely false' (Hayek 1952, p. 168).

What is remarkable is the consilience between Hayek's conclusions and Adam Smith's account of sense-making in his *History of Astronomy*, which concludes with the observation that Newton's system works so well that even he, who has sought 'to represent all philosophical systems as mere inventions of the imagination' has 'been drawn in to make use of language expressing the connecting principles of this one as if they were the real chains which Nature makes use of to bind together her several operations' (Smith 1980, p. 105). There seems to be no indication that Hayek had any knowledge at this time of Smith's analysis of the motivation and the process of knowledge creation.

It is also worth noticing Hayek's recognition of an inherent problem which had been emphasised by David Hume: 'any apparatus of classification must possess a structure of a higher degree of complexity than is possessed by the objects that it classifies; and that, therefore, the capacity of any explaining agent must be limited to objects with a structure possessing a degree of complexity lower than its own. If this is correct, it means that no explaining agent can ever explain objects of its own kind, or of its own degree of complexity, and, therefore, that the human brain can never fully explain its own operations' (Hayek 1952, p. 185).

Smith, Marshall and Hayek all respected the crucial importance of individual human cognition as a scarce resource, unlike proponents of general equilibrium theory who require all goods to be defined not only by their inherent characteristics but also by their location, date and the state of the world at that date, and also require that knowledge of these characteristics is costlessly available to anyone who might be interested in any particular good which is defined in this way.

This shared perspective was recommended, and practised, by Nicholas Stern, who was interviewed in 2014 when he was President of the British Academy. He observed that his own career 'would have been very hard to predict. That is one of the joys of life. It is central to the work of Friedrich Hayek. He and Karl Popper (both Professors at the LSE and Fellows of the British Academy) tried to explain that the inability to predict is central, not just to the human condition, but also to the ways in which economies work and function. Recognising the role of discovery, recognising that we cannot know everything – and it would be a very boring and unproductive world if we did – is key to much of our understanding of the human condition, whether that be through literature, history or economics' (Stern 2014, p. 2). Later in this interview, Stern described Hayek as 'an extraordinarily influential economist and philosopher, who focused on discovery, the role of markets in discovery, the centrality of discovery to the human condition and the human purpose and, indeed, how economies worked' (Stern 2014, p. 5).

Since Stern's interview was designed to be published with ten others in order to reflect the range of scholarly interests within the British Academy, it is not surprising that he made no comparisons between the perspectives of Hayek and those of Smith and Marshall, not only on the use of knowledge in economic systems but also on the crucial role of economic systems, and of systems of economic thought, as creators of knowledge. However, it would be appropriate to conclude by making a fundamental contrast between two perspectives on economics as a field of study. One is that the objective is to construct models which assist the efficient allocation of known resources, and efficient allocation can be ensured only within a closed system: hence the enduring appeal of general equilibrium, in which all possibilities are assumed to be known, as the prime focus of attention. The other is that the objective is to improve our understanding of the processes by which economic systems can create knowledge—not least knowledge which has not yet been imagined. (As we have seen, these processes were explored by Adam Smith both in his *History of Astronomy* and in the *Wealth of Nations*.) Yet 'knowledge' suggests reliability, which in turn suggests equilibrium; hence the attraction of 'partial equilibrium', limited in scope and potentially in duration, to those, like Marshall, who were especially concerned with the improvement and application of knowledge by encouraging the development of differentiated foci of attention, not only within an economy but also between economies, as exemplified by his comparison of France, Germany and the United States in *Industry and Trade* (Marshall 1919).

It is not difficult to see why 'partial equilibrium' should be interpreted as incomplete and therefore unsatisfactory as a basis for understanding. However, since Hume (at least) it has been clear that all human knowledge is necessarily provisional, and certainly incomplete. Smith, having illustrated this in his *History of Astronomy*, subsequently explained how useful knowledge, which is appropriate to particular circumstances, could be generated by the development of differentiated forms of organisation which matched human potential. As Raffaelli has explained, Marshall's understanding of the human mind underpinned his recognition of differences, both between and within trades, as drivers of progress, in ways which seem compatible with Hayek's analysis in *The Sensory Order* as well as Smith's theory of the incentives and processes of knowledge creation. Such differentiation normally permitted an economy to function effectively without fulfilling the strict requirements of a general equilibrium, and, as Smith, Marshall and Hayek all desired, could therefore be a continuing generator of useful knowledge.

References

Barnard, Chester I. (1938) *The Functions of the Executive*. Cambridge, MA: Harvard University Press.

Burns, Tom and Stalker, G. M. (1961) *The Management of Innovation*. London: Tavistock.

Carter, Charles F. (1962) An Experiment in Business Research. *Westminster Bank Review*, February, pp. 2–11.

Coase, Ronald H. ([1972] 1988) *The Firm, the Market and the Law*. Chicago: University of Chicago Press.

Coase, Ronald H. (1991) The Institutional Structure of Production. In Oliver E. Williamson and Sidney G. Winter (eds) *The Nature of the Firm: Origins, Evolution and Development*. Oxford: Oxford University Press.

Cyert, Richard M. and March, James G. (1963) *A Behavioral Theory of the Firm*. Englewood Cliffs, NJ: Prentice-Hall.

Hayek, F. A. (1937) Economics and Knowledge. *Economica* 4, pp. 33–54.

Hayek, F. A. (1952) *The Sensory Order*. Chicago: University of Chicago Press.

Knight, F. A. (1921) *Risk, Uncertainty and Profit*. Boston, MA: Houghton Mifflin.

Marshall, Alfred (1919) *Industry and Trade*. London: Macmillan.

Marshall, Alfred (1961) *Principles of Economics*, 9th (variorum) edn. 2 vols. London: Macmillan.

Raffaelli, Tiziano (2003) *Marshall's Evolutionary Economics*. London and New York: Routledge.

Richardson, George B. (1975) Adam Smith on Competition and Increasing Returns. In A. S. Skinner and T. Wilson (eds) *Essays on Adam Smith*. Oxford: Oxford University Press.

Shackle, George L. S. (1969) *Decision, Order and Time in Human Affairs*, 2nd edn. Cambridge: Cambridge University Press.

Shackle, George L. S. (1970) *Expectation, Enterprise and Profit: The Theory of the Firm*. London: Allen and Unwin.

Skinner, Andrew S. (1996) *A System of Social Science; Papers Relating to Adam Smith*. Oxford: Clarendon Press.

Smith, Adam ([1759] 1976a) *The Theory of Moral Sentiments*. Edited by D. D. Raphael and A. L. Macfie. Oxford: Clarendon Press.

Smith, Adam ([1776] 1976b) *An Inquiry into the Nature and Causes of the Wealth of Nations*. 2 vols. Oxford: Clarendon Press.

Smith, Adam (1980) The Principles Which Lead and Direct Philosophical Enquiries: Illustrated by the History of Astronomy. In Adam Smith, *Essays on Philosophical Subjects*, edited by W. P. D. Wightman and J. C. Bryce. Oxford: Clarendon Press.

Smith, Adam (1983) *Lectures on Rhetoric and Belles Lettres*, edited by J. C. Bryce. Oxford: Clarendon Press.

Stern, Nicholas (2014) Interview in *British Academy Review* 23, pp. 2–9.

Temin, Peter, with Galambos, Louis (1987) *The Fall of the Bell System*. Cambridge: Cambridge University Press.

Williams, Bruce (2004) Charles Frederick Carter, 1919–2002. *Proceedings of the British Academy 124: Biographical Memoirs of Fellows*, pp. 37–47.

Young, Allyn (1928) Increasing Returns and Economic Progress. *Economic Journal* 38, pp. 527–542.

Ziman, John (1978) *Reliable Knowledge*. Cambridge: Cambridge University Press.

Ziman, John (2000) *Real Science*. Cambridge: Cambridge University Press.

Raffaelli on Historical Progress in Smith and in Marshall

Cosimo Perrotta

This paper has a twofold aim. First, to bring together in summary the remarkable analyses that Raffaelli has left us on Smith's and Marshall's views on historical progress. These analyses are now scattered throughout many publications, and having them in a orderly recapitulation may show just how useful they can be for a better understanding of the idea of historical progress.

The second aim is to see how far the similarity between Smith's and Marshall's views on this subject can be seen to go. Raffaelli carried out his analyses of Marshall and Smith side-by-side. Occasionally, he suggested a similarity or a sort of continuity between the two authors, but—with the scientific prudence—went no further.

In Sects. 1–2, we will take a look at Raffaelli's analysis of Smith, with some comments, and, in Sects. 3–4, his pioneering analysis of the young Marshall's philosophical writings. The final section is devoted to a comparison between Smith and Marshall on historical progress.

C. Perrotta (✉)
University of Salento, Lecce, Italy

K. Caldari et al. (eds.), *Marshall and the Marshallian Heritage*,
Palgrave Studies in the History of Economic Thought,
https://doi.org/10.1007/978-3-030-53032-7_3

1 Sympathy and Impersonal Relationships in Smith

Raffaelli's works on Smith are no less insightful than those on Marshall. In a basic article (R. 1994b), our author points out that Smith's interpretation of modern society provides, on the one hand, a brilliant overview of the long series of deliberations of past authors, from Hobbes to Kames and Millar, and, on the other, goes much further than the previous analyses.

One of the key points is the difference between sympathy and benevolence. Raffaelli proves that Smith's commentators have often confused these two attitudes, while they are clearly contrasted with each other in both Hume and Smith.[1] Sympathy is the wish to be appreciated by others. It leads men to envy and imitate the persons who are above in the social ranks (it is the tendency today called imitation or the Duesenberry effect). This sentiment generates competition. Thus, sympathy is far from solidarity or protective feelings. Contrary to benevolence, sympathy goes hand in hand with self-interest and the desire to better one's own condition. This is the very basis of the new economy, which is founded on the competitive pursuit of profit.[2]

This gives rise to a series of consequences. The rise of the bourgeoisie—the class which promotes modern society—advances along with increase in wealth. Wealth is actually produced by the main components of this class: entrepreneurs, merchants, artisans and professionals. The pursuit of wealth is competitive but it takes place in a context of fair rules, in which each can obtain in proportion to what he produces. The context is determined, but the results depend on the respective merits. While—according to Max Weber—wealth is seen by the protestants as a sign of divine grace, in Smith it is the result of human impersonal relationships. Thus, in Smith, the wish to enrich oneself is anthropologically legitimised and morally positive (R. 1994b: 212).

There are some important corollaries to this analysis. First of all, Hume and Smith reject the time-honoured primacy of the contemplative over the active life. This primacy was best expressed by Aristotle and revived by Pascal (but, we may add, it was severely criticised by the humanists, the

[1] See Raffaelli (from now on: R., in the notes) (1994b: 225; 1996a: 13–8).

[2] R. (1994b: 206–8; 1996a: 23).

protestants and finally by the Enlightenment authors).[3] Secondly, Raffaelli does not deny that Smith's metaphor of the invisible hand can imply a providential design, but he claims that it can also be interpreted in a fully naturalistic way. What matters is that the invisible hand metaphor excludes the possibility that the whole process can be the output of a subjective project.

Modern society is based on exchange. For instance, exchange drives landlords to give up their command over men and turn to the possession of material objects, like luxury ornaments, which satisfy their childish vanity (this point is effectively made by Smith and Malthus).[4] From exchange comes the new social order. But all this has nothing to do with benevolence and generosity. As Hume—who inspired Smith—writes in his *Treatise*, benevolence and generosity lead to favouring relatives and friends, while obstructing the objective mechanism of competition and exchange, which is based on self-interest. But only Smith, Raffaelli notes, conceived of the complex social machine that controls the race for enrichment in all its main aspects (R. 1994b: 222).

Thus, the hierarchy of mercantile society no longer depends on privileges and prevarication but derives from the market, the impersonal mechanism which distributes wealth according to self-interest and merit. Steuart too states that individuals in a free society shake off personal dependence to depend only on their own labour, but he fails to see that the mechanism derives from the market. This is why he outlines the evolution of society as following the "natural" order: first agriculture evolves, then the state, then commerce. On the contrary, according to Smith, in real history manufacture preceded the development of agriculture and the state, although this is not the natural order (ibid.: 223).

Sympathy, adds Raffaelli, is also the source of the personal sense of justice on which law is based. Smith, following Montesquieu, states that justice is the substitute for beneficence.[5] It creates "anonymous relations between independent individuals that are promoted by commercial society". In the latter, the "substitution of justice for beneficence is

[3] On this see Perrotta (2004: 22, 92–4, 160–1, and 231–40).

[4] See Perrotta (2018: 28–9, 39).

[5] R. (1996a: 18fn) stresses the difference, already stated by Hume, between benevolence and beneficence as to their social effects. While the former "is ineffective as a motive to human actions", the latter "is very effective in inner circles but inadequate to the wide relations of commercial society".

no accident". As for his moral duties, in the economic sphere "man is dispensed from the requirement of knowledge of the whole system. It is prices which set the rules and afford enough knowledge for economic behaviour" (R. 1996a: 18).

Raffaelli recalls the passage in Mandeville that inspired Smith. It says that money and prices, by measuring the worth of everything, enable society not to overrate itself, as happens to individuals (ibid.: 27–8). Now, in order to establish social distinctions, Hume and Smith look for a similar objective criterion. In commercial society, wealth becomes the best expression of social estimation because it is measurable and impersonal.[6] Finally, the virtue of prudence also has nothing to do with benevolence or altruism. Prudence is the ability to foresee and calculate one's own interest in order to avoid irrational risks.

Having stated so much, Raffaelli notes, Smith's trust in the market is not blind or extreme. For instance, he calls for the state control of the banks and public regulation of the interest rate, against the tendency to speculation (R. 1994b: 223, 228). Thus, Smith provides an overall, coherent and innovative theory of modern society.

2 Development and Historical Progress in Smith

Admittedly, there are some discrepancies in Smith's thought, which Raffaelli records point by point but does not comment on. For instance, as we have seen, Smith revives the ancient and physiocratic idea of the primacy of agriculture. In this connection, he holds that development should start from agriculture because this is the first and most essential sector of production (he keeps in mind the theory of stages, which was very widespread in his time). Only later would development involve manufacture and trade. Moreover, for Smith, landlords should rule society because, due to their "generosity", they can represent the general interest.

However, Smith—showing his independence from any a priori approach—acknowledges that modern development has started with commerce and manufacture, with merchants, artisans and entrepreneurs. It was, as he says, "retrograde". On the other hand, while landlords gave up their natural vocation to rule society for the vanity to possess nice and

[6] R. (1994b: 211–2; 1996a: 20–3).

useless luxuries, merchants prevailed in the long run due to their pettiness and avarice.[7]

We may, then, say that Smith appears passionate and disenchanted at the same time. He has a keen awareness of the progress and civilisation generated by accumulation, but he has no illusion that this means a progress in virtue. He seems to have been inspired by Mandeville much more than he was ready to admit.

Another flaw in modern society that Smith himself recognises is the fact that political society, unlike the economy, functions in an imperfect and non-impersonal way.[8]

But all the threads seem to fall into place with the Smithian theory of the division of labour.[9] First of all, says Raffaelli, Smith wrongly assumes that the division of labour derives from the propensity of men to exchange, and not the reverse. Anyhow, for Smith the division of labour is the crucial factor of progress and development, due to the continual increase in productivity it causes. Productivity, Smith recognises, can grow in manufactures much more than in agriculture.

Smith maintains that the division of labour does not derive from the natural differences among men. On the contrary, it is these differences that are produced, in a large part, by the division of labour which, besides productivity, also enhances mankind's abilities and knowledge. In primitive times there were few different occupations in society but many in the individual. Along with the growth of the division of labour (i.e. of specialisation), occupations in society multiplied while the tasks of an individual diminished. As in the case of the market, this process is not due to a subjective project. It is the spontaneous outcome of resolving a number of technical difficulties in production activity.

From this approach, Raffaelli infers a suggestive parallel between Smith's division of labour and an evolutionary perspective (R. 2001a: 43–5). The first chapter of the *Wealth of Nations*, he says, represents in embryo a very treaty of science of organisation. In the middle of the nineteenth century, the division of labour was explicitly mentioned by Milne-Edwards, a Belgian zoologist, drawing a comparison with the differentiation of functions in an organism.

[7] R. (1994b, passim; 2001a: 197).

[8] See for ex. R. (1996a: 30; 2001a: 196–8).

[9] R. (2001a: 38–47).

This parallel influenced Darwin when he had to solve a crucial point in the theory of evolution: What determines differences in nature and the variety of organisms which derives from them? They were due, Darwin maintained, to the comparative advantage offered by specialisation. It is this that promotes new species. Raffaelli stresses that Darwin derived this view from the economists (he probably refers to Darwin's observation that he was inspired by Malthus's theory of population).[10]

But this was not all. Smith himself, according to Raffaelli, applied the principles of the division of labour to mental activities.[11] Also, the mathematician Prony, when routinising the repetitive calculations of logarithms, was inspired by Smith's description of pin-making and divided his team into groups with different tasks. Finally, Babbage mentioned Prony when stating that the economic division of labour paved the way to high-level research activities in the mind. He set out to mechanise calculations according to the principles of the "mental division of labour".

Loasby confirms Raffaelli's view: what connects Smith to Darwin and Marshall is the twofold process of specialisation and routinisation of learning.[12] Raffaelli writes that Marshall developed this stream of thought to the point of considering organisation as a specific production factor, which puts together specialisation and innovation and makes accumulation a more complex mechanism.

3 Evolution in Marshall

In the 1990s there was a burgeoning of excellent studies which cast new light on Marshall's scientific personality. To this reconsideration Raffaelli, as both Rizzello and Becattini explain,[13] gave a remarkable contribution by showing that, according to Marshall, the evolutionary economic and social processes have their roots in the human mind. They are first of all mental processes.

Raffaelli commented on four manuscripts by the young Marshall, written in the late 1860s, and published them as *Alfred Marshall's Early Philosophical Writings* [1994]: *The Law of Parcimony* (1867); *Ferrier's*

[10] Darwin (1859, Introduction: 4–5).

[11] Probably he refers to Smith (1776, 1.X, Part 1).

[12] Loasby (2003: 211–4).

[13] Rizzello (1997, ch. 3.2), Becattini (2003: 18–9).

Proposition One; *Ye Machine*; and *The Duty of the Logician*. In these works, Marshall explores the possibility of a mechanical and evolutionary interpretation of knowledge. Particularly in *Ye (The) Machine* he imagines an "automaton", i.e. a mechanical construction where connections are established similar to those of the human mind. Raffaelli shows that Marshall arrives at his theses through critical examination of the philosophical/anthropological debate of the 1850s–1860s. Here, we can only describe the essence of Raffaelli's insightful reconstruction.[14]

Marshall was influenced by Mansel, who—following in the footsteps of Kant—had stated the limits of reason. Thus Marshall became aware that science did not rely on an absolute rationality. Science can only contribute to casting light on some limited aspects of reality, although this limit can be ever more extended.

Also, the British empiricist tradition suggests that human actions are external to reason. Reason is a mere instrument which refines pre-rational elements. This view leads to an evolutionary vision. In *The Law of Parcimony*, Marshall describes the growth process of the mind according to the principles of associationism and evolutionism suggested by Darwin.[15] Marshall was increasingly attracted to biological evolutionism, although he retained the principle of self-consciousness—against the absolute empiricism of J.S. Mill—in order to avoid determinism. However, Marshall, at this stage, already held that, except self-consciousness, everything could be explained with the evolution of purely mechanical agents.

In the 1860s–1870s neurophysiologists and philosophers agreed that the nervous system was the source of knowledge. This system consisted of a series of stimulus-feedback circuits of different degrees of complexity, following the chain impressions-sensations-emotions-ideas. However, while the external stimuli cause simple—i.e. automatic—feedbacks, the more complex itineraries of mind produce actions which are automatic on a secondary level. The human automatic feedback can derive from either original or acquired instincts.

The philosopher Bain and the physiologist Carpenter—Raffaelli explains—then maintained that complex actions initially required

[14] See especially sections 2 and 3 of R. (1990). A similar analysis can be found in R. (1991, 1994a).

[15] See Darwin (1871, vol. 1, chs. II, III and V).

conscious attention and active will, but through repetition they became automatic. Spencer provided an evolutionary explanation of the working of the nervous system.

All these authors inspired Marshall in the description of the mental machine. In this machine there are wheels connected by belts which show the process of learning. The latter proceeds by trial and error. At first, effective actions are performed by chance, then they are memorised, retried and finally automatised. Marshall also contemplated the possibility that this association may be hereditary, suggesting a view of instincts as due to evolution.

This process, Raffaelli comments, relieves the machine of the burden of having to devote its attention to performing tasks that can be delegated to automatic feedback (routines). This relief liberates energies that allow the machine to create new routines in circumstances in which those already available do not suffice. Its creativity thus depends on the set of automatic feedback circuits stored in its nervous system, while at the same time creativity modifies the latter and cannot be reduced to it. Here, Marshall resorts to the important notion of "character" in the evolutionary interpretation that Raffaelli traces back to the scientist and mathematician William Clifford, a close friend of Marshall's during this phase. Determined by the range and rapidity of the set of feedback circuits available to the machine, character evolves in reaction to external stimuli by combining "plasticity", i.e. the ability to create new routines in the face of novelties, with "stability"—the ability to store the new routines in its nervous system and thus to progress into a more complex mental organisation.

In this interpretation character means an ability to use routines without completely surrendering to them, an ability that constitutes a sort of mobile capital, which can go in various directions and increase the organism's plasticity. This is why, notes Raffaelli, Marshall in his economic analyses insists on the dangers of excessive specialisation of workers and the necessity of general education (like Smith, we can say).

The notion of character opens the door to another important question: races among men. In those times social scientists used very much the concept of race in outlining the hierarchy among nations.[16] Such hierarchy indicates at the same time the different ranks of the countries in the economy and in civilisation.

Raffaelli retraces the analytical source of Marshall's approach on this subject. In the last part of his reconstruction (R. 1990, section 5) he observes that for Marshall the evolution of the race is based on two interpretations of the notion of character both present in *Ye Machine*: the first is character defined as the power of the subject of anticipating the future and will play an important role in the *Principles* in explaining the willingness to invest in physical and human capital; the other, that Marshall calls "moral character" is identified with sympathy (a concept, notes Raffaelli, taken from the Scottish moral philosophy and from J.S. Mill). Sympathy is a bridge between selfishness and altruism, and it applies first to the family, then to community, nation and race.

It should be stressed that, for Marshall, altruism increases the ability of survival of human societies; then natural selection preserves those races in which the principle of sympathy is more powerful. This is also proved in the so-called social animals, like bees or ants. The same analysis appears in the *Principles of Economics*. This gives Marshall the possibility of stating that utilitarianism as an ethical doctrine is perfectly compatible with evolutionism provided it pursues happiness for all, not only for the individual.[17]

Thus, both tendencies—that which pursues one's own welfare and that aiming at the general welfare—are due to natural selection and evolution. They are developed by a slow accumulation of automatic instincts. Thanks to the automatisation of inferior mental procedures, consciousness and will can extend their influence to the higher tasks. As the creative intellectual actions go beyond the routine associations, in the same way moral creative actions express a degree of sympathy higher that that already fixed in moral instincts.

4 Historical Progress in Marshall

Raffaelli, in a later note (R. 1995), links Marshall's analysis of the working of the mind to his view of social progress more clearly. Through a system of rewards and punishments, the institutions have the task of

[16] This too derived from Darwin (1871, vol. 1, chs. V and VII).

[17] See also R. (1996b, Sect. VII).

making socially useful behaviours increasingly automatic so that altruistic behaviours extend in the market economy. Social progress mainly consists in creative human labour and workers' welfare. This goal is achieved through the two complementary principles of human evolution: the cumulative process of routines and the creativity of the human mind. Thus, "human nature itself is a never-ending process".[18]

In another illuminating article, Raffaelli explains how Marshall explicitly applies his analysis of the working of mind to the organisation of industry and business. He writes: "in order to work effectively, social organization must rely, as far as possible, on automatic mechanisms".[19] And also: "The social equivalent of this mental process is the building up of specialized functions that enable human societies to concentrate their mental energy … on the most difficult and urgent tasks" (ibid.). Then, automatism can also invest the upper levels of organisation, like coordination.

However, the convergence of so many tasks and processes in a harmonised mechanism cannot be the result of some form of conscious, concentrated power, because the variables are too many and subjective direction of them would be overburdened and would fail. Like Smith—says Raffaelli—Marshall believes that this process is the outcome of mechanical selection. Herbert Simon picked up this tradition.

One specific aspect of routinisation was noted in particular by Smith and J.S. Mill. They were worried that automatism and technical progress could depress and dull the minds of workers. Against this danger, Marx maintained that, in order to free the mental potentialities of individuals, a new social organisation was needed. But his approach came up against the impossibility of subjective direction of all the processes (ibid.: 215–7).

Actually, Marshall was aware that the automatic processes do not solve all the problems. He sees the division of labour as a mechanisation process similar to mental working. Standardisation transfers to external things the mental procedures "that simplify the handling of information". However, Raffaelli notes, Darwin himself realised that evolutionary success can have negative side-effects, like damage to the environment. And Marshall admits that the success of a species or of a society is no proof

[18] R. (2000: 19).

[19] R. (2001b: 215).

of their goodness, "but only of their ability to exploit the environment" (ibid.: 218).

The consequence is that Marshall takes a highly problematic view of social evolution,[20] which he sees as "short-sighted"; it works by "local" adaptations, and the final results are not guaranteed. There are numberless cases in which the need for social order sacrifices the mental energies of individuals. One of the most striking examples is to be seen in castes. The trouble is that the division of labour, especially in the Taylorist version, resembles the caste system, insofar as in it, too, the individual is sacrificed to social stability.

Thus, the conflict between order and creativity can arise within the context of technical progress itself. As Raffaelli effectively explains, "like any automatism, machines hinder progress whenever their management requires too much energy and instead of serving human life - that is creativity and freedom - actually becomes a substitute for life itself", while "Automatisms always tend to come out of their proper place and invade life". As Marshall himself graphically summarised, "Progress is the development of order", but at the same time "order is an evil".[21] This antinomy is well expressed by Arena in the relationship between institutions and customs.[22] Arena provides an analysis of the relationship in Marshall between organisation and knowledge which is different from but substantially convergent with that proposed by Raffaelli.

The very cause of the problematic nature of the processes which govern both knowledge and organisation is the fact that Darwinian evolution has no goals. This makes its results uncertain. This is why Marshall asks for subjective intervention by man, to prepare "the next step" of development. For example, in Marshall protection of mental creativity implies that education should avoid excessively early specialisation.[23] Reisman appropriately stresses the central role, for social development, that Marshall attributes to education. He also recalls the many cases in which Marshall

[20] See also Groenewegen (2003: 115–24).

[21] R. (2001b), respectively: 219 and 227, fn. 14.

[22] Arena (2003: 231–5).

[23] See also Perrotta (2018: 108–9).

calls for state intervention to counter market failures.[24] Groenewegen provides other examples of this attitude in Marshall.[25]

Raffaelli remarks that, for Marshall, "the chief aim of the economic system is to preserve and increase the springs of progress, mental energy in particular". Market processes are to be preferred in general, but they must be opposed "whenever they hinder new opportunities for change". Actually, "automatic forces do not converge" (ibid.: 220–1). The same progressive but problematic vision of Marshall emerges in Dardi (1991). Dardi effectively contrasts Marshall's individual, who changes according to the social group and its improvements, with the neo-classical view, especially that of the present times, when the individual is a solitary rational machine aiming only at optimisation of gains.

The same uncertainty regulates the dynamics between economies of scale and external economies. Big and small enterprises have both their own advantages and disadvantages. In general, however, the small business more effectively resists the tendency to bureaucracy of big business, i.e. the tendency to hinder mental energy and creativity due to their organisational needs. Marshall made effective use of this argument in explaining the stability and success of agglomerations of small firms organised in "industrial districts" and other kinds of local productive systems.[26]

5 Comparison Between Smith and Marshall on Historical Progress

Raffaelli has the merit of examining Smith's *Theory of Moral Sentiments* and the *Wealth of Nations* as a homogeneous scientific project. He goes on to confute the imaginary conflicts between the two books (the so-called *Adam Smith Problem*). With this approach, Raffaelli shows that Smith created the matrix—which, more or less unawares, has been used by all the later social scientists—for interpreting both medieval and modern society, with their respective economic and moral structure.

Medieval society was not based on impersonal relationships but on a system of different obligations or exemptions according to the social

[24] Reisman (2003: 64–5).

[25] Groenewegen (2003), especially: 124–30.

[26] See also R. (2003: 254–68).

status of individuals. It was a static society, based on the oppression of producers, on benevolence and charity, in which the wealth of the privileged was not used to acquire comforts but to dominate others.

In modern society, on the contrary, the main values are independence, free labour, possibility of enrichment, merit and competition. Modern society rejects personal relationships as the basic network of society and supplants them with impersonal relationships. This crucial passage is due to economic exchange, which substitutes benevolent or hostile contacts among individuals with relationships based on self-interest. Only modern society can promote ability, industry, knowledge, intelligence and competition based on merit. It creates spontaneous evaluation and selection procedures. The outputs of all this are freedom on the one hand and growing wealth on the other.

Of course, this achievement by Smith is the arrival point of a long process of hard thinking, running through the entire seventeenth century before arriving at the Enlightenment. Thus, for Smith, social evolution is determined by the innate tendency of men to strive for self-betterment. This process is guided by a spontaneous mechanism in which obstacles are overcome by the most efficient attempt to solve a certain problem. Individual self-interest generates exchange, which already implies competition, i.e. regulated conflict. The market, the sum of all exchanges, reduces the individual activities promoted by self-interest to a dimension which is compatible with the interests of others. The tool for this harmonisation is prices, which are settled through agreements among individuals.

The free practice of self-interest triggers the production of wealth and boosts the division of labour. The latter develops in pursuit of higher productivity. All these processes are based on contracts and agreements aiming at fulfilling individuals' self-interest. Each individual realises his own interest only through the mutual realisation of the others' interest. This is why competition—not benevolence—generates respect for others and justice. We owe to Raffaelli this clear and harmonious interpretation of Smith.

Raffaelli also stresses that Smith's vision is not fideistic or extreme. Conflicts continue to be present in all the phases of social evolution. The ruling classes are so keen in pursuing their own interests that they must be checked in order to make them represent or at least respect the general interest. This, according to Smith, opens the way to possible interventions by the state which can supplement or correct the market.

In the end, can we—like Raffaelli—speak of an evolutionary vision in Smith? We certainly can, but not in the same sense the term had subsequent to Darwin. The continuity suggested by Raffaelli refers to the internal logic of the analysis. But on the cultural level, of course things are very different. In Smith, too, social evolution is based on conflict and competition. However, the result of conflict appears more uncertain. Not always can class conflict be settled, and often the state represents the general interest as opposed to the particular interests of groups.

On the contrary, in the Darwinian approach of the late nineteenth century, and especially in Spencer, classes are supplanted by nations and nations are distributed in a sort of hierarchy of civilisation which reflects the different degrees of evolution. That of Spencer was a dubious radicalisation of the approach taken by Darwin himself (see above, fn. 16), giving evolution a deterministic flavour which is not to be found in Smith.

Marshall—like Smith—has a flexible and problematic interpretation of evolution, far from the rigid approach of "social Darwinism". His reading of history owes as much to his evolutionary frame of ideas as to his early meditation of historical-philosophical texts, especially by Maine and Hegel, as is well illustrated by Cook (2009).

Marshall is also worried that routines and bureaucracy, although necessary to evolution, can hinder creativity and mental freedom. This would damage first of all the workers. We perceive in Marshall concern for the spiritual progress of the lower classes as a requisite for their welfare, which is why education is the very driving force of progress in Marshall.

This approach is effectively expressed by Loasby, who writes that efficient institutions "are expected to generate variety", which is—in Marshall's words—"a chief cause of progress". This also includes the variety within a species. On the contrary, "perfect competition is inefficient because it requires homogeneity". The task of institutions is—through variety—"to preserve and enhance what is beneficial and discard what is harmful or merely inferior".[27]

Now, education is the spring of both specialisation and intellectual creativity (variety). Marshall establishes a close relationship between three factors: growth in skill and intellectual labour, improvement of social education and increase of material wealth. He also stresses that the increases in consumption and spending on education by the families have

[27] Loasby (1991: 123–4).

decisive and cumulative effects on the productivity of both the individual and society.[28] For instance, he writes: "No change would conduce so much to a rapid increase of material wealth as an improvement in our schools" (ibid.: 212). And, again, spending on education is "profitable as a mere investment" (ibid.: 216).

Thus, Marshall's social project—just as Smith's—includes increase in welfare, especially for the lower classes, through increase of creativity. This view requires a certain optimism, as aptly remarked by Reisman (1991). See also Caldari (2004).

What actually differentiates Smith and Marshall is the use of history. On this point, both authors give full expression to their own times. Smith has an acute sense of the obstacles that progressive processes have constantly to face. They are hindered by the conservative social forces, which defend the old privileges. Marshall on the contrary, despite his problematic and complex vision and his keen concern for the lower classes, in a sense shares the satisfied optimism of the Victorian bourgeoisie.

He has been criticised for having the idea of a hierarchy between nations and races, but this view was commonplace in his time. Besides, at the time economics was adopting the model of physics, together with methodological individualism and Pareto optimality, i.e. doing away with any historical and social approach, it was Marshall who defended a broader vision for economics and gave truly progressive sense to evolution.

References

Arena, Richard (2003) "Organization and Knowledge in Alfred Marshall's Economics", in Richard Arena and Michel Quéré, eds., *The Economics of Alfred Marshall: Revisiting Marshall's Legacy*, Basingstoke and New York: Palgrave Macmillan: 221–39.

Becattini, Giacomo (2003) "The Return of the 'White Elephant'", in Richard Arena and Michel Quéré, eds., *The Economics of Alfred Marshall: Revisiting Marshall's Legacy*, Basingstoke and New York: Palgrave Macmillan: 13–31.

Caldari, Katia (2004) "Alfred Marshall's Idea of Progress and Sustainable Development", *Journal of the History of Economic Thought*, December: 519–36.

[28] Marshall (1890, book IV, chs. v–vi). See also book VI, chs. iv–v.

Cook, Simon J. (2009) *The Intellectuals Foundations of Alfred Marshall's Economic Science: A Rounded Globe of Knowledge*, New York: Cambridge University Press.

Dardi, Marco (1991) "The Concept and Role of the Individual in Marshallian Economics", *Quaderni di storia dell'economia politica*, IX/2–3: 89–114.

Darwin, Charles (1859) *On the Origin of Species*, London: J. Murray, first ed., online: J. Van Wyhe and S. Asscher eds., 2002, from The Balfour and Newton Libraries, Cambridge.

_____ (1871) *The Descent of Man*, London: J. Murray, first ed., online: J. Van Wyhe ed., 2006, from The Balfour and Newton Libraries, Cambridge.

Groenewegen, Peter (2003) "Competition and Evolution: The Marshallian Conciliation Enterprise", in Richard Arena and Michel Quéré, eds., *The Economics of Alfred Marshall: Revisiting Marshall's Legacy*, Basingstoke and New York: Palgrave Macmillan: 111–33.

Loasby, Brian J. (1991) "Efficient Institutions", *Quaderni di storia dell'economia politica*, IX/2–3: 115–31.

_____ (2003) "Efficiency and Time", in Richard Arena and Michel Quéré, eds., *The Economics of Alfred Marshall: Revisiting Marshall's Legacy*, Basingstoke and New York: Palgrave Macmillan: 202–20.

Marshall, Alfred (1890) *Principles of Economics*, eighth ed., London: Macmillan, 1920, online: Library of Economics and Liberty.

_____ (1994) *Early Philosophical Writings*, T. Raffaelli, ed., Greenwich, CT: JAI Press, Part II: 95–159.

Perrotta, Cosimo (2004) *Consumption as an Investment: I*, London and New York: Routledge.

_____ (2018) *Unproductive Labour in Political Economy*, London and New York: Routledge.

Raffaelli, Tiziano (1990) "Gli studi filosofici del giovane Marshall", Roma: Accademia Nazionale dei Lincei, IX.I: 121–60.

_____ (1991) "The Analysis of the Human Mind in the Early Marshallian Manuscripts", *Quaderni di storia dell'economia politica*, IX/2–3: 29–58.

_____ (1994a) "Marshall's Analysis of the Human Mind", Part 1 of *Early Philosophical Writings of Alfred Marshall*, JAI Press: 53–93.

_____ (1994b) "Dalla teoria delle passioni al nuovo ordine: mercato e capitalismo in Adam Smith", *Moneta e Credito*, giugno 1994: 203–31.

_____ (1995) "Order and Creativity in Marshall's Views of Social Progress", *Kwansei Gakuin University Annual Studies*, Nishnomiya (Japan), XLIV: 199–207.

_____ (1996a) "Human Psychology and the Social Order", *History of Economics Ideas*, 1996/1–2: 5–34.

_____ (1996b) "Utilitarian Premises and the Evolutionary Framework of Marshall's Economics", *Utilitas*, 1996/1: 89–108.

_____ (2000) "The Marshallian Heritage", *Annali della Facoltà di Economia di Cagliari*, Milano: Franco Angeli: 13–20.

_____ (2001a) *La ricchezza delle nazioni. Introduzione alla lettura*, Roma: Carocci.

_____ (2001b) "Marshall on Mind and Society: Neuropsychological Models Applied to Industrial and Business Organization", *European Journal of the History of Economic Thought*, Summer: 208–29.

_____ (2003) "Requirements and Patterns of Marshallian Evolution: The Impact of the Notion of Industrial District", in Richard Arena and Michel Quéré, eds., *The Economics of Alfred Marshall: Revisiting Marshall's Legacy*, Basingstoke and New York: Palgrave Macmillan: 234–68.

Reisman, David A. (1991) "Conservative Capitalism: Alfred Marshall", *Quaderni di storia dell'economia politica*, IX/2–3: 215–33.

——— (2003) "Alfred Marshall on Social Capital", in Richard Arena and Michel Quéré, eds., *The Economics of Alfred Marshall: Revisiting Marshall's Legacy*, Basingstoke and New York: Palgrave Macmillan: 53–66.

Rizzello, Salvatore (1997) *The Economics of Mind*, English ed., Cheltenham, UK and Northampton, MA, USA: E. Elgar, 1999.

Smith, Adam (1776) *Wealth of Nations*, Edwin Cannan, ed., London: Methuen, 1904, online: Library of Economics and Liberty.

Marshall's External Economies: Economic Evolution and Patterns of Development

Neil Hart

1 Introduction

George Stigler, in his influential assessments of Marshall's contributions to economic analysis, made the following observations on the role of external economies in Marshall's *Principles*[1]:

> Of the many concepts which Marshall has contributed to economic analysis, none is in more urgent need of re-examination than the celebrated distinction between external and internal economies. For it is the existence of external economies, and not, as Robertson has suggested, that of the representative firm, which permits reconciliation of competition and decreasing long-run average costs. (Stigler 1941: 68)

[1] Unless otherwise noted, all references to Marshall's *Principles of Economics* (Marshall 1920) refer to the eighth edition as published by Macmillan in 1920.

N. Hart (✉)
School of Economics and Industrial Relations Research Centre,
University of New South Wales, Kensington, NSW, Australia
e-mail: n.hart@unsw.edu.au

Institute of Business Research, University of Economics,
Ho Chi Minh City, Vietnam

K. Caldari et al. (eds.), *Marshall and the Marshallian Heritage*,
Palgrave Studies in the History of Economic Thought,
https://doi.org/10.1007/978-3-030-53032-7_4

> The doctrine of external and internal economies was a major Marshallian contribution. This classification permitted an analytical reconciliation of competition and increasing returns, and thus repaired a major gap in classical price theory. (Stigler 1990: 6)

A similar view was expressed by Paul Romer in relation to Marshall's 'influence' on the ideas which led to the emergence of what became known as New Growth Theory:

> To derive his downward sloping supply curve from an industry with many firms, Marshall introduced the new notion of increasing returns that were external to any individual firm. External effects therefore entered into economics to preserve the analytical machinery of supply and demand curves and price taking in the presence of increasing returns. The analysis of other kinds of external effects - smoke, bees, and so on - came later. (Romer 1994: 14–5)[2]

However, it is argued here that such a characterisation represents a fundamental misrepresentation of the role Marshall intended external economies to play in his analysis. Most importantly, it neglects the essentially evolutionary nature of Marshall's analysis of the organisation of industry and economic progress, a perspective that forms the centrepiece of Tiziano Raffaelli's (2003a) inciteful interpretations of Marshall's writings. Instead, the role of external economies needs to be interpreted in the setting of what Marco Dardi (2010) has referred to as the 'new view' of Marshall's economics, where Marshall's thought is regarded being 'chiefly a scientific treatment of human history, based on a philosophical vision which is almost an outgrowth of a personal variant of evolutionary psychology extended to social and industrial organisation'.[3] Within this setting, the external economies in Marshall's writings take on a completely different role and character than that suggested by Stigler and like-minded

[2] Similarly, Romer (1986: 1004–5) contended that 'With the introduction by Alfred Marshall of the distinction between internal and external economies, it appeared that this [increasing returns] explanation could be given a consistent, competitive equilibrium interpretation'.

[3] Much of the 'new view' has been inspired by Whitaker's (1975) edited volumes of Marshall's early economic writings, Raffaelli's (1994) edited collection of Marshall's philosophical papers and Groenewegen's (1995) definitive Marshall biography. Many of the central themes are presented in the edited volumes Arena and Quéré (2003), Raffaelli et al. (2006, 2011), and Hart (2012).

thinkers, extending well beyond competitive price theory and providing invaluable insights into issues relating to economic growth, industrial organisation and economic geography.

The remainder of this chapter is organised as follows. The deficiencies in the 'traditional' interpretations of Marshall's treatment of external economies, as depicted in the statements by Stigler and Romer, are highlighted in Sect. 2. The *intended* role of external economies in Marshall's analytical framework is established in Sect. 3. Particular attention is placed on the insights to be gained from Marshall's treatment of those external economies associated with the geographical localisation of industry and the formation of what have been termed industrial districts. Section 4 considers how Marshall's treatment of these external economies contrasts to some aspects of the subsequent analysis of similar themes. Some general concluding observations are presented in the final section.

2 External Economies and Competitive Equilibrium: Marshall's Reconciliation Exercise?

The traditional interpretation of Marshall's 'reconciliation exercise', together with his proposed 'solution', has been summarised (though not supported) by Renee Prendergast as follows[4]:

> By the time he published the first edition of his *Principles*, Marshall had formulated an ingenious theoretical solution to the problem of *reconciling increasing returns and competition* within the framework devised by Cournot. The solution involved the introduction of the concept of *external economies which were viewed as the sole cause of increasing returns* within a regime of competition. (Prendergast 1992: 460, emphasis added)

The contention that Marshall assigned the key role to external economies in his attempts to reconcile increasing returns and 'competitive' equilibrium emerges directly from A. C. Pigou's (1927, 1928) treatment of the laws of return and Piero Sraffa's (1926) consequential contribution

[4] Prendergast (1992; 2006: 383) does not support the 'traditional' interpretation, concluding instead that both the life-cycle and external economies were 'necessary for the reconciliation of increasing returns and competition'. The rather different reasons for rejecting the 'traditional view', along the lines argued in this section, are discussed in more detail in Hart (1996).

to the cost controversies of the late 1920s.[5] However, this stands in stark contrast to the conclusion presented by Marshall to Book IV of the *Principles*:

> The general argument of the present Book shows that an increase in the aggregate volume of production of anything will generally increase the size, and therefore the internal economies possessed by such a representative firm; that it will always increase the external economies to which the firm has access; and thus will enable it to manufacture at a less proportionate cost of labour and sacrifice than before. (*Principles*: 318)

Clearly, Marshall does not wish to imply that the existence of external economies limits firm size, or the extent to which internal economies may be realised. Nor does the 'external economy solution' emerge from Marshall's discussion of returns to scale in *Industry and Trade*, where it is observed:

> But with the growth of capital, the development of machinery, and the improvement of the means of communication, *the importance of internal economies has increased steadily and fast*, while some of the old external economies have declined in importance; and many of those which have risen in their place are national, or even cosmopolitan, rather than local. (Marshall 1919: 167, emphasis added)

The notion that Marshall's intended his analysis of external economies to be considered within the confines of 'competitive equilibrium' is, likewise, inconsistent with Marshall's own writings. Marshall frequently warned his readers that a misunderstanding to be guarded against is that 'normal'

[5] Pigou (1928: 195), for example, stated 'The [Marshall's] representative firm must be conceived as one for which, under competitive conditions, there is, at each scale of aggregate output, a certain optimum size, trespass beyond which yields no further internal economies'. Sraffa's perspective was stated most directly in his earlier 1925 paper: 'But when he [Marshall] noticed that a decrease in cost, deriving from the increase in the size of the factories and from a larger division of labour, was incompatible with free competition, he abandoned his original point of view, and instead expanded his theory of external economies, to the extent of considering these *as the sole cause of decreasing costs in a regime of competition*' (Sraffa 1925: 346–7, emphasis added).

economic results are due to the undisturbed action of free competition,[6] and his description of demand and supply schedules for manufacturing industries, where returns to scale were seen to be pervasive, corresponds much more closely with later depictions of 'imperfect competition':

> This may be expressed by saying that when we are considering an individual producer, we must couple his supply curve – not with the general demand curve for his commodity in a wide market, but – with the particular demand curve of his own special market. And this particular demand curve will generally be very steep; perhaps as steep as his own supply curve is likely to be, even when an increased output will give him an important increase of internal economies. (*Principles*: 458n)

Significantly, from his lengthy discussion of the concept of competition in the first chapter of the *Principles*, it is clear that Marshall analysed competition from the perspective of a behavioural activity, in contrast with later definitions of competition specified in terms of market structures. Competition was a form of organisation that evolved through time, with the endless process of adaptation and re-organisation associated with economic change ensuring that market structure itself was a transitory configuration. Most importantly, consideration of the laws of return within the sterile world of free or perfect competition completely distorts the role increasing returns (whether 'internal' or 'external') were intended to play in Marshall's evolutionary account of the structure of industry and economic progress.

If a 'reconciliation problem' is to be designated to Marshall's long-period equilibrium analysis, its genesis must unquestionably stem from the ambition to represent within an equilibrium framework the outcomes of economic actions at a point in logical time which are acknowledged to proceed within an evolutionary setting. The nature of these difficulties was articulated as follows by Marshall:

[6] See, for example, *Principles*: 35, and most notably in Chapter III of Book V, where it is explicitly stated that 'of course Normal does not mean Competitive', with both market and normal prices 'brought about by a multitude of influences, of which some rest on a moral and some on a physical; of which some are competitive and some are not' (*Principles*: 347–8). In a note found in an 1886 printing of Alfred and Mary Paley Marshall's *Economics of Industry* [Marshall and Marshall (1879)] annotated for an envisaged revision, Marshall commented: 'Be careful to strike out everything wh. implies that normal value = competitive value'. Whitaker (1975: 73), Becattini and Dardi (2006: 55–6).

> It must however be admitted that this theory is out of touch with real conditions of life, in so far as it assumes that, if the normal production of a commodity increases and afterwards again diminishes to its old amount, the demand price and the supply price will return to their old positions for that amount... For, when any casual disturbance has caused a great increase in the production of any commodity, and thereby has led to the introduction of extensive economies, these economies are not readily lost. Developments of mechanical appliances, of division of labour and of the means of transport, and improved organisation of all kinds, when they have been once obtained are not readily abandoned. (*Principles*: 807–8)[7]

Consequently, the operational meaning that can be attributed to the long-period supply schedule within an equilibrium framework is called into question. Movements along this supply schedule, occasioned by shifts in demand schedules, could only be envisaged if scale economies can be reversed or reassembled. While these types of adjustments are permitted to occur in the realm of comparative statics, dynamics and evolution do not allow such possibilities. While Marshall's long-period analysis could conceivably indicate equilibrium positions ex-post, it could not describe the process by which the equilibrium positions may be attained or sustained and the theory, when applied to 'the real conditions of life', did not have a meaningful expository role to play in the *determination* of long-period values.[8]

[7] The nature of these issues is discussed further in Appendix H of the *Principles* where Marshall draws a distinction between the 'true' industry supply curve and the 'particular expenses curve'. Here the economies associated with organisation and production on a large scale are explicitly taken as *fixed and constant throughout*. Movements along such curves, in response to shifts in demand schedules, could occur through time, as the irreversibilities associated with organisation and production would not be encountered. Marshall then proceeded to argue that curves drawn under such assumptions had no operational role to play, as it 'is not a true supply curve adapted to the conditions of the world in which we live, but it has properties which are often erroneously attributed to such a curve' (*Principles*: 810). The source of these difficulties is discussed in more detail in Marshall (1898).

[8] Among those who participated in the Marshallian value theory debates of the late 1920s, the nature of these difficulties was most clearly recognised by Allyn Young (1928). Interpretation and the resolution of these difficulties within an evolutionary setting have been developed by writers such as Dardi (2003), Niman (2004), Metcalfe (2007), and Raffaelli (2011).

3 Marshall's External Economies and the Localisation of Industry

The context in which Stigler evaluated Marshall's treatment of external economies in the *Principles* is significant:

> At the outset it should be emphasized that Marshall's external economies form an essentially historical category. The development of knowledge and invention, cross-fertilization, the emergence of subsidiary firms to exploit by-products and to supply equipment, the accumulation of skilled labor, all are characterized by growth. Indeed, the notion of external economies may be a useful interpretive tool in economic history. For the purpose of modern theoretical analysis, however, the question must be raised; Do external economies have any importance in a stationary economy? (Stigler 1941: 71–2).

From Marshall's perspective, the answer to the question posed by Stigler is emphatically in the negative, for as Stigler himself observed:

> A first generalization is that Marshall was so concerned with historical economic developments that he had relatively small patience with the theoretical economics of a stationary state. Almost every important subject in the *Principles* receives its exposition in terms of evolutionary change.... (Stigler 1941: 62–3)

Therefore, in order to place Marshall's treatment of external economies in its intended context, attention needs to be directed away from 'stationary states' to that of Marshall's conceptualisation of 'economic biology'.

As is well known, Marshall proclaimed that the Mecca of the economist lies in economic biology (*Principles*: xiv). Marshall's 'economic biology' epitomised a methodological ideal, reflecting an ambition to introduce a mode of thinking that departed in several important respects from that which Marshall associated as originating from the 'mathematical-physical' sciences, which failed to recognise how liable to change are the habits and institutions of industry (*Principles*: 762–3). Its concrete application can be observed most directly in the portrayal of industry organisation and change found in Book IV of the *Principles*, and in the theme of 'economic movement' that is pervasive throughout the *Principles*. Industrial change is portrayed as a gradual growth of new habits of more or less reflex or automatic action, characterised by cumulative routinisation and specialisation made possible by the division of labour. It was the outcome of the establishment of routines on the one hand and creativity through innovation on the other. This is described by Marshall in the following terms:

> This increased subdivision of functions, or "differentiation," as it is called, manifests itself with regard to industry in such forms as the division of labour, and the development of specialized skill, knowledge and machinery: while "integration," that is, a growing intimacy and firmness of the connections between the separate parts of the industrial organism, shows itself in such forms as the increase of security of commercial credit, and of the means and habits of communication by sea and road, by railway and telegraph, by post and printing-press. ... But we may pass to consider the main bearings in economics of the law that the struggle for existence causes those organisms to multiply which are best fitted to derive benefit from their environment. (*Principles*: 241)

Within this context, external economies were delineated by Marshall as follows:

> Meanwhile an increase in the aggregate scale of production of course increases those economies, which do not directly depend on the size of individual houses of business. The most important of these results from the growth of correlated branches of industry which mutually assist one another, perhaps being concentrated in the same localities, but anyhow availing themselves of the modern facilities for communication offered by steam transport, by the telegraph and by the printing-press. The economies arising from such sources as this, which are accessible to any branch of production, do not depend exclusively upon its own growth: but yet they are sure to grow rapidly and steadily with that growth; and they are sure to dwindle in some, though not in all respects, if it decays. (*Principles*: 317)[9]

[9] While the term external economies was not used explicitly in Marshall's early writing, a clear distinction is made between these economies and internal economies. See, for example, in *Pure Theory of Domestic Values*, where Marshall challenges the proposition that the most important of the advantages of the division of labour can only be obtained by the concentration of large numbers of workmen in vast establishments:

> ...an increase in the total amount of a commodity manufactured can scarcely fail to occasion increased economies in production, whether the task of production is distributed among a large number of small capitalists, or is concentrated in the hands of a comparatively small number of large firms. (Whitaker 1975, II: 198)

External economies arose from the use of specialised skill and machinery depending on the aggregate volume of production in the neighbourhood, and also on the growth of knowledge and the progress of the arts which depend on the aggregate volume of production in the whole civilised world (*Principles*: 265–6). Marshall noted that these economies could often be 'secured by the concentration of many small businesses of a similar character in particular localities', and, as a result, may then result in the 'localisation of industry', occasionally referred to as industrial districts by Marshall, where 'numerous specialized branches of industry have been welded almost automatically into one organic whole' (*Principles*: 266; Marshall 1919: 599). An examination of these 'localised' external economies provides insights into how external economies may potentially affect patterns of development within Marshall's proposed evolutionary framework.

Marshall's interest in the notion of industrial districts emerged in part from his direct observations of the industrial landscape of his times (Groenewegen 1995: 187–9, 206–13) and was also likely influenced by his reading of the works of writers such as Herbert Spencer (1862: 278–9), where the geographical clustering of firms is observed in the detailed discussion of industry organisation.[10] Marshall's reflections on the localisation of industry had been well developed prior to the publication of the first edition of the *Principles*, as observed, for example, in the following passage from the *Pure Theory of Domestic Values*, privately circulated by Henry Sidgwick in 1879:

> For in these trades the advantages of production on a large scale can in general be as well attained by the aggregation of a large number of small masters into one district as by the erection of a few large works. It is true that the disadvantages under which the small masters lie in competition with large firms are increasing more rapidly than are their peculiar advantages; and in most though not in all directions there is a tendency for small masters to be supplanted. But ... the advantages which are generally classed under the heads of the division of labour and production on a large scale can be attained almost as fully by the aggregation into one district of many establishments of a moderate size as by the erection of a few large

[10] See Groenewegen (2009), where the possible influence of W. E. Hearn's *Plutology* is also noted, along with R. M. C. Taylor's writings devoted to the factory system.

> factories. The customary method of treating the advantages of division of labour appears to be defective, inasmuch as it takes little account of this fact. (Whitaker 1975, II: 196)

Marshall then proceeds to outline some explanations for this, of most interest to the current discussion being the following:

> … among the most important of the economies which are available in the production of many classes of commodities are those which are concerned with the education of specialised skill. When large masses of men in the same locality are engaged in similar tasks, it is found that, by associating with one another, they educate one another. To use a mode of speaking which workmen themselves use, the skill required for work 'is in the air, and children breathe it as they grow up'… Each new idea is canvassed and improved upon by many minds; each new accidental experience and each deliberate experiment will afford food for reflection and for new suggestions, not to a few persons, but to many. Thus, in a large localised industry new idea are likely to be started rapidly: and each new idea is likely to be fertile of practical improvements. (ibid.: 197–8)[11]

The territorial aggregation of small firms, whose role was not simply to support the large vertically integrated firms, was seen to be a persistent feature of industry structure, and required explanation within Marshall's evolutionary analysis of industry.

These themes found a place in Marshall's *Principles*, as a significant component of Marshall's depiction of external economies, relating to the emergence of an 'industrial atmosphere', which Marshall described as promoting creativity and innovation and the transfer of knowledge among the geographically connected firms within the evolving industrial district:

> When an industry has thus chosen a locality for itself, it is likely to stay there long: so great are the advantages which people following the same skilled trade get from near neighbourhood to one another. The mysteries of the trade become no mysteries; but are as it were in the air, and children learn many of them unconsciously. Good work is rightly appreciated, inventions and improvements in machinery, in processes and the general

[11] See also in the Marshalls' *Economics of Industry*, where, for example, it is stated that while some of the advantages of the division of labour can be obtained only in large factories, many 'can be secured by small factories and workshops, provided there are a very great number of them *in the same trade*' (Marshall and Marshall 1879: 52, emphasis added).

> organization of the business have their merits promptly discussed: if one man starts a new idea, it is taken up by others and combined with suggestions of their own; and thus it becomes the source of further new ideas. (*Principles*: 271)

As described by Marshall, each of the small firms within an industrial neighbourhood derives benefit from the external economies of scale associated with the locality as a whole. First, the local firms can derive benefit from access to a pool of 'special skilled labour', which is attracted to the locality because of the plentiful local demand for their skills. The use of expensive and specialised equipment may also be rendered more cost effective among the local firms, and the localisation of industries also encourages the growth of subsidiary trades which 'grow up in the neighbourhood, supplying it with implements and materials, organizing its traffic, and in many ways conducive to the economy of its material' (*Principles*: 271). Economies from reduced transportation and communication costs may also arise as a result of the regional proximity of the firms.

Essentially, the formation and development of the industrial districts facilitated the division of labour, enabling the realisation of invention and automation. This fundamentally involved the sharing of knowledge within a socio-economic setting that had evolved from the spatial dispersion of economic and social activities. This emphasises once again Marshall's theme that knowledge and creativity are embodied in the ideas of people, rather than in technologically determined input-output relationships. It is cooperation within the district, combined with competition, which provides the impetus for the self-perpetuation of the 'organic whole'. It is these dimensions that Marshall sought to embed in his category of external economies, and all of this is far removed from questions as to the determination of relative prices in long-period competitive equilibrium characterised by the absence of change.

It can be argued that, most notably in his later writings, Marshall came to place less emphasis on the external economies linked with the formation of industrial districts. In *Industry and Trade*, for example, Marshall observed that 'old external economies have declined in importance; and many of those which have risen in their place are national, or even cosmopolitan, rather than local' (Marshall 1919: 167). This has led some commentators to suggest that Marshall was inclined to 'jettison' the industrial district anomaly, and the associated external economies

(Becattini 2003: 23–4). Perhaps more pointedly, as Brian Loasby (1998: 70) has emphasised, the reader needs to consider more closely Marshall's methodological principle of continuity and not exaggerate the distinctiveness of industrial districts as a pattern of industrial organisation. Industrial districts emerged as a potential outcome of processes in which external economies provided an avenue whereby the evolutionary forces that shaped the pattern of industrial development could manifest themselves.

4 External Economies and Industrial Districts: A 'Post-Marshallian' Analysis?

Subsequent to the writings of Marshall, the analysis of external economies within mainstream economics has largely been confined to its role in price theory, as assigned by the likes of Stigler, and to what Romer referred to as the 'smoke, bees, and so on' setting. Following Glaeser et al. (1992), there is frequent reference to Marshall-Arrow-Romer externalities within the geography of economic growth literature. Here, the Marshall-Arrow element allows for the existence of a variety of regionally based technology or knowledge spillovers, leading to 'knowledge rents' to be shared within the region. The proximity of firms within an industry influences how well knowledge is shared among firms to facilitate innovation and growth. However, within the Romer setting, these regionally based external economies must accede through time to an economy-wide diffusion process, if they are to ultimately generate long-run growth. Therefore, regional differences play an important role during a limited time period, but must ultimately diminish through time, completing the development cycle from innovation-driven divergence to diffusion led convergence and economy-wide growth. As Michael Storper's (2009) critical account of this approach highlights, Romer has come to overshadow Marshall in the so-called Marshall-Arrow-Romer version of external economies.[12]

In a similar manner, Paul Krugman, in his influential contributions that inspired the 'new' economic geography movement, referred directly to Marshall's work on localised external economies. In Krugman's scheme, the ('centripetal') forces that promote geographical concentration are equated directly with what are termed the 'three classic Marshallian

[12] Storper's own contributions to the geography of economic development have been significant; see, for example, Storper (2013).

sources of external economies': market size effects, thick labour markets (especially for specialized skills) and pure external economies' (Krugman 1998: 3). Those opposing localisation include immobility in factors of production, land rents and 'pure external diseconomies' (congestion being the example put forward). The forces that promote and oppose the spatial concentration of activities collectively come together to constitute a form of regional competitiveness that provides an economic rationale for the localisation of industry. Most significantly, Krugman's 'pure external economy effects' are equated with 'information spillovers' associated with the local concentration of economic activity and are linked directly with Marshall's original analysis through the usage of his expression: 'The mysteries of the trade become no mystery, but are, as it were, in the air'.

A key objective of Krugman's work was to place geographical analysis squarely in the economic mainstream, allowing for the construction of formal models that were 'fully general equilibrium', based on aggregate behaviour from individual maximisation. Consequently, while Krugman's perception of 'pure external economies' appears to resemble Marshall's notion of knowledge-based external economies, they were to play little or no role in his analysis:

> To conduct analytical work on economic geography, however, it is necessary to cut through the complexities of the real world and focus on a more limited set of forces... This is especially true because much of the analysis we will want to undertake involves asking how a changing economic environment alters economic geography... This will be an ill-defined task if the forces producing that geography are inside a black box labelled 'external effects'. So, the pure external economies and diseconomies are put on one side, in favour of forces that are more amenable to analysis. (Krugman 1998: 8–9)

Within Krugman's setting, it is industry that chooses locations, with the forces that nurture the 'industrial atmosphere' playing a passive role. Marshall's observation of instances where 'social forces co-operate with economic' in the realisation of external economies in local regions (*Principles*: 276) is jettisoned, along with any notion of evolutionary processes in operation. Krugman (2010: 5) argued that 'the new economic geography was designed to attract the attention of mainstream economists', and the failure to integrate Marshall's 'pure external economies' within this formal modelling once again highlighted the difficulties associated with representing Marshall's insights within an equilibrium framework.

The methodological approach adopted within the 'new' economic geography framework has been heavily criticised by a number of those working within geographical economics, who contend that geography has not been taken seriously enough and argue that the 'untraded interdependencies' excluded by the Krugman approach are the key drivers of the external economies that shape regional development and industry location. A particularly forceful critic has been Ron Martin, whose views succinctly capture the thrust of what are judged to be the inadequacies of the Krugman approach:

> ... another serious flaw in the 'new geographical economics', namely its neglect of real places. This neglect is most obvious in the mathematical models of spatial agglomeration. Here 'regions' or 'locations' are often just points along a linear economy, or concentric circles in a von Thunen-type landscape, or point-patterns in a Christaller-type surface. Real communities in real historical, social and cultural settings with real people, going about the 'ordinary business of life' (as Marshall once described economics) are completely bypassed. (Martin 1999: 77)[13]

Consequently, the conceptual basis of economic geographers' work on regional economies has not been equilibrium location theory, but instead approaches that emphasise the political, economic, institutional and social bases of regional development and industrial agglomeration. Not surprisingly, these notions have attracted the attention of geographers working within the emerging field of evolutionary economic geography.[14] Here, for example, geographical proximity facilitates knowledge spillovers, and history forms the basis for new dynamics. Cumulative and collective

[13] Similar arguments were developed assertively by Wilkinson (1983), who observed that sociopolitical forces are either assumed not to affect outcomes or are held to distort the operation of the market, in which case they need to be adjusted to make them compatible with the postulates of economic theory. As a result, the traditional approaches fail to recognise the central role of institutions in economic development and the inextricable link between social, political and economic forces in determining how economies function. The influence of the historical and institutionalist schools of economic thought on Marshall's industrial economics is noted. The latter point is considered in some detail in Jensen (1990).

[14] See the edited volumes Boschma (2012), Kogler (2016), along with Frenken (2007), for an overview of the evolutionary economic geography literature.

learning embedded in a region, with the local accumulation of intangible human capital, knowledge, information linkages, network externalities and supportive institutions lead to a comparative advantage which is hard to copy and difficult to transfer to other areas (Boschma and Lambooy 1999). While there is very little direct recognition of Marshall's contributions within this literature, the connections are clearly observed in the following concluding observation from the aptly titled 'Marshall's disciples':

> The reference to Alfred Marshall is not only motivated by his work on industrial districts (Marshall 1890/1920, Book IV.10) but also by his deep insights into the nature of economic processes... However, we argue that, as research on how knowledge and innovation influence regional development and growth is to a large extent research into process, it is indispensable to take an evolutionary perspective, which allows for this kind of analysis. On the other hand, research taking an equilibrium perspective might be dispensable, because it is mainly concerned with outcomes and not with processes. (Werker and Athreye 2004: 521)

In his critique of the 'new' economic geography, Martin (1999: 79) referred favourably to what he termed neo-Marshallian industrial district economics emanating from a small group of Italian economists. While it was observed that spatial agglomeration modellers rarely alluded to this work, it was noted that the Italian industrial districts literature has encouraged economic geographers to focus on the networks of trust, cooperation, competition and governance that characterise such areas, aspects that had been neglected in the Krugman approach. It is not possible here to provide an overview of the industrial districts literature, however, the following description provided by Giacomo Becattini, a pioneering contributor, aptly captures the general tenor of this approach:

> Now, with the industrial district, the human community undergoes a transition from a passive entity into an actor, for what are the industrial atmosphere and the internal-external economies if not ways through which the local society affects the productivity of labour. The concept of a local society as an additional productive factor, together with accumulation and technical progress is understandable only within a dynamic conception of the learning process and with a consideration of the economic function of a 'modern brotherhood' (i.e., a sense of belonging). These last two

> aspects are present only in Marshall, and in no other economist of his time. (Becattini 2003: 21–2)[15]

Beccattini's reference to Marshall is significant, for, as noted by Raffaelli (2003b: 254), Marshall's analytical idea of localised external economies provided the kernel around which district studies came to be organised.[16] In the tradition of Marshall, the modern treatment of industrial districts focuses on the social, rather than the narrower economic nature of industrial districts, with emphasis placed on process rather than on inputs and outputs (Piore 2009: 267–8). The unit of analysis became the district, rather than an industrial sector, on which much of the 'new' economic geography focused its attention. This has been reflected in a convergence of interest in many disciplinary perspectives to assemble a distinctly interdisciplinary theory of local development (Trigilia 2009; Becattini 2011).[17]

Interestingly, however, Becattini (2006: 669–70) found it rather paradoxical that much of the attention on Marshall's industrial districts clung stubbornly to Chapter 10 of book IV of the *Principles*, which, it is argued, is devoted neither to the productive specialisation of an existing community nor to the process of urban-industrial proliferation, but rather to the criteria that rule over the spatial distribution of the firms that belong to a given industry. Here, Becattini contrasts Marshall's perspective in the *Principles* with that of his earlier writings, such as in *The Economics of Industry*, where the main focus was on the 'factory', which was seen as being part of the community's productive structure, as opposed to a

[15] Much of Becattini's early work was published in Italian, however, the nature of his contributions can be observed in Becattini (1990, 2004). A comprehensive overview of the literature has been provided by the contributors to Becattini et al. (2009) and Konzelmann and Wilkinson (2016). García-Lillo et al.'s (2018) bibliometric review is indicative of the growth in subsequent research on this and related themes. Interesting examples of recent work include Bellandi et al.'s (2018) development of a conceptual framework on knowledge accumulation and depletion in industrial districts.

[16] A more detailed discussion of the connections between the industrial districts literature and Marshall's external economies is developed in Raffaelli (2003b), Bellandi (2003), Belussi and Caldari (2009), Hart (2009) and Loasby (2009).

[17] The work of Porter and his followers on industrial clusters should also be recognised; see Porter and Ketels (2009) for a discussion of the similarities and differences between Porter's treatment of industrial clusters and the themes emphasised by Marshall and in the subsequent industrial district literature.

cluster of firms. Becattini's criticism of Marshall in this respect resembles in part, the criticisms noted earlier with respect to Krugman's approach:

> Putting the cluster in the socio-cultural dress of the district, Marshall sells the primogeniture of the 'interdisciplinary' concept of the industrial district, which forms part of the 'study of man', for the mess of pottage of a theory of industrial localization. A theory, moreover, that muddied as it is by the presence of metaeconomic concepts derived from the industrial concept approach, such as the already quoted 'industrial atmosphere', is not even deemed worthy of consideration by economic geographers and theoreticians of industrial localization! (ibid.: 670)

Nevertheless, and following in the footsteps of Raffaelli (2003b), the industrial district is increasingly placed in an evolutionary setting, perceived to have features of evolutionary processes that, under favourable circumstances, favour constructive evolution, thereby fostering the creation and sharing of knowledge. Bellandi et al.'s (2019) modelling, which places Marshall's conceptualisation of industrial districts in an explicitly evolutionary framework, is a recent example of how Marshall's notion of localised external economies lends itself to techniques associated with evolutionary economic geography. Likewise, Konzelmann et al. (2018), recognising that by their very nature districts are evolutionary, illustrate how Marshall's methodological and theoretical approach to understanding this form of industrial organisation helps to explain the dynamism of contemporary British industrial districts, with important implications for Britain's industrial revitalisation. It is in this sense, that the industrial districts literature, along with the evolutionary geography approach, can truly be classified as 'post-Marshallian', with respect to the treatment of external economies.

5 Concluding Comment

It is sometimes argued that there are (at least) two sorts of Marshallians; the book-5 Marshallian who see Marshall's legacy in his time period analysis, and the book-4 Marshallian who instead find in Marshall something much more dynamic, Darwinian, and empirically based (Collard 2004: 401). However, as Stanley Metcalfe (2007: S2) has maintained, the two theories are inextricably linked, and the subsequent attempt to separate them has made it impossible to appreciate the role Marshall gave to innovation, and its corollary, the growth of knowledge and organisation, in the workings of a market economy. This is particularly apparent when the nature and role of external economies in Marshall's writings are examined. It is only when the analysis escapes the confines of equilibrium theory and ventures into the evolutionary framework envisaged by Marshall as portrayed in Raffaelli's writings, that the role of external economies can be fully appreciated and extended to provide useful insights into the forces that shape the patterns of economic development.

Acknowledgements I am thankful to Geoff Harcourt and Peter Kriesler, from the University of New South Wales, Australia, for their helpful comments and suggestions.

References

Arena, R., and Quéré, M. (eds) (2003) *The Economics of Alfred Marshall* (London: Palgrave Macmillan).

Becattini, G. (1990) 'The Marshallian Industrial District as a Socio-Economic Notion', in F. Pyke, G. Becattini, and W. Sengenberger (eds) *Industrial Districts and Inter-Firm Co-operation in Italy* (Geneva: IILS, ILO).

Becattini, G. (2003) 'The Return of the "White Elephant"', in R. Arena and M. Quéré (eds) *Revisiting Marshall's Legacy* (New York: Palgrave Macmillan).

Becattini, G. (2004) *Industrial Districts: A New Approach to Industrial Change* (Cheltenham, UK: Edward Elgar).

Becattini, G. (2006) 'The Industrial District and Development Economics', in T. Raffaelli, G. Becattini, and M. Dardi (eds) *The Elgar Companion to Alfred Marshall* (Cheltenham, UK: Edward Elgar).

Becattini, G. (2011) 'Introduction: From the Wanderjahre to the Revival of Marshall's Industrial Districts', in T. Raffaelli, T. Nishizawa, and S. Cook (eds) *Marshall, Marshallians and Industrial Economics* (London: Routledge).

Becattini, G., Bellandi, M., and De Propris, L. (eds) (2009) *A Handbook of Industrial Districts* (Cheltenham, UK: Edward Elgar).

Becattini, G., and Dardi, M. (2006) 'The Economics of Industry', in T. Raffaelli, G. Becattini, and M. Dardi (eds) *The Elgar Companion to Alfred Marshall* (Cheltenham, UK: Edward Elgar).

Bellandi, M. (2003) 'Some Remarks on Marshallian External Economies and Industrial Tendencies', in R. Arena and M. Quéré (eds) (2003) *The Economics of Alfred Marshall* (London: Palgrave Macmillan).

Bellandi, M., De Propris, L., and Santini, E. (2019) 'An Evolutionary Analysis of Industrial Districts: The Changing Multiplicity of Production Know-How Nuclei', *Cambridge Journal of Economics*, 43 (1), 187–204.

Bellandi, M., Santini, E., and Vecciolini, V. (2018) 'Learning, Unlearning and Forgetting Processes in Industrial Districts', *Cambridge Journal of Economics*, 42 (6), 1671–85.

Belussi, F., and Caldari, K. (2009) 'At the Origin of the Industrial District: Alfred Marshall and the Cambridge School', *Cambridge Journal of Economics*, 33 (2) 335–55.

Boschma, R. A. (ed) (2012) *The Handbook of Evolutionary Economic Geography* (Aldershot: Edward Elgar).

Boschma, R. A., and Lambooy, J. G. (1999) 'Evolutionary Economics and Economic Geography', *Journal of Evolutionary Economics*, 9 (4), 411–29.

Collard, D. A. (2004) 'Review of The Economics of Alfred Marshall: Revisiting Marshall's Legacy', *History of Political Economy*, 36 (2), 401–3.

Dardi, M. (2003) 'Alfred Marshall's Partial Equilibrium: Dynamics in Disguise', in R. Arena and M. Quéré (eds) *The Economics of Alfred Marshall* (London: Palgrave Macmillan).

Dardi, M. (2010) 'The Intellectual Foundations of Alfred Marshall's Economic Science: A Rounded Globe of Knowledge' [Review of Cook (2009)], *European Journal of the History of Economic Thought*, 17 (3), 521–35.

Frenken, K., (2007) *Applied Evolutionary Economics and Economic Geography* (Aldershot: Edward Elgar).

García-Lillo, F., Claver-Cortés, E., Marco-Lajara, B., Úbeda-García, M., and Seva-Larrosa, P. (2018) 'On Clusters and Industrial Districts: A Literature Review Using Bibliometrics Methods, 2000–2015', *Regional Science*, 97 (4), 835–61.

Glaeser, E., Kallal, H., Scheinkman, J., and Shleifer, A. (1992) 'Growth in Cities', *Journal of Political Economy*, 100 (6), 1126–52.

Groenewegen, P. D. (1995) *A Soaring Eagle: Alfred Marshall 1842–1924* (Aldershot: Edward Elgar).

Groenewegen, P. D. (2009) 'Forerunners of Marshall on the Industrial Districts', in G. Becattini, M. Bellandi, and L. De Propris (eds) *A Handbook of Industrial Districts* (Cheltenham, UK: Edward Elgar).

Hart, N. (1996) 'Marshall's Theory of Value: The Role of External Economies', *Cambridge Journal of Economics*, 20 (3), 353–69.

Hart, N. (2009) 'External and Internal Economies', in G. Becattini, M. Bellandi, and L. De Propris (eds) *A Handbook of Industrial Districts* (Cheltenham, UK: Edward Elgar).

Hart, N. (2012) *Equilibrium and Evolution: Alfred Marshall and the Marshallians* (Houndmills, UK: Palgrave Macmillan).

Jensen, H. (1990) 'Are there Institutionalist Signposts in the Economics of Alfred Marshall?', *Journal of Economic Issues*, 24 (2), 405–13.

Kogler, D. (2016) *Evolutionary Economic Geography: Theoretical and Empirical Progress* (Abingdon: Routledge).

Konzelmann, S. J., Fovargue-Davies, M., and Wilkinson, F. (2018) 'Britain's Industrial Evolution: The Structuring Role of Economic Theory', *Journal of Economic Issues*, 52 (1), 1–30.

Konzelmann, S. J., and Wilkinson, F. (2016) 'Co-operation in Production, the Organization of Industry and Productive Systems: A Critical Survey of the "District" Form of Industrial Organization and Development', *Cambridge Centre for Business Research Working Paper 481.* Cambridge: Cambridge Centre for Business Research, September 2016.

Krugman, P. (1998) 'The Role of Geography in Development', paper prepared for the Annual World Bank Conference on Development Economics, Washington, DC, April 20–21, 1998.

Krugman, P. (2010) 'The New Economic Geography, Now Middle-Aged', paper prepared for presentation to the Association of American Geographers, April 16, 2010.

Loasby, B. J. (1998) 'Industrial Districts as Knowledge Communities', in M. Bellet and C. L. Harmet (eds) *Industry, Space and Competition: The Contribution of Economists of the Past* (Cheltenham, UK: Edward Elgar).

Loasby, B. J. (2009) 'Industrial Districts in Marshall's Economics', in G. Becattini, M. Bellandi, and L. De Propris (eds) *A Handbook of Industrial Districts* (Cheltenham, UK: Edward Elgar).

Marshall, A. (1898) 'Mechanical and Biological Analogies in Economics', in A. C. Pigou (ed) (1925) *Memorials of Alfred Marshall* (London: Macmillan), 312–18.

Marshall, A. (1919) *Industry and Trade* (London: Macmillan).

Marshall, A. (1920) *Principles of Economics*, Eighth Edition (London: Macmillan).

Marshall, A., and Marshall, M. P. (1879) *The Economics of Industry*, First Edition (London: Macmillan).

Martin, R. (1999) 'The New "Geographical Turn" in Economics: Some Critical Reflections', *Cambridge Journal of Economics*, 23, 63–91.

Metcalfe, J. S. (2007) 'Alfred Marshall's Mecca: Reconciling the Theories of Value and Development', *Economic Record*, 83, S1–S22.

Niman, N. B. (2004) 'The Evolutionary Firm and Cournot's Dilemma', *Cambridge Journal of Economics*, 28, 273–89.

Pigou, A. C. (1927) 'The Laws of Diminishing and Increasing Cost', *Economic Journal*, 37, 188–97.

Pigou, A. C. (1928) 'An Analysis of Supply', *Economic Journal*, 38, 238–57.

Piore, M. J. (2009) 'Conceptualizing the Dynamics of Industrial Districts', in G. Becattini, M. Bellandi, and L. De Propris (eds) *A Handbook of Industrial Districts* (Cheltenham, UK: Edward Elgar).

Porter, M., and Ketels, C. (2009) 'Clusters and Industrial Districts: Common Roots, Different Perspectives', in G. Becattini, M. Bellandi, and L. De Propris (eds) *A Handbook of Industrial Districts* (Cheltenham, UK: Edward Elgar).

Prendergast, R. (1992) 'Increasing Returns and Competitive Equilibrium—The Content and Development of Marshall's Theory', *Cambridge Journal of Economics*, 16 (4), 447–62.

Prendergast, R. (2006) 'Increasing and Diminishing Returns', in T. Raffaelli, G. Becattini, and M. Dardi (eds) *The Elgar Companion to Alfred Marshall* (Cheltenham, UK: Edward Elgar).

Raffaelli, T. (ed) (1994) 'The Early Philosophical Writings of Alfred Marshall', *Research in the History of Economic Thought and Methodology*, 4 (Archival Supplement).

Raffaelli, T. (2003a) *Marshall's Evolutionary Economics* (London: Routledge).

Raffaelli, T. (2003b) 'Requirements and Patterns of Marshallian Evolution: Their Impact on the Notion of Industrial District', in R. Arena and M. Quéré (eds) *The Economics of Alfred Marshall* (London: Palgrave Macmillan).

Raffaelli, T. (2011) 'Marshall's Evolutionary Model and Its Bearing on Business Organization and Size', in T. Raffaelli, T. Nishizawa, and S. Cook (eds) *Marshall, Marshallians and Industrial Economics* (London: Routledge).

Raffaelli, T., Becattini, G., and Dardi, M. (eds) (2006) *The Elgar Companion to Alfred Marshall* (Cheltenham, UK: Edward Elgar).

Raffaelli, T., Nishizawa, T., and Cook, S. (eds) (2011) *Marshall, Marshallians and Industrial Economics* (London: Routledge).

Romer, P. M. (1986) 'Increasing Returns and Long Run Growth', *Journal of Political Economy*, 94 (5), 1002–37.

Romer, P. M. (1994) 'The Origins of Endogenous Growth', *Journal of Economic Perspectives*, 8 (1), 3–22.

Spencer, H. (1862) *First Principles*, Sixth Edition (London: Williams and Norgate).

Sraffa, P. (1925) 'Sulle relazioni fra costo e quantità prodotta (On the Relations Between Cost and Quantity Produced)', *Annali di Economia*, 2, 277–328, in L. Pasinetti (ed) (1998) *Italian Economic Papers*, Volume III (Bologna: Il Mulino and Oxford University Press).

Sraffa, P. (1926) 'The Laws of Returns Under Competitive Conditions', *Economic Journal*, 36, 535–50.

Stigler, G. J. (1941) *Production and Distribution Theories* (New York: Macmillan).

Stigler, G. J. (1990) 'The Place of Marshall's Principles in the Development of Economics', in J. K. Whitaker (ed) *Centenary Essays on Alfred Marshall* (Cambridge: Cambridge University Press).

Storper, M. (2009) 'The Economics of Context, Location and Trade: Another Great Transformation?' in G. Becattini, M. Bellandi, and L. De Propris (eds) *A Handbook of Industrial Districts* (Cheltenham, UK: Edward Elgar).

Storper, M. (2013) *Keys to the City: How Economics, Institutions, Social Interaction, and Politics Shape Development* (Princeton, NJ: Princeton University Press).

Trigilia, C. (2009) 'Introduction to Section 3', in G. Becattini, M. Bellandi, and L. De Propris (eds) *A Handbook of Industrial Districts* (Cheltenham, UK: Edward Elgar).

Werker, C., and Athreye, S. (2004) 'Marshall's Disciples: Knowledge and Innovation Driving Regional Economic Development and Growth', *Journal of Evolutionary Economics*, 14 (5), 505–23.

Whitaker, J. K. (1975) *The Early Economic Writings of Alfred Marshall*, Volumes I and II (London: Macmillan).

Wilkinson, F. (1983) 'Productive Systems', *Cambridge Journal of Economics*, 7 (3–4), 413–42.

Young, A. A. (1928) 'Increasing Returns and Economic Progress', *Economic Journal*, 38, 527–40.

Economic, Ethical and Political Aspects of Wellbeing: Some Marshallian Insights from His Book on Progress

Katia Caldari and Tamotsu Nishizawa

1 Introduction

Marshall's *Principles of Economics* opens with the following sentences: "Political economy or Economics is a study of mankind in the ordinary business of life; it examines that part of individual and social action that is most closely connected with the attainment and with the use of the material requisites of wellbeing. Thus, it is on the one side a study of wealth; and on the other, and more important side a part of the study of man" (1920: 1). Three aspects of these sentences are worth being underlined here: the first is that Marshall's economics is to be understood as political economy which is far from being the neutral science that the Marginalist revolution brought about; accordingly, and we come to the second aspect, in his writings Marshall deals not only with abstract and analytical issues

K. Caldari (✉)
Dipartimento di Scienze Economiche e Aziendali, Università di Padova, Padua, Italy
e-mail: katia.caldari@unipd.it

T. Nishizawa
Faculty of Economics, Teikyo University, Tokyo, Japan
e-mail: nisizawa@ier.hit-u.ac.jp

K. Caldari et al. (eds.), *Marshall and the Marshallian Heritage*, Palgrave Studies in the History of Economic Thought,
https://doi.org/10.1007/978-3-030-53032-7_5

but rather with practical problems which he wanted to solve, first of all the problem of poverty (see on this Caldari and Nishizawa 2011, 2014, 2016): in fact for him, the main aim of economics as a science is to find out the ways to attain and increase human wellbeing. The third aspect is that wellbeing is to be conceived in its two dimensions: on the one hand, the material dimension which is "wealth" and on the other hand the moral, ethical and mental dimension which is more closely connected with the complex nature of man. These two dimensions are both important, but they do not lie on the same plane because as stressed by Marshall "wealth exists only for the benefit of mankind. It cannot be measured adequately in yards, nor even as equivalent to so many ounces of gold; its true measure lies only in the contribution it makes to human wellbeing" (Marshall in Pigou 1925: 366, emphasis added).

All Marshall's writings pivot on these three main aspects as distinctive of his approach to economics, distinguished from say Jevons and Edgeworth (see *Principles of Economics*, *Industry and Trade*, *Money Credit and Commerce* and his main articles collected in Pigou 1925). But it is his last unfinished book on economic progress which gives particularly interesting insights on his conception of wellbeing and allows us to shed a new light into Marshall's economic thought on the fundamental conditions of economic progress including state intervention. The notes left for his last volume allows us to frame better his complex approach to economics which goes far beyond the analytical apparatus developed particularly in Book V of *Principles of Economics*, and to understand his main concerns as economist, among them the question of how to prompt human wellbeing has a paramount importance.

2 The Choice of *Economics*

Marshall's gradual evolution into economics would help to better understand the presence of those three dimensions in his approach. As is well-known, he got great distinction in the Mathematical Tripos. Then he gave much time to mental science, philosophy and psychology. While ethical and psychological issues were vivid in his mind, transition to economics was forced by academic needs ("I taught economics because Pearson did not wish it", see below). A reluctant economist at first, later recollected how "gradually …the increasing urgency of economic studies as a means toward human wellbeing grew upon me", and that "economics grew and grew in practical urgency, not so much in relation to the growth of wealth as to the quality of life" (Whitaker 1996, II: 285; Coats and Raffaelli 2006: 183).[1]

As John K. Whitaker remarks, plunging headlong into philosophy "the newly-awakened Marshall came to ethics, psychology and – rather reluctantly – political economy; that is to the study on a secular basis of the possibilities for man's mental and material development and the factors frustrating such development" (1975, I: 5). As recalled by Marshall himself, "Psychology seemed to hold out good promise of constructive and progressive studies of human nature and its possibilities: and I thought that it might best meet my wants. .....I taught economics because Pearson did not wish it but repelled with indignation the suggestion that I was an economist 'I am a philosopher straying in a foreign land: I will go home soon'" (Marshall's manuscript fragment, quoted in Whitaker 1975, I: 6–7).

Marshall's passage into economics is described in his own words in some pages, written about 1917 and designed for the Preface to *Money, Credit and Commerce*:

> About the year 1867 (while mainly occupied with teaching Mathematics in Cambridge), Mansel's Bampton Lectures came into my hands and caused me to think that man's own possibilities were the most important subject for his study. So I gave myself for a time to the study of Metaphysics; but soon passed to what seemed to be the more progressive study of Psychology. Its fascinating inquiries into the possibilities of the higher and more rapid development of human faculties brought me into touch with the question: how far do the conditions of life of the British (and other) working classes generally suffice for fullness of life? Older and wiser men told me that the resources of production do not suffice for affording to the great body of the people the leisure and the opportunity for study; and they told me that I needed to study Political Economy. I followed their service, and regarded myself as a wanderer in the land of dry facts; looking forward to a speedy return to the luxuriance of pure thought. (Keynes 1924: 171)

However, a certain measure of regret for that choice remained always with him. As it is recollected by Keynes: "Near the end of his life, when the intellect grew dimmer and the preaching imp could rise nearer to the surface to the protest against its lifelong servitude, he once said: 'If

[1] For "economic science and applied economic ethics" in Marshall, see Coats (1990).

I had to live my life over again I should have devoted it to psychology. Economics has too little to do with ideals.' These notions had always been with him. ....Meanwhile I got a good deal interested in the semi-mathematical side of pure economics, and was afraid of becoming a mere thinker. But a glance at my patron saint seemed to call me back to the right path. ...I despised them, but the *instinct of the chase* tempted me towards them'" (Keynes 1924: 200–1).

After his commitment to economics, Marshall "seems to have abandoned any serious attempt to do work in psychology or philosophy. But his early ambitions in these directions did leave significant effects" (Whitaker 1975, I: 9). This explains pretty well why his economics is imbued with ethical, psychological and philosophical elements, often severely criticized (Parsons 1937; Samuelson 1967; Blaug 1997) and why it is not reducible to pure economics. But, according to Marshall, economics is not even to be taken as merely abstract in so far as it has a part which is unavoidably applied.[2] This latter aspect largely explains the definition Marshall gave to economics and with which we have opened this paper.

3 Wellbeing as a Matter of Progress

For Marshall, the possibilities of economic and social progress with prospects of the elimination of human poverty were major motives which took him from philosophical studies to economic studies. This emphasis on progress and human wellbeing stayed in his thoughts and remained all along his life. The projected volume on economic progress was the final stage in this lifelong endeavour. Eliminating poverty, progress would provide means for all the people to develop their faculties and activities; this message is often repeated as for instance in *Industry and Trade* where he refers to "the distant goal where the opportunities of a noble life may be accessible to all" (1919: 665), or in *Principles of Economics* where from

[2] "Some parts of economics are relatively abstract or pure, because they are concerned mainly with broad general propositions: for, in order that a proposition may be of broad application it must necessarily contain few details: it cannot adapt itself to particular cases; and if it points to any prediction, that must be governed by a strong conditioning clause in which a very large meaning is given to the phrase 'other things being equal'. Other parts are relatively applied, because they deal with narrower questions more in detail; they take more account of local and temporary elements; and they consider economic conditions in fuller and closer relation to other conditions of life" (1920: 37 fn).

the fifth edition of 1907 he added a final new chapter "Progress in relation to standards of life", which has given the *Principles* "a higher, ethical note" (Groenewegen 2005; Nishizawa, forthcoming).

Economic progress was to be the subject of Marshall's last book, after his three main works (*Principles of Economics, Industry and Trade*, and *Money Credit and Commerce*). Elected as Professor of Political Economy at the University of Cambridge in December 1884, Marshall was asked to address to the Industrial Remuneration Conference towards the end of January 1885a. Here, referring to "the first aim of every social endeavour", he concludes his speech as follows:

> ...no one can lay his head on his pillow at peace with himself, who is not giving of his time and his substance to diminish the number of the outcasts of society, and to increase the number of those who can earn a reasonable income and have the opportunity of living, if they will it, a noble life. (1885b: 183, emphasis added)

This opinion is repeated with the same words in the last concluding paragraph of his last published book, *Money, Credit and Commerce* (1923), which was "the third of a group" of a series (i.e. first, *Principles*, second, *Industry and Trade*) to be followed by a fourth volume (the one on Economic Progress). In *Money Credit and Commerce*, Marshall mentions "the causes which govern the richness of the reward of the work"—a subject already partly developed in the first volume of the series, that is the *Principles*. Those causes are considered "the deepest concern to the student of the conditions of social well-being" and, accordingly, they were to "be designed to have a prominent place in the final volume of the present series" (1923: 234), namely to that last never published volume to which he optimistically refers to in the Preface: "although old age presses on me, I am not without hopes that some of the notions, which I have formed as to the possibilities of social advance, may yet to be published" (1923: v–vi).

That final volume never appeared but several notes written for it survive and are preserved at the Marshall Library of Economics. These notes focus on the concept of economic progress and on the main elements that could foster it. The theme of economic progress is indeed the constant background of any Marshall's reflection and references to it are present also in all his published writings. However—although part of that material consists of a number of reprints (some of them partly modified) and a few manuscript notes have recently been published by some Marshallian scholars (for instance, Dardi 2010; Groenewegen 2005; Raffaelli 2011)—the interest of these unpublished notes lies in the particular emphasis given to certain elements that according to Marshall were the driving force of economic progress (Caldari and Nishizawa 2020).

Economic progress is for Marshall something highly complex which involves several different factors and implies both quantitative and qualitative changes. Progress is not to be identified with a mere increment of "wealth", it does not coincide with economic growth but it involves other and far more important factors; as Marshall underlines in *Principles*: "the production of wealth is but a means to the sustenance of man; to the satisfaction of his wants; and to the development of his activities, physical, mental and moral[3]" (1920: 173). This explains the reason why Marshall prefers the terms "development" or "progress" rather than "growth", which is barely used in his writings. The term growth suggests in fact mainly a quantitative meaning, while "development" and "progress" connote more a qualitative dimension. True progress unavoidably implies a certain level of material wealth—"a certain minimum of means is necessary for material wellbeing", he writes (undated, Marshall library Archive, Folder 5.3.1)—but it is mainly marked by other features.

Human wellbeing is the true aim of progress and it has to be conceived as something extremely complex and multifaceted in so far as it includes material, physical, mental and moral components. As suggested in the title of this paper, following Marshall, when reasoning in terms of wellbeing, three main different aspects have to be taken into consideration.

[3]Though the power of sustaining great muscular exertion seems to rest on constitutional strength and other physical conditions, yet it also depends on force of will, and strength of character: as recalled in *Principles*, "this strength of the man himself, this resolution, energy and self-masterly, or in short this 'vigour' is the source of all progress" (Marshall 1920: 193–94). In his late notes, Marshall remarks that: "The ideal is not comfort but life, vigour. The comfort of the masses is to be thought for: they ought not to [be] robbed of their sugar, or their tobacco. But it is their life, the physical mental & moral vigour for which we ought to care" (undated, Marshall Library Archive, folder 5.9). This is why for him it was necessary to "Use public money freely in order to increase vigour rather than diminish suffering" (dated 7.9.11; 5.1.12 and 18.1.12, Marshall Library Archive, folder 5.39). A concept that is repeated in a letter written to Helen Bosanquet (28 September 1902), where Marshall stresses: "I have always held that poverty & pain, disease & death are evils of much importance than they appear, except in so far as they lead to weakness of life & character; & that true philanthropy aims at increasing strength more than at diminishing poverty" (Whitaker 1996, II: 399).

Wellbeing has in fact (1) an important economic connotation, insofar as it necessarily implies a certain degree of wealth; a true wellbeing also implies (2) many elements that are more connected with the ethical, moral and mental sphere, insofar as it relies to human beings; wellbeing, finally, entails (3) a political involvement insofar as it cannot be guaranteed by the simple free play of the market but it requires a certain degree of state intervention. When inquiring into these different aspects connected to wellbeing and therefore to economic progress, Marshall, especially in his unpublished notes, underlines what are, in his view, the most important elements to foster.

4 The Economic and Ethical Levers of Progress and Wellbeing

In a handwritten note, Marshall stresses that "great advance in material wellbeing is attainable only by those nations, whose industries are progressive, and whose men are strong in character and in action" (undated, Marshall Library Archive, Folder 5.3.1). Accordingly, when dealing with the material, economic wellbeing Marshall focuses on two main strictly interconnected questions: (a) how to promote productivity and industrial efficiency; (b) how to strengthen people's character and foster their activity, which depend on living and working conditions and circumstances.

How to increase productivity, industrial efficiency and national production is the central question in *Industry and Trade* (1919), where Marshall deals with the problem of the decreasing competitiveness of British industries (Belussi and Caldari 2011; Nishizawa 2001). In his notes on progress, Marshall devotes a large attention to industrial and labour efficiency; starting from a number of reflections on the characteristics of British economy and its transformation (Marshall Library Archive, folders 5.37; 5.42), he inquiries into the factors that may foster industrial efficiency and competitiveness. Free enterprise, initiative and the capacity to tackle uncertainty—considered "an inevitable result of progress, but also a condition necessary for it" (dated 13.11.03, Marshall Library Archive, folder 5.42), "eagerness on the part of .. experienced m[e]n of business" (undated, Marshall Library Archive, folder 5.8) are considered among the most important aspects on the production side. References are also made to the role of small size firms and the possible negative effects of advertising, on which Marshall largely dwells on in *Industry and Trade*

(Caldari 2007). However, in the notes on progress, it is the labour side that is more analysed: hours of labour, level of wages, productive efficiency and work conditions. If on the one hand productive efficiency of labour requires an appropriate industrial organization (Caldari 2007), on the other hand it is fundamentally based on labour conditions and their possible effects on workers considered both as working people and human beings.

According to Marshall, "the progress of man's nature" (or character) is "the centre of the ultimate aim of economic studies" (1961: 75)[4] and a crucial importance is recognized to the interaction between *economic* wellbeing (economic environment) and *moral* wellbeing (character formation). These two aspects of what he calls "organic growth" (Nishizawa, forthcoming) could not, in his view, be separated:

> partly through the suggestions of biological study, the influence of circumstances in fashioning character is generally recognized as the dominant fact in social science. Economists have accordingly now learnt to take a larger and more hopeful view of the possibilities of human progress. They have learnt to trust that the human will, guided by careful thought, can so modify circumstances as largely to modify character; and thus to bring about new conditions of life still more favourable to character; and therefore to the economic, as well as the moral, wellbeing of the masses of the people. (1920, 48: emphasis added)

In his view, the progress of society would annihilate the distinction between working man and gentleman; here he recognizes as decisive factor the influence which an occupation exerts on human character: since "work, in its best sense, the healthy energetic exercise of faculties, is the aim of life, is life itself", ideally no man "should have any occupation which tends to make him anything else than gentleman" (1873a: 115 and 110). The important influence of work and labour conditions on human character is often underlined by Marshall, as in *Principles* where he writes that "man's character [is] formed by the way he uses his faculties in his work, by his thoughts and feelings which it suggests, and by his relations to his associates in work, his employers and his employees" (1920: 2).[5]

[4] For the attention given to "human character", see Raffaelli's "Character and capabilities" in Raffaelli et al. (2006).

[5] A clear echo of this Marshallian opinion is in Pigou's *Economics of Welfare* where the author notes: "Non-economic welfare is liable to be modified by the manner in

Marshall pays great attention to the conditions of different occupations. Those employments that promote sense of responsibility and mental wideness also ameliorate the character of employees; they "demand powers and activities of mind in various kinds; the faculty of maintaining social intercourse with a large number of persons; and, in appearance, at least, the kindly habit of promptly anticipating the feelings of others on minor points, of ready watchfulness to avoid each trivial word or deed that may pain or annoy. These qualities are required for success, and they are therefore prepared in youth by a careful, long and continued education. Throughout life they are fostered and improved by exercise and by contact with persons who have similar qualities and require them of their associate" (1873a: 103–104). On the contrary, those occupations that require many hours of hard work, tire and restrict mental faculties, and take place in unhealthy environments, are absolutely prejudicial to employees.

Marshall gives also much attention to the question of wages (Caldari 2006b, 2015) and he deeply inquiries into the ("limited") relation between efficiency and remuneration. In a typewritten text left for his volume on progress, he underlines that:

> the personal efficiency of a worker is a group of qualities inherent in himself. It is likely to have been largely influenced by his surroundings; and when brought to bear in action its potency is dominated by his surroundings: but it is at any one time his own, whatever be his surroundings. The elements of which it may be made up are very numerous; and their relative importance varies with the occupation and other circumstances of the individual....[and therefore] the social value of a man's efficiency is almost as incapable of measurement as is the aggregate of qualities of which it is composed...[Because] such a measure *for it* ignores morbid and other unworthy pleasures; *and it* takes no account of the needs of *posterity; for only* a small share of the contributions to social wellbeing made by *a creative mind, such as Aeschylus, or* Beethoven, Archimedes or Watt accrued to *the* own country or the generation *to which the genius belonged. Also the*

which income is earned. For the surroundings of work react upon the quality of life. Ethical quality is affected by the occupations.... In the relations between employers and workpeople in ordinary industry the non-economic element is fully as significant. ... Employers and the employed became more distant in station,......This spirit of hostility was an obvious negative element in non-economic welfare due to an economic cause; and the partial suppression of it through the Boards of Conciliation, Whitley Councils and Co-partnership arrangements is an equally obvious positive element. ..." (1920: 14–17).

> *measure* fails to recognize *such* benefits *as* result from the labours of a great musician among a people whose musical faculties are dormant *so* that they care little for the education which he is giving them: or *from* those of a civil engineer whose efforts to develop the natural resources of a backward country meet with *little* support. (undated, Marshall Library Archive, Folder 6.21.1)[6]

This long quotation brings into focus the complexity of human nature, which Marshall bears always in his mind, and moreover the connected difficulty to foster at best man's potentialities. Indeed, although Marshall is the first economist to largely underline the importance of and systematically inquire into industrial organization and is far from overshadowing its effects in terms of productiveness, nonetheless it is man rather than industrial organization which is for him the most powerful and precious engine of progress.[7] The man Marshall refers to is not homo œconomicus typified by extremely simple behaviours but a social being characterized, as the quotation above suggests, by several intricate actions and reactions. Tiziano Raffaelli's works on Marshall's early philosophical studies (1994, 2003) allow us to properly pin-point this important element and to fully understand Marshall's whole economic reasoning and his apparently odd (for an economist) arguments.[8]

[6] Among the elements that shape individual efficiency we find: "the qualities of physical and constitutional strength, the mental qualities of manual dexterity and skill: and beyond these they include patience, resolution, energy and self-mastery; knowledge and intelligence and artistic instincts; versatility and adaptability; initiative, inventiveness, sense of proportion, and the power of rising to emergency; honesty, solidity of character; order, unselfishness and affection in family life; patriotism; ethical, social, and aesthetic idealism" (undated, Marshall Library Archive, folder 6.21.1).

[7] Since his early *Lectures to Women* (1873b), Marshall had underlined that man is "the finest instrument of production in the world", "the most important productive machine" warning that "we must regard a man as intelligent capital" and "mental and moral capital" (Raffaelli et al. 1995: 98, 117–19).

[8] It is Tiziano Raffaelli (1994) who, first, has underlined the importance of some Marshall's early philosophical studies on mind (especially "Ye Machine") to understand his approach to economic science and in particular his idea of the growth of knowledge, understood as the product of a mix of routine and innovation, his rejection of the neoclassical concept of *homo oeconomicus* in favour of 'a man of flesh and blood'; his view of industrial and social organizations; the use of partial equilibrium analysis; his critical position towards some political and social issues such as socialism, trade unions and bureaucracy; the idea that progress must advance slowly (see on this Caldari 2015, 2018).

One of them is the emphasis that Marshall gives to "education" in all his writings including his notes on progress. Education is crucial insofar as it promotes mental progress, as clearly depicted in the manuscript Ye Machine, first published by Raffaelli in 1994. In its turn, mental progress allows for improvements in man's occupations, wages, style of life, productivity and efficiency. Education is therefore a crucial element for production, wealth and wellbeing. According to Marshall, the only true and incisive remedy to poverty is education[9] to be understood as something complex and multifaceted. As underlined in a late note dated 25.6.22, the chief purpose of education is

> to cause mental activities to be thorough. These [activities in order of time are: observation, memory, reasoning, imagination, creation. 'Observation' is to be taken broadly so as to include every method of acquiring knowledge. Similarly, 'reasoning' is to include appropriate arrangement of knowledge in relation to the particular problem in hand. 'Creation' is the product of the application of reasoning to and imagination to material supplied by observation and memory. (undated, Marshall Library Archive, Folder 5.6)

Education stimulates previously unused human resources, and in this way it increases production. It is therefore a form of investment on man, the subtlest instrument of production, and the most important productive machinery.[10] Moreover, education helps distributive justice because it raises the wages of unskilled workers: on the one hand it reduces their number, making that kind of work scarce, on the other it improves the quality of work and increases production.

[9] In a letter to Bishop Brooke Foss Westcott (24 January 1900), he writes: "There is only one effective remedy that I know of, and that is *not* short in its working. It needs patience for the ills of others as well as our own. It is to remove the sources of industrial weakness: to improve the education of home life, and the opportunities for fresh-air joyous play of the young; to keep them longer at school; and to look after them, when their parents are making default, much more paternally than we do. Then the Residuum should be attacked in its strongholds. We ought to expend more money, and with it more force, moral and physical, in cutting off the supply of people unbale to do good work, and therefore unable to earn good wages" (Whitaker 1996, II: 263).

[10] As such education plays an essential part in social (and economic) progress so that Marshall has been recognized as a forerunner of human capital theory (see Bowman 1990, see also Nishizawa 2002).

For all these reasons, as Marshall explains: "the best investment of the present capital of the country is to educate the next generation and make them all gentlemen" (1873b: 106). A low level of education is considered a problem which affects not only the people directly involved but the whole society and nation. As underlined in a long note dated 4.9.12 with many pieces pasted from *Principles*:

> ..in the lower ranks of society the evil is great. For the slender means and education of the parents, and comparative weakness of their power of distinctly realizing the future, prevent them from investing capital in the education and training of their children ...*And* this evil is cumulative. The worse fed are the children of one generation, the less will they earn when they grow up, and the less will be their power of providing adequately for the material wants of their children; and so on. And again, the less fully their own faculties are developed, the less will they realize the importance of developing the best faculties of their children, and the less will be their power of doing so. (dated 4.9.12, Marshall Library Archive, Folder 5.40)

As we will see in the next section, this is one of the grounds for state intervention and taxation: "funds [to guarantee a certain level of education] should be obtained by a graduated income tax; from which savings should be exempted: + a property tax which would of course be highly graduated; but a less percentage on funds carried from income to property, than if they had been consumed" (dated August 1920, Marshall Library Archive, Folder 5.6).

5 Government and Welfare

Once pinpointed the main conditions for progress and wellbeing, in considering how to encourage and stimulate them, Marshall underlines the crucial role of government. His attitude towards state activity has changed over time (Caldari 2016) and especially in his late notes on progress Marshall considers as indispensable and unavoidable a certain (not so small indeed) degree of state intervention since it is only in an ideal order that "we [may] postulate ... a perfection of human nature so absolute that every one cares for the wellbeing of his neighbour as much as for his own; and therefore there exists no justice or injustice, no law and no compulsion" (dated 27.4.22, Marshall Library Archive, Folder 5.7). On the contrary, in the "world as it is", far from any ideal perfection, public intervention is considered the only means to face, partly at least, those elements that may prevent a true progress of the whole nation. In the real world, progress has also produced important wealth inequalities among people.[11] These inequalities for Marshall may have serious consequences on the trend of progress itself. Far from endorsing the more extreme socialist conclusions with collectivist flavour (McWilliams Tullberg 1975, 2006), Marshall reputes that if a certain degree of inequality is unavoidable, natural and even beneficial, it may also act—beyond a certain level—as a dangerous brake on progress: this is the case when considerable wealth inequalities imply that some strata of population are cut out of any possibility to properly contribute to the wellbeing of the nation. He often recalls that there is "one waste product, so much more important than all others", that is called "THE WASTE PRODUCT": it is the higher abilities of many of the working classes, "the latent, the undeveloped, the choked-up and wasted faculties for higher work, that for lack of opportunity have come to nothing" (Marshall 1889: 229). This is one of the main reasons why the state has to intervene.

Government—at both the central and local level—does in fact play a crucial role in promoting progress and therefore wellbeing, and indeed a number of cases justify its intervention. As Marshall put it in a note written in a very late manuscript[12]:

> Everyone has duties to himself and to others. Duties to himself are connected with the development of strength of character, of mind and physique. Duties to others call for the avoidance of actions that may injure them; and the rendering on occasion of service to them ..... But the reach of an individual in such matters is necessarily narrow; and many of his duties to his fellow creatures must be rendered through powerful agencies to the support of which he contributes his share. (undated, Marshall Library Archive, Folder 5.36)

[11] As stressed by Marshall "The existence of grave inequalities of wealth is an integral part of the progress of mankind, as we know it. Another world may be more prosperous than our own, without any similar inequalities. Everyone in it may be intent on the advance of general wellbeing, and care but little how much of it falls to his share" (undated, Marshall Library Archive, Folder 5.8).

[12] Although this manuscript is undated it is bound together with a note by his wife Mary in which she writes: "These pages were written during the last few months when his memory was failing". Marshall's handwriting evidences his old age.

Where by "powerful agencies" he means governmental agencies that are distinguished, according to their scope, between national and local.

Among the most important functions which Marshall attributes to government we find: a) "to provide for weal at home and for defense against external force" (undated, Marshall Library Archive, 6.18.2) and especially b) "To clear the way for [progress]: to strengthen those who may take part on it, and to provide security" (undated, Marshall Library Archive, 5.26). Moreover, state has to intervene when

(a) [...] individuals concerned are of a lower order than the average man, and are in fact not fit for freedom: this justifies the constraint of madmen, idiots, and perhaps habitual drunkards
(b) [...] private action is injurious to public weal; e.g. sanitary nuisances
(c) [...] the individuals concerned are acting injuriously to members of their own family and through them of the State .....
(d) [...] the individuals concerned are sacrificing higher ends in order to increase their material gains in such a way as indirectly to compel others to do the same ....
(e) [...] the individuals concerned are reaping too much for themselves of what is really collective property: that the State is therefore justified in demanding some concession to public interest...(note with several dates written on—10.10.03, 13.8.04, 27.2.12, Marshall Library Archive, Folder 5.36).

Here we find not only the idea of a state that must take care of individuals' wellbeing and provide important public goods (such as defence), but also of a state that may interfere in people's private lives for reasons of public benefit. According to Marshall:

> It is a urgent social duty, which must be performed at any cost, to put a stop as soon as may be to those conditions of work, which are incompatible with a wholesome life. Whenever the home of children is such that there is no considerable chance of their growing up to be good citizens, healthy in mind and body, the State is bound as a duty and for self-preservation to intervene. It may improve the home; or close it, and take charge of the family. In the rare cases in which when the wages of any kind of adult male labour are so low that, even when supplemented by the utmost earnings that wife and children are likely to bring in, they would not suffice to

> maintain a wholesome family life, then it may conceivably be advisable to prohibit such low wages. (undated, Marshall Library Archive, Folder 5.37 emphasis added)

Taxation is a fundamental means for raising funds to be used to achieve government's main purposes. Although it is a crucial topic in Marshall's reflections, "he never wrote a general treatise on taxation and failed to complete the segment on tax foreshadowed for Book X of Volume 2 of *the Principles*" (Groenewegen 1990: 91). There exist, nonetheless, "interesting fragments of taxation" (Groenewegen: ibid.), most notably notes left for the book on progress, and other writings (academic notes and reprints)[13] that enable us to frame Marshall's view on the subject.[14]

Among its main aims, state has also that of an equitable distribution of wealth and application of the principle of equity. The "equity of the distribution of the burden of obtaining these services" (undated, Marshall Library Archive, Folder 6.18.1) is indeed considered a fundamental principle for taxation, along with that of equality, to be understood as "equality of sacrifice, and in proportion to ability or in proportion to the services rendered" (undated, Marshall Library Archive, Folder 5.40). Equity and equality are not, however, important principles to follow only in collecting taxes, but also in using the money collected from taxation. In a very amended note, Marshall underlines that among the fundamental principles of taxation there should be the following rule:

> Take off taxes from the poorer classes as far as is practicable without encouraging wastefulness in the public expenditure, which will come ever more and more under their control: and use public money freely in order to increase vigour rather than to diminish suffering. Take the least attractive course...... (dated 7.9.11; 5.1.12 and 18.1.12; Marshall Library Archive, Folder 5.39)

Taxes are to be used in an efficient and not wasteful way, where "efficient" is to be understood as able to foster progress and wellbeing. To this end,

[13] Two major works by Marshall on taxation are in fact to be recalled: The Memorandum on the Classification and Incidence of Imperial and Local Taxation (1897) and National Taxation after the War (1917).

[14] For a comprehensive explanation of the British tax system and its evolution over time during Marshall's life, see Groenewegen (1995).

both the richer and poorer classes have, for Marshall, the duty—according to different proportions—to cooperate with the state.

Particular attention is paid to some specific taxes, including the taxes on coinage, luxuries, houses and land, motor cars, savings, income and wages and natural resources. They are all considered for their effects in terms of equity, efficacy and consequences for wellbeing. In relation to these important aspects, Marshall distinguishes between beneficial and onerous taxes:

> A tax is "onerous" to any class of persons, if it directly or indirectly takes from them any income or property, which they would otherwise [have] possessed; and is expended in such a way as not to give them an equivalent return. On the other hand if a special tax, levied on wet land, is spent on a drainage system which added much more than it costs to the value of the land, then it is not "onerous" but beneficial to those owners.
> Similarly a tax levied on the whole people and spent on education, sanitation, etc. in such a way as to confer on them benefits in the health and energy and earning power which are more than equivalent to the charge levied on them is "beneficial". In so far as it is levied mainly on the well-to-do and spent mainly in the service of the working classes, it is onerous to the well to do in the first instance: though it may be in the long run beneficial even to them, if it greatly increases the supply of efficient labour; while it makes the country stronger against invasion, and more abounding in the amenities of life...... (undated, Marshall Library Archive, Folder 6.17)

A tax is, therefore, considered "onerous" or "beneficial" not on the basis of its immediate effect on the people that pay it but mainly on the ground of its effects in terms of progress and public wellbeing. Every tax is, therefore, to be considered "beneficial" if it is used to increase and promote the conditions of progress (education, sanitation, health, quality of labour and so forth).[15]

[15] In the last chapter of *Principles* ("Progress in relation to standards of life", contending the chief remedy to fit more of the children of the unskilled for higher work), Marshall notes: "Education must be made more thorough. ...It is to educate character, faculties and activities; so that the children even of those parents who are not thoughtful themselves, may have a better chance of being trained up to become thoughtful parents of the next generation. To this end public money must flow freely. And it must flow freely to provide fresh air and space for wholesome play for the children in all working class quarters. Thus the State seems to be required to contribute generously and even lavishly to that side of the wellbeing of the poorer working class which they cannot easily

6 Concluding Remarks

Economic progress is the underlining issue and concern in all Marshall's writings. Moreover, it was to be the main subject of his last never published book.

Marshall's idea of economic progress is to be understood as an extremely multifaceted question which involves—along with the strictly economic elements—social, ethical and political aspects.

Progress means an increase of human wellbeing, but the latter is by no means only connected with material wealth: it implies also a number of elements that contribute to a high level of quality of life (education, health, unpolluted environment and so on).

Progress needs all the people's effort and contribution according to their best potentialities but also and moreover state intervention. If progress in fact implies to take the best from people and to put to good use their potentialities and capabilities, it is up to the state to pave the way for that.

In the notes left for his volume on progress, Marshall clearly define what are in his view the responsibilities of each person and the role of the state in promoting progress and therefore wellbeing. More than in other writings, in these notes Marshall underlines that a true long-lasting prosperity of a society is based on wealth but also and moreover on the quality of its people and the activity of its government and that wellbeing is to be considered as a common aim.

provide for themselves" (1920: 717–18). See also fn. and Appendix G, whose §9 referred to "fresh air rate" (see on this Caldari 2004). In a note written for his book on progress, he underlines: "The chief sources of water supply should be declared national property; and they should be leased, ...to local authorities. The same is true of fresh air. The central government should see to it that towns and industrial districts do not continue to increase without ample provisions for that fresh air and wholesome play which are required to maintain the vigour of the people and their place among nations; this is, perhaps, the most important financial responsibility which has not yet been faced" (undated, Marshall Library Archive, folder 6.32.1).

References

Belussi F. and Caldari K. (2011), "The Lancashire Industrial District: Its Rise, Prosperity and Decline in the Analysis of British Economists", in T. Raffaelli, T. Nishizawa, and S. Cook (eds), *Marshall, Marshallians and Industrial Economics*, Abingdon, Oxon: Routledge: 135–162.

Blaug M. (1997 [1962]), *Economic Theory in Retrospect*, V ed., Cambridge: Cambridge University Press.

Bowman R.S., (1990), "Smith, Mill, and Marshall on Human Capital Formation", *History of Political Economy*, 22(2): 239–259.

Caldari K. (2004), "Alfred Marshall's Idea of Progress and Sustainable Development", *Journal of the History of Economic Thought*, 26(4): 519–536.

Caldari K. (2006a), "Progress", in T. Raffaelli, G. Becattini, and M. Dardi (eds), *The Elgar Companion to Alfred Marshall*, Aldershot: Edward Elgar: 483–487.

Caldari K. (2006b), "Labour and Wages", in T. Raffaelli, G. Becattini, and M. Dardi (eds), *The Elgar Companion to Alfred Marshall*, Aldershot: Edward Elgar: 328–336.

Caldari K. (2007), "Alfred Marshall's Critical Analysis of Scientific Management", *European Journal of the History of Economic Thought*, 14(1): 55–78.

Caldari K. (2015), "Marshall and Complexity: A Necessary Balance Between Process and Order", *Cambridge Journal of Economics*, 39(4): 1071–1085.

Caldari K. (2016), "Marshall's Reflections on War Through His Economic Writings", in *OEconomia* 6(4): 475–485.

Caldari K. (2018), "Alfred Marshall", in J. Conlin (ed), *Great Economic Thinkers*, Reaktion: University of Chicago Press.

Caldari K. and Nishizawa T. (2011), "Marshall's Ideas on Progress: Roots and Diffusion", in H.D. Kurz, T. Nishizawa, and K. Tribe (eds), *The Dissemination of Economic Ideas*, Cheltenham: Edward Elgar: 125–157.

Caldari K. and Nishizawa T. (2014), "Marshall's 'Welfare Economics' and 'Welfare': A Reappraisal Based on his Unpublished Manuscript on Progress", *History of Economic Ideas*, XXII(1): 51–67.

Caldari K. and Nishizawa T. (2016), "Progress Beyond Growth: Some Insights from Marshall's Final Book", *European Journal of the History of Economic Thought*, 23(1): 226–245.

Caldari K. and Nishizawa T. (2020), *Alfred Marshall's Last Challenge: His Book on Economic Progress*, Newcastle: Cambridge Scholars Publishing.

Coats A.W. (1990), "Marshall and Ethics", in R. McWilliams Tullberg (ed), *Alfred Marshall in Retrospect*, Cheltenham: Edward Elgar: 153–177.

Coats A.W. and Raffaelli T. (2006), "Economics and Ethics", in T. Raffaelli, G. Becattini, and M. Dardi (eds), *The Elgar Companion to Alfred Marshall*, Aldershot: Edward Elgar: 182–189.

Dardi, M. (2010), "Three Manuscripts on Ideal Social Orders", *Marshall Studies Bulletin*, vol. 11, online: http://www.disei.unifi.it/vp-100-marshall-studies-bulletin-vol-11-2010.html.

Groenewegen, P.D. (1990), "Marshall on Taxation", in R. McWilliams Tullberg (ed), *Alfred Marshall in Retrospect*, Aldershot: Edward Elgar: 91–112.

Groenewegen P. (1995), *A Soaring Eagle: Alfred Marshall, 1842–1924*, Aldershot: Edward Elgar.

Groenewegen P. (2005), "A Book That Never Was: Marshall's Final Volume on Progress", *History of Economic Review*, no. 42: 29–44.

Keynes, J.M. (1924), "Alfred Marshall", in *Essays in Biography*, in *The Collected Writings of John Maynard Keynes* (1972), vol. X, London: Macmillan: 161–231.

McWilliams Tullberg R. (1975), "Marshall's Tendency to Socialism", *History of Political Economy*, 7(1): 75–111.

McWilliams Tullberg R. (2006), "Socialism", in T. Raffaelli, G. Becattini, and M. Dardi (eds), *The Elgar Companion to Alfred Marshall*, Aldershot: Edward Elgar: 517–521.

Marshall A. (1873a), "The future of the working classes", in A.C. Pigou (ed.) (1925), *Memorials of Alfred Marshall*, London: Macmillan: 101–118.

Marshall A. (1873b), "Lectures to Women", in T. Raffaelli, R. McWilliams Tullberg, and E. Biagini (eds) (1995), *Lectures to Women*, Aldershot: Edward Elgar: 85–132.

Marshall A. (1885a), "The Present Position of Economics", in A.C. Pigou (ed.) (1925), *Memorials of Alfred Marshall*, London: Macmillan: 152–174.

Marshall A. (1885b), "How far do remediable causes influence prejudicially (a) the continuity of employment, (b) the rates of wages?", in *Industrial Remuneration Conference. The Report of the Proceedings and Papers,* London: Cassel & Company Limited: 173–199.

Marshall A. (1889), "Co-operation", in A.C. Pigou (ed) (1925), *Memorials of Alfred Marshall*, London: Macmillan: 227–255.

Marshall A. (1919), *Industry and Trade*, London: Macmillan.

Marshall A. (1920 [1890]), *Principles of Economics*, London: Macmillan.

Marshall A. (1923), *Money, Credit and Commerce*, London: Macmillan.

Marshall A. (1961), *Principles of Economics*, Variorum Edition, 2 vols., C.W. Guillebaud (ed), vol. 2 Notes, London: Macmillan.

Nishizawa T. (2001), "Alfred Marshall on Britain's Industrial Leadership—With Special Reference to Industrial Organization", *Economic Review* (Hitotsubashi University), 52(3): 239–252.

Nishizawa T. (2002), "Alfred Marshall on Human Capital and Future Generation", *Economic Review* (Hitotsubashi University), 53(4): 305–324.

Nishizawa, T. (forthcoming), "Alfred Marshall on Progress and Human Wellbeing", in R.E. Backhouse, A. Baujard and T. Nishizawa (eds), *Welfare Theory,*

Public Action and Ethical Values: Revisiting the History of Welfare Economics. Cambridge: Cambridge University Press.

Parsons T. (1937), *The Structure of Social Action: A Study in Social Theory with Special Reference to a Group of Recent European Writers*, New York: The Free Press of Glencoe.

Pigou A.C. (1920), *The Economics of Welfare*, 4th ed., 1932, London: Macmillan.

Pigou A.C. (ed) (1925), *Memorials of Alfred Marshall*, London: Macmillan.

Raffaelli T. (1994), "Marshall on Machinery and Life", *Marshall Studies Bulletin* 4: 9–22.

Raffaelli T. (2003), *Marshall's Evolutionary Economics*, London: Routledge.

Raffaelli T. (2006), "Character and Capabilities", in T. Raffaelli, G. Becattini, and M. Dardi (eds), *The Elgar Companion to Alfred Marshall*, Aldershot: Edward Elgar: 488–494.

Raffaelli T. (2011), "Two Manuscripts on Competition", *Marshall Studies Bulletin*, 12. http://www.dse.unifi.it/CMpro-v-p-141.html.

Raffaelli T., McWilliams Tullberg R., and Biagini E. (1995), *Lectures to Women*, Aldershot: Edward Elgar.

Samuelson P.A. (1967), "Monopolistic Competition Revolution", in R.E. Kuenne (ed), *Monopolistic Competition Theory: Studies in Impact: Essays in Honor of Edward H. Chamberlin*, New York: Wiley: 105–138.

Whitaker J.K. (1975), *The Early Economic Writings of Alfred Marshall, 1867–1890*, 2 vols, London: Macmillan.

Whitaker J.K. (1996), *The Correspondence of Alfred Marshall*, J.K. Whitaker (ed), 3 vols., Cambridge: Cambridge University Press.

Jevons and Marshall as Humboldtian Scientists

Harro Maas

In *The Philosophical Breakfast Club*, Laura Snyder recently discussed the work of the mathematician Charles Babbage, the astronomer John Herschel, the political economist Richard Jones, and the polymath William Whewell as "Baconian."[1] But in her analysis of their scientific endeavors, Snyder somewhat brushed over the difficulties in classifying all of them as strictly "Baconian," even when Snyder is of course correct in signaling the great interest her cast of characters showed in Francis Bacon's work. Perhaps with the exception of Richard Jones, they were all moving towards a different understanding of the meaning of induction and the scientific method and to a different research practice.

It is exactly for this reason that the historian of science Susan Faye Cannon coined the notion of "Humboldtian science" in a famous essay in her *Science in Culture: The Victorian Period*. Cannon questioned the usefulness of the term "Baconian science" to characterize the inductive

[1]Laura J. Snyder, *The Philosophical Breakfast Club: Four Remarkable Friends Who Transformed Science and Changed the World* (Portland: Broadway Books, 2011).

H. Maas (✉)
Centre Walras-Pareto for the History of Economic and Political Thought, Institute for Political Studies, University of Lausanne, Lausanne, Switzerland
e-mail: Harro.maas@unil.ch

K. Caldari et al. (eds.), *Marshall and the Marshallian Heritage*, Palgrave Studies in the History of Economic Thought,
https://doi.org/10.1007/978-3-030-53032-7_6

approach to science in the Victorian period.[2] Her puzzle was that many Victorian scientists did not merely heap up facts to then draw conclusions; they also formed hypotheses along the way which were then loosely put to the test. For lack of a proper term, she proposed the notion of "Humboldtian science," after the famous German polymath Alexander von Humboldt, who is well-known for his daring voyages through the Amazon and the Andes to which he sailed with several ships, loaded with scientific instruments. From his measurements, he constructed comparisons between ecosystems (a word he coined) in different regions of the world. In his most daring and voluminous book, *Cosmos*, Humboldt tried to see how all the different spheres of nature were part of one unified whole, regulated by encompassing laws. Cannon emphasized Humboldt's *approach* to science. A plethora of scientific instruments, innumerable field observations, a commitment to precise measurements, the use of visuals such as charts, diagrams, and graphs, hypotheses that were developed on the go—Humboldt used all of those in an effort to render the data he collected in a coherent and preferably mathematical form.[3]

As Cannon was an expert on the Cambridge network of the early nineteenth century, it may come as no surprise that she considered to what extent some of its towering members, William Whewell and John Herschel in particular, could be considered as Humboldtians. William Whewell championed the inductive method; but in his history of philosophy of the inductive sciences and in his practical research, he gave induction a twist that made it differ substantially from what was at the time perceived as "Baconianism." Herschel preached his Baconian faith in his book on scientific method as well, but his scientific work at least partly passed Cannon's test. His astronomical sojourns in India and South-Africa, the (Imperial) project to observe and measure the transit of Venus, certainly can be analyzed as Humboldtian science. The same can be said of Whewell's studies on the tides, for which he constructed detailed tidal maps, or of his expedition with George Biddell Airy to the Dalcoath Mine in Cornwall to measure the mean density of the earth, a project that failed because of a "rascally piece of machinery of steel deviating

[2] Susan Faye Cannon, *Science in Culture: The Early Victorian Period* (New York, 1978).

[3] For a recent engaging, though somewhat overly heroic intellectual biography, see Andrea Wulf, *The Invention of Nature: Alexander von Humboldt's New World* (Knopf, 2015).

1/10,000th of an inch from a straight line."[4] Precision measurement and large-scale, collaborative projects are all there, and it is a question whether one should see these projects as *imperial* science, that is, enabled by the British Empire, as *empirical*—fact-finding—science, or as Humboldtian in not only striving to collect exact numerical data, but also searching for explanations by visual means and large-scale projects.

Probably, they are all three, but for this essay I would like to concentrate on the elements of *precision measurement* and *visualization*, as well as on the attempt to understand the world as an encompassing whole. I will discuss these elements in relation not to the natural sciences, but to the science of political economy, for which I will look at the work of two Victorian political economists, Stanley Jevons and Alfred Marshall. Hence, the question driving this essay is if we can consider Jevons and Marshall as Humboldtians, that is, as scientists approaching their subject with instruments of precision measurement and visualization that help to establish a web of mathematical laws explaining the economy as an interconnected whole. I will start my inquiry with a letter of thanks that Sidgwick received from Jevons for sending him Marshall's essay on international trade. In this essay, Marshall introduced his method of diagrams, the method that would become the workhorse of twentieth-century economics. Focusing primarily on their empirical work, I will discuss Jevons's use of graphic visualizations and Marshall's distinction between the method of diagrams and the method of graphs, along with his move away from mathematics and statistics as modes of expressing empirical economic research. In conclusion, I will reflect on the usefulness of the label of Humboldtian science to understand their ways of working.

1 Jevons on the Method of Diagrams

In a letter of 28 February 1879, Jevons thanked Sidgwick for sending him Marshall's paper on international trade. Jevons pointed out the close relation between graphs and mathematics, implicitly moving empirical statistics close to mathematical theory:

[4] Todhunter 2:93, letter of 9 September 1828 to Richard Jones, cited from Harro Maas, *William Stanley Jevons and the Making of Modern Economics* (Cambridge University Press, 2005).

> I notice … that you speak of the method of diagrams as being opposed to that of symbols, whereas I should not attribute this meaning to Marshall's remarks … I should prefer to say that if not ultimately the same methods they are parallel methods, the difference being one of convenience of apprehension.[5]

In Sidgwick's view, Marshall had drawn a clear distinction between symbols and diagrams. Marshall had pointed out that in contrast to mathematics, the method of diagrams was a visual method of proof and demonstration that was particularly appropriate for economics because of its subject matter. Jevons correctly argued that Marshall had considered the method of diagrams "more convenient" for reasoning in economics than mathematics, but as we will see, this did not make Marshall's use of the method the same as Jevons's. Especially Whitaker's work on Marshall's early mathematical manuscripts and Mary Morgan's recent work on economic modeling have uncovered the usage of the method of diagrams in Marshall's mental experiments.[6]

In contrast with Sidgwick and Marshall, Jevons considered the method of diagrams as a stepping-stone in the search for the mathematical laws governing data. As Michael White has recently argued, for Jevons these laws were, at the end of the day, rooted in natural phenomena.[7] Put otherwise, for Jevons there was a causal sequence from the natural to the social, and the task of the economist was to trace economic phenomena back to their natural causes, be they the choices made by individuals in the marketplace, commercial fluctuations, or otherwise. Inductive research was for Jevons a form of reverse engineering the natural and the social.

[5] Sidgwick archives TCC Add.Ms.c.94.59, cited in Maas, *Stanley Jevons*, p. 293.

[6] John K. Whitaker, "The Evolution of Alfred Marshall's Economic Thought and Writings Over the Years 1867–90," in *The Early Economic Writings of Alfred Marshall, 1867–1890* (London and Basingstoke: Macmillan, 1975), 1–113; Mary S. Morgan, *The World in the Model: How Economists Work and Think* (Cambridge: Cambridge University Press, 2012); See also Hsiang-Ke Chao and Harro Maas, "Engines of Discovery: Jevons and Marshall on the Methods of Graphs and Diagrams," in *Research in History of Economic Thought and Methodology* (Emerald Publishing, 2017), 35–61, https://doi.org/10.1108/S0743-41542017000035A003.

[7] Michael V. White, "Riders on the Storm: W. Stanley Jevons, Meteorology and the Analysis of 'Commercial Fluctuations'" (The usage of metaphors in the theorization of crises, cycles and equilibrium, Lausanne, 2019); See also Michael V. White, "Bridging the Natural and the Social: Science and Character in Jevons's Political Economy," *Economic Inquiry* 32, no. 3 (1994): 429–44.

In that sense, there was no difference between Jevons's search for the natural causes of commercial fluctuations and his remark in his *Principles of Science* that he hoped that one day, all phenomena of mind and matter would be reduced to changes in chemical components like phosphorus and nitrogen. For Jevons, relations between cause and effect were rooted in natural causes, and these relations could be expressed mathematically.

White gives the example of Jevons's comparison of grain prices in the thirteenth and fourteenth centuries, on the one hand, and in the nineteenth century, on the other.[8] Jevons used a set of grain prices from 1259 to 1400 that was produced by Thorold Rogers, first Tooke professor at King's College, London, to bring out the relation between commercial fluctuations and, as Jevons conjectured, sunspots. The starting point for Jevons's investigation was the "well-known principle of mechanics that the effects of a periodically varying cause are themselves periodical."[9] Using this principle, Jevons traced commercial fluctuations to the fluctuations in sunspot activity. He argued that commercial fluctuations could be traced to fluctuations in the prices of agricultural produce. These prices, in turn, depended on the yearly success of harvests, which depended on variations in the weather. These variations depended on variations in the sun's radiation. Sunspots provided an indication of the variations in the sun's activity. Hence, variations in the sun's activity, measured by sunspots, were the final causes of commercial fluctuations. Jevons read his paper on sunspots to the meeting of the British Association for the Advancement of Science in Bristol in 1875, but did not publish it because he discovered afterward that Rogers's data did not only fit the cycle of sunspots (of around eleven years), but several shorter cycles as well (Jevons 1884, 225).[10]

Not included in his 1875 paper was a diagram he made to compare the periodicity of Rogers's data with nineteenth-century grain prices.

Figure 1 shows Jevons's comparison between the movements in both data sets. White argues convincingly that the comparison was important for Jevons, because he considered that he could thus isolate the underlying law governing the data, a law that would not be "masked by 'all

[8] White, "Riders on the Storm."

[9] William Stanley Jevons, *Investigations in Currency and Finance* (London: Macmillan, 1884), 194.

[10] For details, see White, "Riders on the Storm."

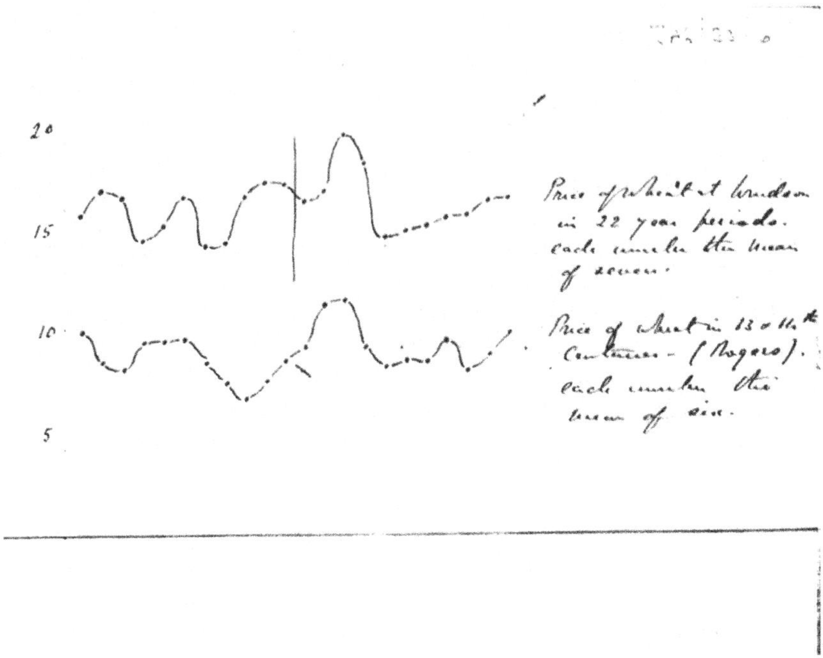

Fig. 1 Jevons's comparison of average prices of wheat in London for 22 year periods with the price of wheat in the thirteenth and fourteenth centuries. JA6/23/6 (Copyright of The University of Manchester)

kinds of political and social events', including wars, inventions, 'great industrial discoveries' and inflation at the turn of the century."[11]

There are many other examples of Jevons's efforts to reduce statistical data to law-like regularities that can be expressed in mathematical form, most famously his mathematical treatment of the so-called King-Davenant price-quantity table in his *Theory of Political Economy*, but one can also find snippets of papers that are not always easy to trace to one of his published articles in which Jevons is searching for the mathematical form of the data. Figure 2 provides an example in which Jevons is using the method of differences to search for the fit of a polynomial to what are most likely statistical data.

[11] White, 22 quoting Jevons 1875.

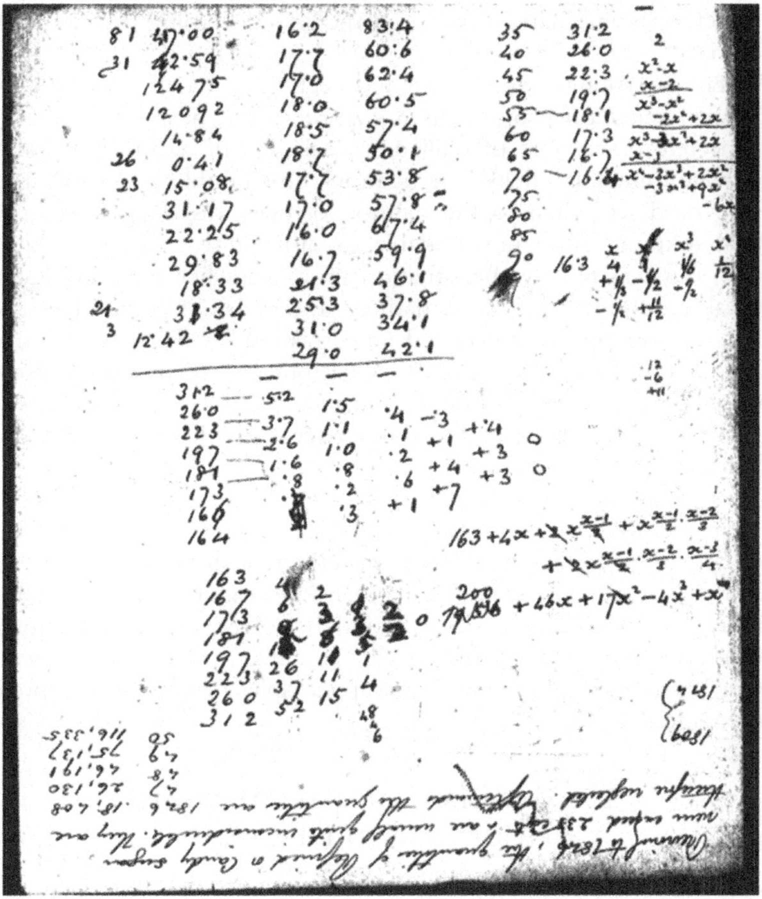

Fig. 2 Paper scrap on which Jevons compressed statistical data to a polynomial through the method of differences. JA6/23/11 (Copyright of The University of Manchester)

The point of these illustrations is that Jevons was shifting smoothly between the method of curves and the reduction of statistical data to mathematical form. For Jevons, there was no difference indeed between the use of diagrams and the effort to turn economics into a mathematical science. As I have argued elsewhere, the driving force of these efforts was his belief in the mechanical nature of the laws governing the natural and the social.[12]

When the young Jevons started collecting materials for his largest, unfinished statistical project, his *Statistical Atlas*, he referred as might be expected to the work of William Playfair, but he also included a citation from John Herschel's investigations into double stars that argued for the need to switch to the method of diagrams if rigorous mathematical solutions were not available or difficult to find. According to Jevons, this was exactly the situation in sciences like meteorology and political economy, where the nature of the data was—in Herschel's words—"uncertain, irregular, and embarrassing."[13] The "solid foundation" of scientific knowledge was to be found in mathematics, but for "half sciences" such as economics and meteorology, exact mathematical foundations were hard to find, and inference to law-like regularities could be made by means of graphs.[14]

Thus, when Jevons in reply to William Guy's presentation on the "tabular method" to the London Statistical Society in 1879 pleaded for more attention to William Playfair's method of diagrams, this was not intended to merely promote a visual method of inquiry, but to promote a method of imaging data that would be effective in finding mathematical regularities driving the data.[15] For Jevons, the final goal was to ground these regularities in mechanical principles that could be expressed mathematically.

2 Marshall on the Methods of Curves and Diagrams

Thanks to Tiziano Raffaelli's careful work on the remaining early manuscripts of Marshall, especially "Ye Machine," we now know how Marshall from an early age searched for ways to conceptualize the human

[12] Maas, *Stanley Jevons*.

[13] Jevons Archive, JA6/6/133b.

[14] William Stanley Jevons, *Letters and Journal of W. Stanley Jevons Edited by His Wife Harriet Jevons* (London: Edinburgh Printed, 1886), 48 entry of the 5th of January 1855.

[15] William A. Guy, "On Tabular Analysis," *Journal of the Statistical Society of London* 42, no. 3 (1879): 644–62; Harro Maas and Mary S. Morgan, "Timing History: The Introduction of Graphical Analysis in 19th Century British Economics," *Revue d'histoire Des Sciences Humaines*, no. 2 (2002): 97–127.

mind and society within an evolutionary framework.[16] But however ingenious Raffaelli's interpretation of Marshall's quasi-mechanical mental experiment is, it is in my view undeniable that there was something clumsy to Marshall's idea of a self-learning machine that to a certain extent seemed to mimic the inner mechanics of a textile mill.[17] Well-known is Pierre Duhem's complaint about such experiments, which to him meant that whenever he was expected to read theory, he found himself in a factory. According to Duhem, "the English mind" always confronted the reader with a "mechanical contrivance," where there was nothing but "strings which move around pulleys, which roll around drums, which go through pearl beads, which carry weights, and tubes which pump water while others swell and contract, toothed wheels which are geared to one another and engage hooks."[18]

While Jevons was perfectly comfortable with the idea that the world in its final analysis was governed by mechanical laws, it is no coincidence that Marshall's youthful mental experiment remained unpublished. This did not mean, as Raffaelli and others have emphasized, that Marshall abandoned his search for an evolutionary theory. Marshall's quasi-mechanical experiment just did not tally with his evolutionary vision. The question can be asked if the different attitudes of Jevons and Marshall towards mechanical explanations also entailed a different attitude towards the relation of mathematics and economics. Remember that Jevons closely linked mathematics, the graphical method, and empirical statistical data through his belief in a mechanical world order. Measurement of data secured the link between these stages. In the absence of such a belief, did Marshall maintain similar links?

The answer is that Marshall downplayed the role of statistical measurement and mathematics. Most famous, and probably best known among historians of economics, is Marshall's endorsement of the "method of diagrams" as an "engine of discovery," first in his article on the

[16] Tiziano Raffaelli, *Marshall's Evolutionary Economics* (Routledge, 2003); Tiziano Raffaelli, "Marshall on 'Machinery and Life'," *Marshall Studies Bulletin* 4 (1994): 9–22; Tiziano Raffaelli, *Alfred Marshall's Early Philosophical Papers*, vol. 4 (Jai Press, 1994).

[17] This does not mean Marshall's mental experiment was nonsensical as implied by Philip Mirowski in *Machine Dreams: Economics Becomes a Cyborg Science* (Cambridge University Press, 2002).

[18] Pierre Maurice Marie Duhem, *The Aim and Structure of Physical Theory*, vol. 13 (Princeton: Princeton University Press, 1991).

pure theory of international trade, and subsequently in his *Principles of Economics* of 1890. In the previous section, we saw how Jevons fitted Marshall's defense of this method into his own approach to empirical statistics. For an understanding of Marshall's use of the method, the *locus classicus* in my view is not so much Marshall's explicit defense of the method of diagrams in his theory of pure trade, but Peter Groenewegen's reproduction of the two pages of Marshall's own copy of John Stuart Mill's *Principles of Political Economy*. On the left of Fig. 3, we read Mill's narrative counterfactual experiments in which he reasons through what might happen with production and distribution if technical

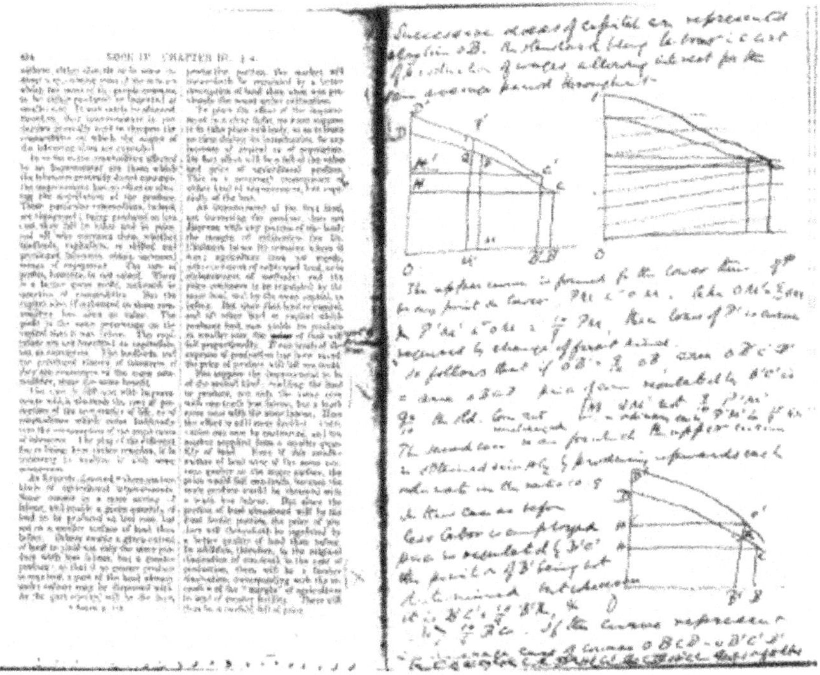

Fig. 3 Marshall's Diagrammatic Annotation of Mill's Principles of Political Economy (*Source* Reproduced with the kind permission of the Marshall Librarian, Marshall Library, Cambridge. *Note* From Marshall's personal copy, Cambridge University Library, Rare Books call mark Marshall.d.61)

or economic conditions were to change.[19] The right-hand page shows Marshall's translation of Mill's narrative experiment in geometric form.

Marshall read Mill's *Principles* in the 1860s. In his autobiographical fragments, Marshall wrote that during this period of his life, he felt more at ease in mathematics than in English, a not altogether strange self-assessment if one considers that Marshall had finished as Second Wrangler in the Mathematics Tripos at Cambridge. Simon Cook has examined the geometric tradition of mathematics at Cambridge, a tradition that, as Marco Dardi in his first Raffaelli lecture has shown, went back to William Whewell's defense of the Cambridge mathematics tradition at Cambridge, and in a liberal education in general.[20] After the short-lived Analytical Society of which Charles Babbage and John Herschel had been important initiators, Cambridge never fully embraced the mathematical innovations of the Continent, but remained, as shown by Weintraub, a mathematical backwater.[21]

Whether Cambridge was a mathematical backwater or not is, however, immaterial to understanding Marshall's way of approaching a classical political economist like John Stuart Mill. Whitaker's collection of Marshall's early mathematical manuscripts has provided historians of economics a much better grasp of the extent and importance of Marshall's diagrammatic experiments.[22] Marshall persistently experimented with diagrams in what Judy Klein has labeled "logical space."[23] He drew a Cartesian space and then curves of various shapes which he subsequently shifted in position. The drawings were accompanied by small commentaries in which Marshall reasoned on his diagrammatic experiment. Some

[19] Peter Groenewegen, *A Soaring Eagle: Alfred Marshall, 1842–1924* (Aldershot: Elgar, 1995).

[20] Simon J. Cook, *The Intellectual Foundations of Alfred Marshall's Economic Science: A Rounded Globe of Knowledge* (New York: Cambridge University Press, 2009); Marco Dardi, "The Pattern/Invention Scheme in Marshallian Economics," *History of Economic Ideas* 27, no. 1 (2019): 161–75, https://doi.org/10.19272/201906101009. See also Marco Dardi, "Mathematics and Statistics," in *The Elgar Companion to Alfred Marshall* (2006), 153–61.

[21] E. Roy Weintraub, *How Economics Became a Mathematical Science* (Durham, NC: Duke University Press, 2002).

[22] Judy L. Klein, "The Method of Diagrams and the Black Arts of Inductive Economics," in Ingrid H. Rima (Ed.), *Measurement, Quantification and Economic Analysis* (London: Routledge, 1995), 89–139.

[23] Klein, "The Method of Diagrams."

diagrammatic experiments remained sketchy, unfinished as a diagram or in its accompanying comment, while others found their way to Marshall's "Pure Theory of International Trade," or to his *Principles of Economics*, its footnotes and appendices.

Marshall distinguished this method of diagrams from the "method of curves" or "curvilinear method." In contrast with the method of diagrams which organized concepts, Marshall perceived the method of curves as a method that organized empirical data. Elsewhere, I investigated how Marshall during his early years of study, the same years he presented "Ye Machine" and other visionary papers to the Grote Club, felt lost in how to deal with the "dry facts" of economic history, but then started organizing his empirical data at what at first sight very much looked like Jevons's *Statistical Atlas* project.[24] He collected these data, mostly from secondary sources, in a large folio-like bounded volume, his so-called *Red Book*, but started doing so at increased pace after he traveled for several months to the United States in 1875, collecting political, economic and juridical data. While Jevons's aim was to document the history of Great Britain in some thirty-nine diagrams, Marshall set himself the more ambitious goal of covering not just the history of Great Britain, but world history. He started several pages on the Chinese and Moghul empires to then move to the present, covering the United States and Great Britain in greatest detail.

Just like Jevons, Marshall presented most of this data in the form of graphs. But in contrast with Jevons, Marshall never attempted to reduce this data, nor these curves, to mathematical form. For Marshall, there was a clear distinction between mathematics and the method of diagrams on the one hand, and the method of curves on the other. With diagrams, Marshall experimented conceptually: How did the interaction of economic concepts play out *logically*? Jevons was correct in his judgment that the method of diagrams was the same if not identical with mathematics. But this did not make Marshall's use of graphs and diagrams similar to Jevons's. Instead, Marshall's "method of curves" started with the collection of empirical data which he then graphed and compared by turning the pages of his *Red Book*, as he remembered in a letter to his former student Arthur Bowley, "backwards and forwards, backwards

[24] Harro Maas, "'A Wanderer in the Land of Dry Facts': Marshall's Struggles with History in the Concrete," *History of Economic Ideas* 27, no. 3 (2019): 129–54; See also Chao and Maas, "Engines of Discovery."

and forwards from one correlated group to another."[25] The diagrams of Marshall's mental experiments never had its scales specified; the scales of his graphs were always specified.

Marshall relied largely on the work of others for the data he represented in his curves; he never systematically engaged in measurement projects himself. Marshall thus followed the nineteenth-century separation of the work of the statistician and the economist as expressed most explicitly in Nassau Senior's address to the Statistical Society of London in 1860.[26] The work of the statistician was that of the data collector and constructor; the work of the economist was to flesh out causal connections between them. This did not mean Marshall never engaged in fact-finding, but he did so rather by fieldwork and personal inquiries, not by means of statistics. When touring the Continent with his wife, they visited factories and interviewed local workmen. In Cambridge, he invited workmen to his home to hear about their working conditions. His travel through the United States may have served as a catalyst for his fieldwork, but it fits into the inductive way of inquiry in political economy that had been encouraged at Cambridge by William Whewell, who considered conversations with countrymen on equal footing with the collection of statistical data. Whewell considered both part of the first steps to reach general conclusions about "laws of phenomena."[27] Simon Cook has examined in great detail how Marshall's reading of Hegel informed his conception and conceptualization of history and society. Whether it was his reading of Hegel, growing up in an intellectual climate in which Whewell's views on scientific method were an important reference point, or a larger understanding of the evolutionary concatenation of various spheres of life which Marshall conceived in "Ye Machine," in his own search for the laws governing the phenomena, Marshall was not searching for reductive mathematical laws governing society. Marshall aimed to

[25] Arthur Cecil Pigou, *Memorials of Alfred Marshall* (London: Macmillan, 1925), 421–23 letter of early 1901 to Bowley.

[26] Nassau W. Senior, "Opening Address of Nassau W. Senior, Esq., as President of Section F (Economic Science and Statistics), at the Meeting of the British Association, at Oxford, 28th June 1860," *Journal of the Statistical Society of London* 23, no. 3 (1860): 357–61.

[27] Maas, *Stanley Jevons*; Harro Maas, "'A Hard Battle to Fight': Natural Theology and the Dismal Science, 1820–50," *History of Political Economy* 40, no. 5 (2008): 143–67, https://doi.org/10.1215/00182702-2007-064.

conceive "the One in the Many, the Many in the One"—Marshall's elliptic description of the great chain of being. Law-like knowledge of the economy was to be gained, not from uncovering a mechanism mathematically rooted in nature, but from comparing movements in empirical data, which should be brought in an overarching relation to one another. This empirical data could consist of quantitative statistics and a variety of qualitative data, ranging from historical facts to anecdotes.

The distinction between Marshall's method of diagrams and his method of curves has to my knowledge not sufficiently been noticed. Scholarship has shown great enthusiasm for Marshall's plea to use diagrams "as an engine of discovery," but Marshall made the exact same plea for the method of curves, which perhaps, but wrongly, gave reason to think they are the same. In his contribution to the jubilee issue of the London (now Royal) Statistical Society of 1885, he used the logo of the society, a bound wheatsheaf encircled with the words "*aliis exterendum*," to explain how individual graphs could produce a coherent understanding of economic phenomena.[28] Marshall ignored the accompanying Latin words, "to be thrashed out by others," and concentrated on the meaning of the bound wheatsheaf itself. The virtue of the method of curves did not reside in its separate curves, but in the possibility of making systematic comparisons between graphs to thus begin to understand the causal structure governing them. As I noted above, Jevons made a comparison between the prices of grain in very different periods of history, but this was to exclude confounding factors to isolate a common, natural cause. Even though Marshall is famous for his use of the *ceteris paribus* clause, the aim of his comparisons was not to exclude confounding factors, but to begin to see how different phenomena were causally connected by including such confounding factors. Marshall did not search for a causal connection rooted in natural causes that could be expressed mathematically. In correspondence with his former student Arthur Bowley, to which I will turn in the next section, he emphasized precisely the importance of his *Red Book* for generating causal explanations by comparing different kinds of data.

[28] Alfred Marshall, "On the Graphic Method of Statistics," *Journal of the Statistical Society of London*, Jubilee issue (1885): 251–60.

3 Marshall's Move from Graphs to Narrative

In the previous sections, we looked at Jevons's and Marshall's use of the methods of graphs and diagrams. We have seen that Jevons used the *empirical* method of graphs as a stepping-stone to find the mathematical laws governing the phenomena. Marshall used the ***analytical*** method of diagrams as a tool to perform mental experiments on concepts and theories of his own and of his precursors. The *empirical* method of graphs was used by Marshall to compare different phenomena, not to find a mathematical law that governed them, but to put these phenomena themselves into causal connection. These efforts moved Marshall in a distinctly different direction than Jevons. In this section, I will use two examples from Marshall's work to show how this different orientation played out in Marshall's later published work. I will first take an example from Marshall's *Red Book* and then a fragment from a large plate which served as a script to think about the causal concatenation of specific events through time. The fragment tallies with the explanation Marshall gave in *Industry and Trade* about why the repeal of the Corn Laws did not immediately have the expected effect on wheat imports in Britain.

Figure 4 shows a fragment of a graph of the price of government bonds ("consols") which I take from Marshall's *Red Book.* Marshall added to the individual high and low values specific causes that were clearly designed to explain the specific highs and lows (e.g., "Napoleon returns from Elba"). Doing so was in no way peculiar for Marshall. Jevons similarly annotated one of the plates of his *Statistical Atlas* project. In this plate, Jevons noted, for example, that the extraordinary spikes in wheat prices in the years around 1800 coincided with the Napoleonic wars, thus similarly correlating a specific event to this rise in prices. But when Jevons made the comparison between nineteenth-century grain prices and those of the thirteenth and fourteenth centuries, he did so to *exclude* such specific causes from consideration; fundamental explanations of movements in economic prices and quantities were to be sought in a mechanical common cause.

Building on his *Red Book*, Marshall by contrast organized his comparisons in ways that departed from the use of graphs and moved to summarizing data as events. He wrote these events on a large plate that enabled him to view them at a glance and to see their relative placement in time. He thus could start to see the causal relations between them which he then presented in a running causal narrative.

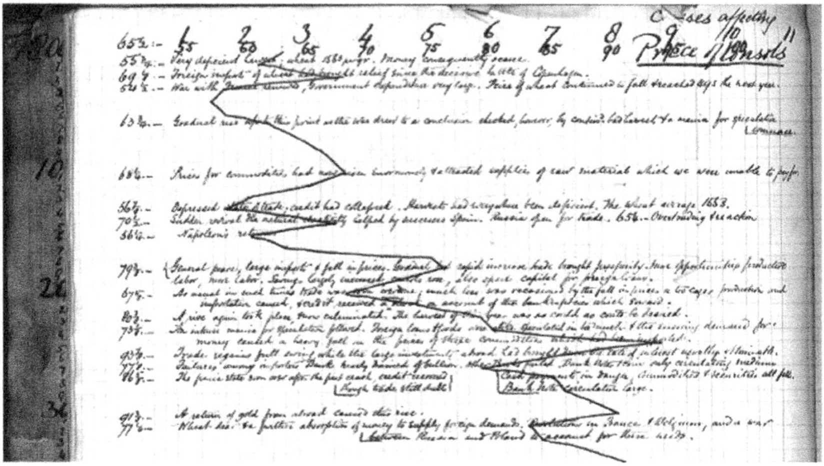

Fig. 4 Fragment of page from Marshall's *Red Book* showing the "causes affecting the price of consols" (government bonds). The curves show the price of consols and the discount rate, respectively. Marshall inserted comments on the specific causes of specific price changes, which he connected to general causal patterns (*Source* Reproduced by kind permission of the Marshall Librarian, Marshall Library, Cambridge. Marshall archives identity code Marshall 7/5)

Marshall thus moved away from the comparison of graphs to the comparison of specific, heterogeneous events.

Figure 5 shows a large plate on which Marshall marked such heterogeneous events from 1820 until around 1903. These events could be quantitative as well as qualitative; they were all put in the same space. Marshall listed categories vertically, ranging from (from top to bottom) "revolutions," "wars and tariffs" (which he connected by curly brackets), "prime ministers," "English general history," "harvest year prices," agricultural events that he connected on the horizontal timeline with accolades to these prices, such as "good" or "bad" harvests, "mining, manufacture, transport," all three connected by an accolade, thus suggesting that even though these were three different economic categories, they were nevertheless closely connected. Then followed foreign "trade, credit, and commercial fluctuations," which were also closely put together though not connected with an accolade. Subsequently came "Money," followed by "Public Borrowing," and then "Labour conflicts, Factory Acts," and

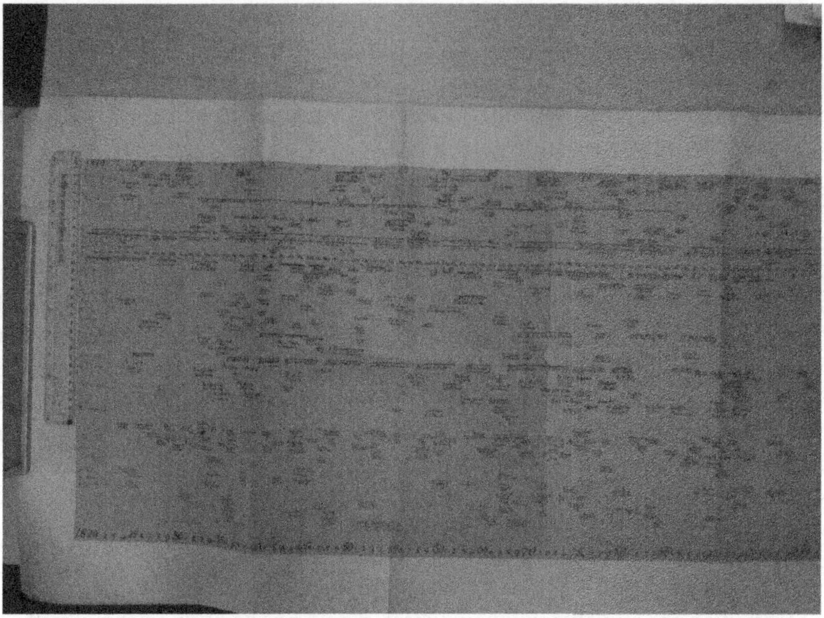

Fig. 5 Large Plate Marshall Designed to Organize Historical Facts and Events from 1820 to 1903. The full plate measures a rough 17 by 35 inches. Marshall's last entries are for 1903 (*Source* Reproduced by kind permission of the Marshall Librarian, Marshall Library, Cambridge. Marshall archives identity code 7-7)

"Other Labour Legislation." These categories (most in red, some in black) were then sequenced in time. On the timeline, Marshall noted either specific data (prices of wheat), combinations of data and events (good or bad harvests, famines, railway or commercial crises, gold discoveries), specific wars (Crimean War), and the names of prime ministers. Marshall exchanged a curve of wheat prices for its time series data, and instead of making a crisis or upturn visible graphically, he noted remarkable changes with accolades and a verbal reference, for example "crisis" as a noteworthy commercial event. Graphs made way for the facts of history that were labeled and presented through time and in spatial relation to one another. We will presently see how Marshall used this plate as a script that enabled him to construct a narrative by going back and forth between the different kinds of events—wars, political administrations, commercial crises, famines, etc. That narrative did not attempt to isolate one single causal thread (the relation between sunspots and commercial fluctuations) but aimed to put historical events in their place by constructing the interrelations between them.

Figure 6 is a detail of Marshall's large plate that we can find in narrative form in Marshall's *Industry and Trade*, in which appears the famous epigraph "The Many in the One, The One in the Many."[29] On pp. 741–742 Marshall discussed why the repeal of the Corn Laws did not have an "immediate effect." In other words, *ceteris paribus* the repeal should have led to a rise in grain imports. The sequel reads as an explanation of all disturbing causes that prevented this immediate effect from happening (and that an economist might expect to happen on the basis of the "laws of supply and demand"). But a simple enumeration of these disturbing causes is not the same as an explanation. With this purpose, Marshall stitched them together into a reasoned, explanatory, sequential order. He writes,

> Therefore the full effect, which the opening of England's ports to wheat exerted on the available supply of wheat, would not be likely to show itself for many years; and meanwhile prices in the world's market for wheat were disturbed by the *new gold supplies beginning about 1850*, by a *series of wars* and *by some exceptional harvests*. In many years indeed these disturbances exerted a much greater influence on the price of wheat than had been exerted by the rather low import duties levied in England after 1843. [p. 741, my italics]

Marshall continued by "going into particulars." He explained that after the "great war" (i.e., the Napoleonic wars), harvests were sufficiently abundant to feed the home market, making the import duty "inoperative" and wheat prices sufficiently low "despite of it." But this was different for the years preceding the repeal. "Moderate harvests," followed by "rain" in 1845 and then "potato disease" forced Prime Minister Peel to a "complete repeal" of the laws in 1846. Marshall continued to explain why also afterward the effect of the repeal did not come into full force, adding that

[29] Alfred Marshall, *Industry and Trade: A Study of Industrial Technique and Business Organization* (London: Macmillan, 1919).

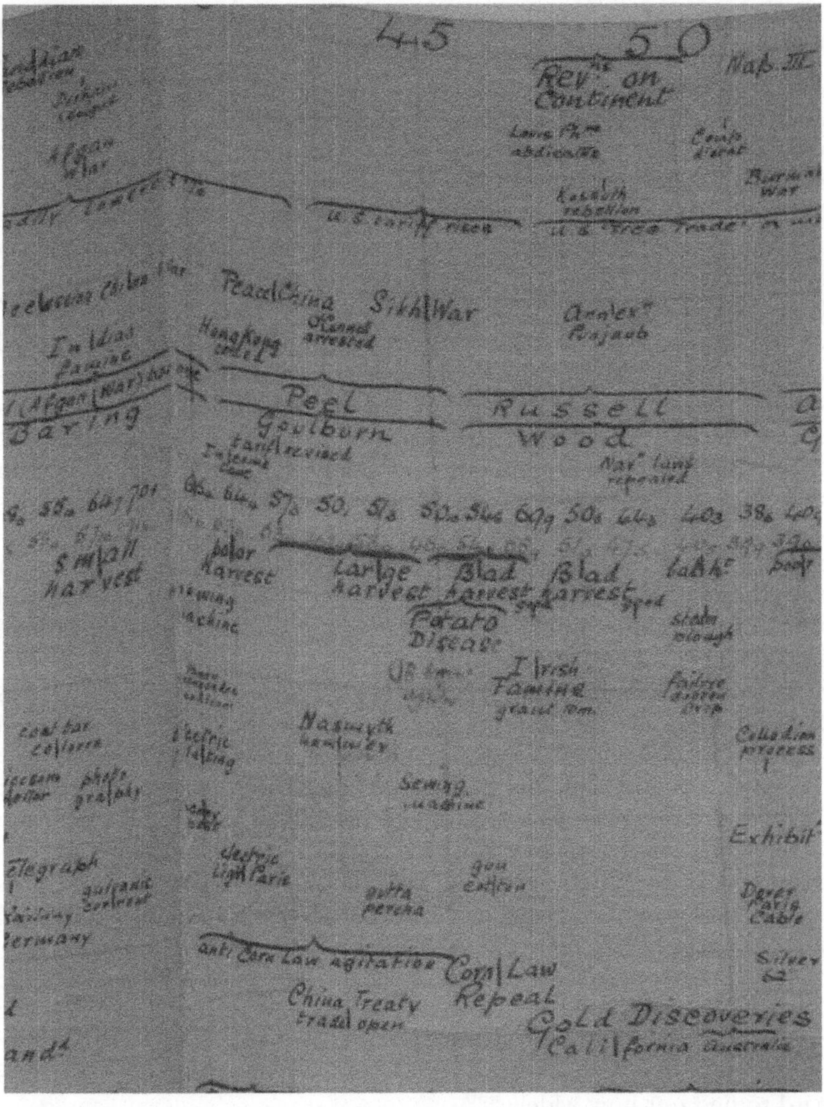

Fig. 6 Fragment of same plate. The fragment shows various quantitative and qualitative events (*Source* Reproduced by kind permission of the Marshall Librarian, Marshall Library, Cambridge. Marshall archives identity code 7-7)

the improvement of the railway infrastructure also helped to keep wheat prices low.

If we compare this fragment from *Industry and Trade* with Fig. 6, we recognize the words I italicized in the quoted fragment (new gold supplies, series of wars, exceptional harvests) and the more detailed causal factors (moderate harvests, rain, potato disease, Prime Minister Peel). Marshall clearly used his plate as a *script* to help him tell the narrative of all disturbing and contributing causes to the final effect on wheat prices and imports that should or might never follow the repeal of the Corn Laws. In contrast with Jevons, Marshall was not searching for a "deeper" causal structure but was organizing the daily business of life into a causal whole. While Marshall in his younger years had considered mathematics and the method of diagrams helpful to understanding and explanation in economics, in his later years, his sustained indulgence in empirical data, initially largely collected in the form of graphs in his *Red Book*, made him shift back to the narrative form of economics he had known from his years of study. But instead of moving back to John Stuart Mill's verbal causal mental experiments, in which Mill mentally isolated the effect of one changing variable, Marshall came close to the writings of the historical school, in which a number of causes were put into a logical pluri-causal story.

In correspondence with Arthur Bowley from 1901, Marshall was explicit about his reservations against mathematics and statistics and implicitly recommended a historical approach. His reservations had little or nothing to do with his understanding of mathematics or the lack thereof—Marshall was very clear about his limited knowledge and grasp of the newly developing mathematical statistics—but rather with his fears that neat mathematical and statistical concepts were unable to help us grasp the messiness of the concrete events an economist was confronted with. He gave the example of his "'field work' in the workingmen's quarters of many German towns" and his "conversations with Germans in the Tyrol," on which he had always relied more than on statistics: "For the Statistics seems to me specially full of traps. 'Arbeitslosigkeit' for instance means something very widely removed from 'Unemployment,' and it is hard to find out how widely."[30]

[30] Letters of Alfred Marshall to Arthur Bowley of 7 and 15 May 1906, in Pigou (1925, 428–30).

Economics was not about neat concepts that lend themselves to mathematical-statistical analysis; it was about history in the concrete, about the interconnections between manifold events. The task of the economist was to sort these out.[31] Mathematics and statistics were unfit or even misleading instruments for this goal. In earlier correspondence with Bowley, Marshall wrote:

> In my view every economic fact, whether or not it is of such a nature as to be expressed in numbers, stands in relation as cause and effect to many other facts: and since it *never* happens that all of them can be expressed in numbers, the application of exact mathematical methods to those which can is nearly always a waste of time, while in the large majority of cases it is positively misleading; and the world would have been further on its way forward if the work had never been done at all. It is chiefly when the mathematical method is used not for direct construction, but to train sound instinctive habits (like that of practicing of scales on the piano), that it seems to me generally helpful.[32]

In his explanation of how to gain insight into how "facts" stand "in relation as cause and effect to many other facts" Marshall invoked his *Red Book*:

> You know my old "Red" curve book in which any important economic or semi-economic fact (in figure form or other) which occurred in any year, say 1867 or 1889, will be pierced through by a pin put on the proper spot and run through the book. A very great part of my work has been the study of that book, or more recently of lecture diagrams on a similar scheme. On each page or wall diagram there will be the history of from two to ten correlated movements. But I scarcely ever get any instruction worth having from a single page: I learn only by turning backwards and forwards, backwards and forwards from one correlated group to another.[33]

This intensive study of his *Red Book* had not been a personal affair, but something he had practiced with his students, among whom was Bowley. It is noteworthy that Marshall's essay on the pure theory of international

[31] Harro Maas, "Sorting Things Out: The Economist as an Armchair Observer," in *Histories of Scientific Observation* (Chicago: University of Chicago Press, 2011), 206–29.

[32] Pigou, *Memorials*, 422 letter of 3 March 1901 to Bowley.

[33] Pigou, *Memorials*, 422 Letter of 3 March 1901 to Bowley.

trade figured as an appendix in *Money, Credit and Commerce*, but not in its main text; Marshall did not dismiss its content, but it had moved to the fringes of his mature approach to the explanatory work of the economist.[34] Based on diagrammatic reasoning, one could have expected a rise in corn prices and imports. He needed his scripted table to explain why this did not happen immediately. If such more complete explanations were impossible, what use were the analytical insights?

The same was true for the "correlation of curves," of which he was "ashamed to admit" not to fully understand the mathematical details. Giving the example of bimetallism, he held against its proponents (even though he was a proponent himself) that

> [o]ut of a hundred things which I think are causally connected, and which—by continually turning from one page of my "red book" to another—I have got to regard as but manifestations of one broad, many-sided movement, the writers of the [Bimetallist HM] League select two. Without proof they assert that *A* is the cause of *B*, when it seems to me that it would be less untrue to say that *B* is the cause of *A*, and they deluge the public with these correlated curves to prove it. No doubt they can be fought with their own weapons: their own methods can be made to bring out exactly the opposite results in every particular: but that is a dreary soul-sickening waste of time. Surely *the* thing to do is to build the basis of our economic structure soundly and not to put a varnish of mathematical accuracy to many places of decimals on results the premises of which are not established within 20 or 50 per cent: many not even so far as to put beyond dispute the question whether *A* is the cause of *B*, or *B* the cause of *A*, or *A* and *B* are the results of $a + b + c + d + \ldots$. Surely *the* thing to do is to seek the Many in the One, the One in the Many.[35]

Burn the Mathematics was about Marshall's "growing feeling" that a "good mathematical theorem" was "very unlikely" to be good economics.[36] That feeling, which had been building up over the years, pertained to the limited usefulness of mathematico-statistics, including his method of diagrams and the emerging correlation analysis which Jevons pioneered in his sunspot studies. In contrast, Marshall aimed to get at a coherent explanation of all contributing causes to the structure of our

[34] Alfred Marshall, *Money, Credit & Commerce* (Macmillan, 1923).

[35] Pigou, *Memorials*, 423 letter of 3 March 1901 to Bowley.

[36] Pigou, *Memorials*, 427 letter to Bowley of 27 February 1906.

economy. For that explanatory work, he considered different tools and a different, narrative exposition more appropriate.

4 Jevons and Marshall as Humboldtians

In this essay, I followed Cannon's lead by trying the label of Humboldtian scientist to capture a scientist's ways of world-making; it is a label that is concerned with a scientist's methods in finding things out. Cannon's stellar example of a Humboldtian scientist was no less than Charles Darwin, but Cannon was well aware that Darwin did not tick all of her boxes. She acknowledged that her efforts to epitomize by a generic label the specific way a scientist worked might ultimately well miss or distort an individual style of reasoning that fits uneasily with neat classifications.

That problem is not unknown to historians of economics. After all, historians of economics have long made it their stock in trade to classify individual economists in "schools of thought" or as adherents of specific economic "paradigms" to thus find unity or disunity in their "visions" on the economy and in their epistemic and ontological commitments. And in most cases the label one tries to impose on the individual economist does not quite fit. This certainly holds for Stanley Jevons and Alfred Marshall, who have been considered as neoclassical economists, as founders of the "marginalist revolution," and as frontrunners in the mathematization of the discipline, and for all these labels there have been arguments pro and con. What is gained with yet another label?

There are obviously circumstances not covered in the preceding that make Jevons *not* a Humboldtian scientist. Alexander von Humboldt was a scientific entrepreneur, brother of the famous ambassador Wilhelm von Humboldt who designed the blueprint for the nineteenth-century *Bildungsuniversity* named after him. The Prussian king Frederic Wilhelm II was his godfather. The death of his mother left him with a substantial fortune, but even then, his large-scale scientific projects were so expensive that he would never have managed to even begin them, if he had not had royal financial support for his wide-ranging plans. Humboldt set out for well-equipped scientific expeditions, with clear scientific goals (though uncertain outcomes).

Things were very different for Jevons. Jevons, it is well-known, traveled to Sydney to take up the position as gold-assayer at the newly established Sydney Mint, in 1854. Son of a middle-class iron merchant from Liverpool who became bankrupt in the aftermath of the great railway crisis of 1845, Jevons benefited from no equivalent of Humboldt's fortune. Jevons did not embark on a scientific expedition but traveled to New South Wales to take up a job for a living and to support his siblings. His scientific work in Sydney is not even remotely of the same order as what Humboldt accomplished on his spectacular expeditions. Indeed, it is not surprising that of all of the Victorians, Cannon considered only Charles Darwin's voyage on the *Beagle* to coming near Humboldt's projects in breadth and scope. Yet, the kind of projects Jevons engaged himself with tick quite some of Cannon's boxes. During his voyage to Australia, Jevons kept a record of his readings of the barometer and thermometer, and it is likely he used the captain's meteorological register as well. He ardently collected meteorological data which he plotted on maps that he juxtaposed on weather maps of Europe to get to an understanding of the weather and climate of Australia. He made observations on cloud formation that he translated into experiments to begin to understand its mechanism. He made systematic observations on the social conditions of the working poor in Sydney, his Social Survey of Sydney.[37] Jevons made similar observations when he traveled for several weeks through New South Wales, drawing maps of the settlements he passed through, taking photographs of gold-diggers and aboriginals. Such endeavors were part and parcel of learned societies in Britain, which was well-known to him from his middle-class Unitarian culture. For Cannon, to be a Humboldtian did not mean to conduct similar grandiose projects as Humboldt, but to endorse a similar approach and attitude towards scientific inquiry. Though conducted on his own and on a far smaller scale than Humboldt, these projects add to the image of Jevons as someone who performed projects of data collection and measurement to then map and graph the data with the aim of scientific understanding and explanation. That is what Cannon defined as Humboldtian science. It is best exemplified in Jevons's *Statistical Atlas* project and in his strong belief that the vast collection of statistical data would turn economics into an exact mathematical science. I discussed at some length how Jevons used the method of graphs for these purposes. Not Humboldtian were Jevons's efforts to isolate singular causal chains instead of searching for an encompassing, comprehensive understanding of the natural and social realm.

[37] Graeme Davison, "The Unsociable Sociologist: W.S. Jevons and His Social Survey of Sydney 1856–8." *Australian Cultural History* (1998): 127–50.

Marshall outshone Jevons as an economist. Historians of economics have for a long time regarded his *Principles of Economics* as a book of wider scope and importance than Jevons's *Theory of Political Economy*. That is undeniably the case, if only for the diagrammatic method it introduced into economics (even when there were predecessors). But that is not the kind of wide-ranging scientific endeavor Cannon would have labeled Humboldtian. The *Principles* was not about measurement nor about empirical research. It may have been an ingenious and important book, and historians of economics may for good reasons consider its enduring importance to outshine Marshall's other work. But there was nothing Humboldtian about it. How different things are for his *Red Book*. It would be overstretching to claim that all of Marshall's later writings followed from it, but Marshall himself gave an indication of its importance for his later approach to economics. The *Red Book* did not open a program of measurement and mathematization, but it did fit into another important characteristic of Humboldtian science: the commitment to see the connections between disparate data and events. *Ceteris paribus* was exchanged for an understanding of data and events as parts of wholes. We have seen how Marshall used maps to construct such connections. Perhaps more than anything else did the famous epigraph to *Industry and Trade*, "The One in the Many, the Many in the One," betray Marshall as a Humboldtian.

It is legitimate to ask if anything is gained with the label "Humboldtian" instead of pointing out Marshall's indebtedness to German historicism. I think there is. By thinking about Jevons and Marshall as Humboldtians, the attention shifts from their philosophical tenets toward their research practices. Cannon invites us to not ask about their theories, but about their ways of working, about how they came to write the way they did. Too often, in my view, historians of economics forget that studying the work of economists is not just studying their ideas. At the end of the day, it is *work* that finds its way to print, and to understand how it is done, we not only need to understand the ideas that may have guided them in producing it, but also their actual mode of production.

References

Cannon, Susan Faye. *Science in Culture: The Early Victorian Period*. New York: Science History Publications, 1978.

Chao, Hsiang-Ke, and Harro Maas. "Engines of Discovery: Jevons and Marshall on the Methods of Graphs and Diagrams." In *Research in History of Economic Thought and Methodology*, 35–61. Bingley: Emerald Publishing, 2017. https://doi.org/10.1108/S0743-41542017000035A003.

Cook, Simon J. *The Intellectual Foundations of Alfred Marshall's Economic Science: A Rounded Globe of Knowledge*. New York: Cambridge University Press, 2009.

Dardi, Marco. "Mathematics and Statistics." In *The Elgar Companion to Alfred Marshall*, 153–61. Cheltenham: Edward Elgar, 2006.

———. "The Pattern/Invention Scheme in Marshallian Economics." *History of Economic Ideas* 27, no. 1 (2019): 161–75. https://doi.org/10.19272/201906101009.

Davison, Graeme. "The Unsociable Sociologist: W.S. Jevons and His Social Survey of Sydney 1856–8." *Australian Cultural History* 16 (1998): 127–50.

Duhem, Pierre Maurice Marie. *The Aim and Structure of Physical Theory*. Vol. 13. Princeton: Princeton University Press, 1991.

Groenewegen, Peter. *A Soaring Eagle: Alfred Marshall, 1842–1924*. Aldershot: Elgar, 1995.

Guy, William A. "On Tabular Analysis." *Journal of the Statistical Society of London* 42, no. 3 (1879): 644–62.

Jevons, William Stanley. *Investigations in Currency and Finance*. London: Macmillan, 1884.

———. *Letters and Journal of W. Stanley Jevons Edited by His Wife Harriet Jevons*. London: Edinburgh Printed, 1886.

Klein, Judy L. "The Method of Diagrams and the Black Arts of Inductive Economics." In Ingrid H. Rima (Ed.), *Measurement, Quantification and Economic Analysis*, 89–139. London: Routledge, 1995.

Maas, Harro. "'A Hard Battle to Fight': Natural Theology and the Dismal Science, 1820–50." *History of Political Economy* 40, no. 5 (2008): 143–67. https://doi.org/10.1215/00182702-2007-064.

———. "'A Wanderer in the Land of Dry Facts': Marshall's Struggles with History in the Concrete." *History of Economic Ideas* 27, no. 3 (2019): 129–54.

———. "Sorting Things Out: The Economist as an Armchair Observer." In *Histories of Scientific Observation*, 206–29. Chicago: University of Chicago Press, 2011.

———. *William Stanley Jevons and the Making of Modern Economics*. New York: Cambridge University Press, 2005.

Maas, Harro, and Mary S. Morgan. "Timing History: The Introduction of Graphical Analysis in 19th Century British Economics." *Revue d'histoire Des Sciences Humaines* 7, no. 2 (2002): 97–127.

Marshall, Alfred. *Industry and Trade: A Study of Industrial Technique and Business Organization*. London: Macmillan, 1919.

———. *Money, Credit & Commerce*. London: Macmillan, 1923.

———. "On the Graphic Method of Statistics." *Journal of the Statistical Society of London*, Jubilee issue (1885): 251–60.

Mirowski, Philip. *Machine Dreams: Economics Becomes a Cyborg Science*. Cambridge: Cambridge University Press, 2002.

Morgan, Mary S. *The World in the Model: How Economists Work and Think*. Cambridge: Cambridge University Press, 2012.

Pigou, Arthur Cecil. *Memorials of Alfred Marshall*. London: Macmillan, 1925.

Raffaelli, Tiziano. *Alfred Marshall's Early Philosophical Papers*. Vol. 4. Greenwich, CT: Jai Press, 1994.

———. "Marshall on 'Machinery and Life'." *Marshall Studies Bulletin* 4 (1994): 9–22.

———. *Marshall's Evolutionary Economics*. Routledge, 2003.

Senior, Nassau W. "Opening Address of Nassau W. Senior, Esq., as President of Section F (Economic Science and Statistics), at the Meeting of the British Association, at Oxford, 28th June, 1860." *Journal of the Statistical Society of London* 23, no. 3 (1860): 357–61.

Snyder, Laura J. *The Philosophical Breakfast Club: Four Remarkable Friends Who Transformed Science and Changed the World*. Portland: Broadway Books, 2011.

Weintraub, E. Roy. *How Economics Became a Mathematical Science*. Durham, NC: Duke University Press, 2002.

Whitaker, John K. "The Evolution of Alfred Marshall's Economic Thought and Writings Over the Years 1867–90." In *The Early Economic Writings of Alfred Marshall, 1867–1890*, vol. 1, 1–113. London and Basingstoke: Macmillan, 1975.

White, Michael V. "Bridging the Natural and the Social: Science and Character in Jevons's Political Economy." *Economic Inquiry* 32, no. 3 (1994): 429–44.

———. "Riders on the Storm: W. Stanley Jevons, Meteorology and the Analysis of 'Commercial Fluctuations.'" Lausanne, 2019.

Wulf, Andrea. *The Invention of Nature: Alexander von Humboldt's New World*. New York: Knopf, 2015.

Utilitarianism, the Moral Sciences and Political Economy: Mill-Grote-Sidgwick

Keith Tribe

> Mr. Marshall also gave a course on Moral and Political Philosophy scattered over the years 1873-4. This was chiefly on Bentham and Mill's Utilitarianism.... He also said that Bentham had more influence on Economics than any other non-economist, his contribution being the stress laid on measurement. (Marshall 1947: 18–19)

In 1868, Alfred Marshall was appointed Lecturer in Moral Sciences for St John's College, Cambridge. His chief interest in the developing Moral Sciences Tripos lay initially in psychology, but he was soon asked to provide intercollegiate lectures on political economy for the

This essay originated as an Istvan Hont Memorial Lecture presented at the University of St. Andrews, 11 May 2015, and was written up and revised with the support of Estonian Research Council Grant (PRG 318).

K. Tribe (✉)
Department of History and Archaeology, University of Tartu, Tartu, Estonia
e-mail: tess@dircon.co.uk

K. Caldari et al. (eds.), *Marshall and the Marshallian Heritage*,
Palgrave Studies in the History of Economic Thought,
https://doi.org/10.1007/978-3-030-53032-7_7

Tripos, and so he began to study the subject.[1] As Simon Cook emphasises, this inevitably implied an engagement with Mill's *Principles of Political Economy*; but then, while Marshall's understanding of contemporary political economy was slowly developing, in 1871 Stanley Jevons published his *Theory of Political Economy*. This book elaborated the utilitarian framework that had first been exposed in Jevons's 1862 paper for the annual meeting of the British Association for the Advancement of Science; by the 1880s Jevons's book would be widely recognised as a new version of political economy that moved on from that of John Stuart Mill, setting the standard for advanced argument in the subject. Edgeworth began his economic studies from the work of his Hampstead neighbour Jevons; Wicksteed turned to Jevons's text having had his interest in political economy fired by Henry George. It was, for instance, Wicksteed who coined the term "marginal utility" as a translation of von Wieser's *Grenznutzen* and so replaced what Jevons had in 1871 referred to as "final utility".

In the introduction to his edition of Marshall's early economic writings John Whitaker presents a synopsis of Marshall's later comments on this period of his intellectual development, first summarising Marshall's own (retrospective) account. Whitaker notes that in 1883 (the year after Jevons drowned in a swimming accident) Marshall wrote to Léon Walras that

> I cannot be said to have accepted Mr Jevons doctrine of 'final utility'. For I had taught it publicly in lectures at Cambridge before his book appeared. ... But following the lead of Cournot I had anticipated all the central points of Jevons book and had in many respects gone beyond him. (Whitaker 1975 Vol. I: 38–39; Marshall to Walras, 1 November 1883: Whitaker 1996 Vol. I: 169)

Whitaker is sceptical of the claims Marshall later made of his path into political economy, and he follows the synopsis with a critical assessment (Whitaker 1975 Vol. I: 40–44). It is however certainly true that Marshall read Cournot's *Recherches sur les principles mathématiques de la théorie des richesses* (1838) at this time and made notes that are reprinted in Whitaker's collection (Whitaker 1975 Vol. 2: 240–48). The problem is however that there is no independent demand function in Cournot's

[1] See for a narrative of the development of Marshall's interest in political economy (Cook 2009: Ch. 5).

model of two producers of bottled water, only "sales"[2]; and so there is no way Marshall could have followed "the lead of Cournot" to anticipate Jevons's account of an economic agent making decisions on the basis of the resulting pleasure or pain. This account was a fiction. And as will be suggested below, it is very unlikely that Marshall was teaching anything like "Mr Jevons doctrine of 'final utility'" before 1871.

Marshall was given to fictional narratives, as Mike White has documented in the case of the non-existent "Giffen Good" (White 2015). But lacking anything other than Marshall's own later recollections of his path into political economy, to understand this path we must examine what Marshall was seeking to achieve with his fabrications, rather than treat them as direct evidence of how he had come to be an economist. We can understand that he would by the 1880s seek to belittle the significance of Jevons, given how long it was taking him to realise his own, actually very different, vision of what economics should be. But he had reviewed Jevons's *Theory of Political Economy* in *The Academy* for 1 April 1872, and so we do have clear evidence of how he thought about Jevons during the early years of his turn to political economy.

Marshall's critique turned essentially on the idea that Jevons was saying nothing new: "We may ... read far into the present book without finding any important proposition which is new in substance. ... The main value of the book ... does not lie in its more prominent theories, but in its original treatment of a number of minor points, its suggestive remarks and careful analyses" (Marshall 1925: 93, 95). In a note appended to the reprinted article Marshall came back again to the formative influence upon him of Cournot and Thünen (1925: 99), writers who could have given him what he later said he took from them. Marshall's diffuse attempts to associate Jevons's arguments about value with those of Ricardo betray not only his *penchant* for seeing continuity where there was little, they

[2] Cournot (1980) Ch. IV is "The Law of Sales"; hence we could say that, for Cournot, "demand" is something that enables producers to sell things. Whitaker (1975 Vol. 2: 245) has Marshall's notes on competitive equilibrium in Cournot's Ch. VII, "On Competition among Producers". Here Cournot explains the stability of an equilibrium by the behaviour of producers (of a generic product) with respect to each other (61): that if, deceived as to their real interests, they try to break away from the existing equilibrium, they will be brought back to it by a series of reactions. This is the core idea of what, as eventually developed by Edwin Chamberlin, became the modern theory of oligopoly as a market in which producers, seeking to retain market share in the sales of functionally similar products, seek to differentiate their product in some way from those of their competitors.

amount to a misdirection that related to the role of political economy in the Moral Sciences Tripos. For if we turn to Jevons's 1862 British Association paper, we find Millian utilitarianism rewritten as an account of economic action and subjective choice. This was the theoretical core of what Jevons later developed; a core that Marshall in his 1872 review overlooked, either because he had at that time not realised its significance, or because he did sense its significance and sought to redirect his readers' attention.

We can shed light on Marshall's curious treatment of Jevons by considering what Mill represented in the later 1860s and early 1870s. The slow path that Marshall trod in his detachment from Mill is illuminated by the textbook that Alfred Marshall wrote with his wife Mary Paley, who had been commissioned to write a textbook suitable for use in extension classes. As eventually published in 1879, this had become chiefly the work of Alfred Marshall, as John Whitaker notes (1975 Vol. I: 67), and it is reasonable to suppose that he sought in the 1890s to suppress the book not primarily because of any latent misogyny, which is the motive usually cited, but precisely because in its confused presentation a continuing reliance on Mill was all too obvious. This was an introductory textbook that was in places hard to follow, unless the reader had a prior understanding of Mill (Backhouse and Tribe 2018: 190–93). Nonetheless, this does bring to our attention an important point: How could Mill's work of synthesis provide the foundation upon which a very different approach to economic argument and analysis was built, an approach which then consigned this prior foundation to history?[3]

As Roger Backhouse has shown, an important part in this story was played by Henry Sidgwick (Backhouse 2006). From 1883, he was Knightbridge Professor of Moral Philosophy at the University of Cambridge and also the guiding spirit of the Moral Sciences Tripos, which in the mid-1880s combined teaching in political philosophy, ethics, political economy, the history of modern metaphysical philosophy, psychology, and logic.[4] This provided the framework for Alfred Marshall's teaching

[3] Aligning my argument here with Stanley Jevons's remarks about "that able but wrong-headed man, David Ricardo", and not with Alfred Marshall's implausible pleas for continuity—see Jevons (1957: li). Like Edgeworth, Jevons seems to have by-passed Mill's *Principles* altogether in sketching out his approach to economic analysis.

[4] The scheme of lectures for the Special Board for Moral Science 1884–1885; *Cambridge University Reporter* 15 October 1884 p. 79. At this time, Foxwell gave

in Cambridge from 1885 until 1903, when the new Economics Tripos was initiated and the Moral Sciences Tripos soon became the Philosophy Tripos. And by understanding rather better Marshall's relationship to Jevons we can gain some insight into why it was that he sought to detach the teaching of economics from the Moral Sciences Tripos, given the synthesis of Jevons and Mill that Sidgwick's own *Principles of Political Economy* represented.

Roger Backhouse noted (2006: 28) that Marshall reacted badly to news that Sidgwick would publish in 1883 his own *Principles of Political Economy*, leading to a deterioration in hitherto good relations between Sidgwick and Marshall. Not least, Sidgwick had been indirectly responsible for finding Marshall his wife; Mary Paley had become a Cambridge student of political economy who was able to study in Cambridge and sit examinations through the dedication of Sidgwick and others to the cause of women's education.[5] That in 1883 Sidgwick also became Knightbridge Professor meant that it was now less likely that he would present any real obstacle to Marshall's ideas for the development of the teaching of economics, if he were able to return to Cambridge. Which he did in early 1885, following the premature death of Henry Fawcett, Professor of Political Economy. Then in 1890 Marshall finally published his own *Principles of Economics*, providing a framework for the teaching of political economy in Cambridge that displaced Sidgwick's book, a second edition of which had appeared in 1887.

It had been the appearance in 1874 of Sidgwick's *Methods of Ethics* that provided the platform for his appointment to the Knightbridge chair, and so also a platform from which he could direct the Moral Sciences Tripos.[6] *Methods of Ethics* has a more direct connection to contemporary political economy than might at first appear, since it presented a version of the utilitarianism that Jevons had embraced in 1862 then written up in 1871 as

the political economy lectures for the Tripos; Fawcett's own Professorial lectures were primarily directed at poll men, students seeking an ordinary rather than an honours degree. Mary Paley, for example, as a moral sciences student, did not attend Fawcett's lectures, but was taught by Sidgwick and Marshall (1947: 18).

[5] See Rita McWilliams Tullberg (1995); at Marshall's suggestion, Mary Paley sat the Moral Sciences Tripos examination informally in December 1874 (pp. 55–56).

[6] Not least through covering several of its topics by publishing books: besides *Methods of Ethics* and *Principles of Political Economy*, in 1888 he published *Outlines of the History of Ethics for English Readers* and in 1891 *The Elements of Politics*. See Backhouse (2006: 17–21) for a summary of *Methods of Ethics*.

The Theory of Political Economy, in which version it then became incorporated into Sidgwick's own *Principles of Political Economy*. Indeed, part of any difference between Sidgwick and Marshall in the 1880s was the Jevonian cast of Sidgwick's political economy and Marshall's own efforts to overcome the priority that Jevons enjoyed during the 1880s as the exponent of a modern economics. This connection between Jevons, Sidgwick and contemporary political economy, and Marshall's efforts to disconnect them, is less obvious today since Sidgwick has been enjoying a revival of interest among moral philosophers, who presume *Methods of Ethics* to be a work of a moral philosophy of the kind they themselves pursue. Consequently, they consider it quite unproblematic to approach the book with their own problems, seeking ways in which Sidgwick might have contributed to their formulation and resolution. This is something that should sound familiar to historians of economics: as what economists long did to Adam Smith, and still occasionally do.[7] Ironically, Adam Smith practised moral philosophy too, and so one strand in current commentary is to do to Smith exactly what has been done to Sidgwick: presume that his moral philosophy is an entity continuous with whatever it is modern moral philosophers think they are doing.

In the case of Sidgwick, the moral sciences of which he was a part did turn into a philosophical enterprise of a modern kind. When in 1903 Alfred Marshall took political economy and politics out of the Moral Sciences Tripos and established the Economics Tripos, this left a rump Moral Sciences Tripos now dedicated only to moral philosophy and logic: and so Marshall's efforts also brought about what then became the Cambridge Philosophy Tripos. The story of this division has always been told from the point of view of Marshall: that, dissatisfied with the compromises forced upon him by teaching economics within the Moral Sciences Tripos, he struggled for many years first to enlarge the scope of political economy within the Tripos, and then to create an independent vehicle for the training of economists. His eventual success in creating the first three-year undergraduate degree in economics did create much

[7] At the time of the bicentenary of *Wealth of Nations* in 1976 this was the dominant tendency: the collection *Essays on Adam Smith* had very few contributions that would today be considered properly historical, and in its second half chapter after chapter places Adam Smith in relation to modern economic ideas. See Skinner and Wilson (1976); this was a companion volume to the new Glasgow editions of *Theory of Moral Sentiments* and *Wealth of Nations*.

ill-feeling, resulting in the elimination of economics from the teaching of history and moral philosophy in Cambridge. In Oxford, on the other hand, the tide flowed the other way: in 1920 a PPE degree was created in which economics shared a degree with philosophy and politics. It is also worth noting that when Marshall complained of the ineffectiveness of teaching economics within the Moral Sciences Tripos, all of those men whom he considered his best students, up to and including Pigou, were directly or indirectly products of this Tripos.[8] Not until the 1930s did the Economics Tripos begin producing economists with whose names we might today be familiar.

If we are to properly appreciate how Sidgwick could in 1883 become the Cambridge Professor of Moral Philosophy, and in the same year publish a large and interesting treatise on political economy, we need to establish quite what the moral sciences represented in Cambridge in the last quarter of the nineteenth century, and so recalibrate what Marshall's ambition for the teaching of economics meant. To do so, I seek to restore a perspective upon *Methods of Ethics* as a product of Cambridge Moral Sciences, and not as a canonical work of modern moral philosophy.[9] In so doing, I will demonstrate that the construction of *Methods of Ethics* owes a great deal to a book by a predecessor of Sidgwick in the Knightbridge Chair, John Grote[10]—his posthumous *An Examination of the Utilitarian Philosophy*. When this was published in 1870, Grote had been dead four years; the book was put together by Joseph Mayor,[11] one-time St. Johns

[8] Including Nicholson, Foxwell, J. N. Keynes, Chapman, Flux, Macgregor as well as Pigou.

[9] Here I should note that by far the best account of Sidgwick's moral philosophy, Schneewind (1977), does recognise the significance of the Tripos, and it opens by acknowledging that the very modernity of Sidgwick's "tone and content" fosters the kind of approach which I criticise above. Schneewind's purpose is to place Sidgwick with respect to the philosophical field of mid-nineteenth-century England, which he does very successfully; here I am concerned to suggest that this field was, in Sidgwick's work, inflected by the framework provided by the Moral Sciences Tripos.

[10] Sometimes confused with his brother George Grote, banker, MP and historian of ancient Greece; see the index entry in Crisp (2015: 250).

[11] Mayor entered St. John's College, Cambridge in 1847 and graduated in 1851 with the second-placed First in Classics. He was the author of "The Moral Sciences" in the first *Student Guide to the University of Cambridge* (1862: 140–52), and in 1863 one of the candidates for the chair of political economy, alongside Leonard Courtney and Henry Dunning Macleod. In October 1863, the post had been made permanent by the Senate, and it became a paid University appointment; following lobbying by Leslie

College Lecturer in Moral Sciences, from notes made by Grote in the early 1860s. This had been the time of the "Grote Society", a discussion group in which Sidgwick and Grote were the leading lights. It also coincides with Stanley Jevons' move into political economy, with his paper "Brief Account of a General Mathematical Theory of Political Economy" presented at the Section F session of the British Association meeting in Cambridge in the summer of 1862.[12] There is then a common factor uniting the separate endeavours but common interests of Sidgwick, Grote and Jevons: the publication, in the autumn and winter of 1861, of John Stuart Mill's essay on utilitarianism in *Fraser's Magazine*.

In order to make sense of these relationships, we need to turn our attention away from Mill's *Principles of Political Economy* and towards his various statements of the utilitarian position. Linked to this, we can examine the early history of the Moral Sciences Tripos and quite what Grote, Sidgwick and Mayor made of it. This also necessarily involves some reconstruction of how teaching was actually conducted in Cambridge in the mid-nineteenth century, for it was not then organised in the way it is today. Central to Oxbridge undergraduate teaching today is the relationship between University lectures and college supervision/tutorial, in which a reading list defines the scope of material to be covered. However, the weekly supervision or tutorial is a twentieth-century innovation, in Cambridge linked to the reorganisation of the University on a Faculty basis in the 1920s, realigning the functions of University and colleges. For much of the nineteenth-century University Professors had lectured very sporadically, if at all; as already noted Henry Fawcett, Marshall's predecessor as Professor of Political Economy from 1863 to 1884, lectured exclusively to Pass Men until at least 1876; that is, to students pursuing an ordinary degree and more interested in collecting credits than in higher learning. To understand why the Moral Sciences Tripos existed, what it was supposed to do, and what it actually did do, we first need to step back into the Cambridge of the early nineteenth century.

Stephen, Henry Fawcett, who had also published his *Manual of Political Economy* that year, was appointed.

12 Subsequently published as Jevons (1866). Jevons did not attend the meeting, but his paper was read out.

1 Teaching and Its Reorganisation Before the Moral Sciences Tripos

In the early nineteenth century, the University of Cambridge was, as the historian of the University put it, "practically a preserve of the Church of England" (Winstanley 1940: 82). College fellows, tutors, professors and readers were all obliged to conform to the liturgy of the Church of England and were not permitted to marry, reinforcing the sense of seminary life. To graduate, students had to swear allegiance to the Thirty-Nine Articles of Anglican faith printed in the *Book of Common Prayer*[13]; but a significant proportion of students never got as far as this and left college without graduating from the University, suggesting both the centrality of college life and a greater emphasis on sociability than education. Broadly speaking, as the century progressed emphasis did shift from college-based teaching and learning towards lectures by university appointees; but well into the second half of the twentieth-century college life dominated not only the social existence of the undergraduate, but progress towards a university degree as well.

The curriculum was in the early nineteenth century dominated by mathematics. This formed the main part, along with some Paley and Locke, of the Senate House Examination, which in time became known as the Mathematics Tripos. While this four- to five-day written examination was taken by a majority of students, this also meant that very many did not sit the exam. A distinction emerged between "Pass" or "Poll" men, and those competing for honours in an examination aimed not primarily at classification, but a rank ordering of all candidates. Reforms in 1822 introduced a Classical Tripos open only to those who had already gained honours in mathematics; and an elementary examination called the "Previous Examination" was introduced in the fifth term of residence, for which the Gospels or Apostles, Paley's *Evidences of Christianity*, a Greek or Latin prescribed author formed the subject matter. By mid-century, with divinity, mechanics and hydrostatics added in 1837, this had become the ordinary degree, for which attendance and examination at one course of Professorial lectures was also required. It had not been that usual in the early part of the century for Professors to lecture: in 1809, the Professor of Divinity "broke a well-established tradition of his chair by delivering a course of lectures", and when Whewell became Knightbridge Professor in

[13] For a summary of these and their significance see my (2017).

1838 he ended its status as a sinecure by delivering at least twelve lectures annually, apart from the year in which he was Vice Chancellor.[14]

Teaching students was a college matter; as is evident from the description of teaching on the Moral Sciences Tripos in the 1893 edition of the *Student's Guide*, this was still the case at the end of the century (1893: 70–71). Throughout the century, college lectures were more like school classes, students being called upon to construe a passage or prove orally a mathematical proposition. Given the broad scope of the ordinary degree, colleges sometimes lacked appropriate or sufficient tutors, and a system of private coaching developed which in turn contributed to a low academic standard, since more rigorous examination would only increase the demand for private tutoring and encourage cramming for the ordinary degree.[15]

The appointment of Prince Albert as Chancellor of the University in 1847 lent a focus to existing arguments in Cambridge for reform. Albert had studied law, philosophy and the history of art during 1837 and 1838 at the University of Bonn.[16] Having been given a list of Cambridge teaching by the Vice Chancellor, Albert concluded that the existing provision was very incomplete and advocated an extensive broadening of subjects that found some support among Cambridge fellows. However, given that teaching was a college matter and that the colleges were already beholden to an extra-collegiate network of private coaches, something other than a simple extension of college teaching was required. The result was a proposal in February 1848 that all students for the ordinary degree be required to attend for at least one term lectures given by one or more University Professors and be certified by the appropriate Professor

[14] Winstanley (1940: 80–81, 175). Winstanley goes on (179) to emphasise that Whewell was not an advocate of University lectures in themselves, but wished to improve the standing of professorial lectures so that they might be linked to subjects for examination, and also reduce the reliance on private tutors.

[15] The role of coaching for the Mathematics Tripos was different; here it was the private coaches who supplied the specialised teaching needed for a first-class degree that the colleges could not. While the Mathematics Tripos was very important in shaping Marshall's thinking about the teaching of economics, that is not my immediate object here. On the role of coaches however see Clark (2008).

[16] The previous academic year Karl Marx had followed the same courses. Albert had studied in Brussels before attending Bonn, and he later corresponded with Quetelet about the latter's *On the Social System and the Laws which Regulate It* (1848)—Palfrey (2002: 106, fn. 44).

as having passed an examination in the subject of the lectures. Implicit was therefore a requirement that Professors provide regular courses of lectures. Additionally, two new Triposes were added, in Natural Sciences and in Moral Sciences. Corresponding to the new function of professorial lectures, the component subjects for the new Moral Sciences Tripos were simply derived from existing professorial chairs: moral philosophy, history, political economy, English law and general jurisprudence. Admission to the Tripos no longer required that a Senate House Examination be sat first, as had been the case when the Classics Tripos was introduced in 1822. Instead, students were admitted only if they had already gained an ordinary degree: so when established the Moral Sciences Tripos was a supplementary one-year graduate degree. Only in 1860 did it become a free-standing three-year honours undergraduate course, when the content was altered, professorial control loosened, and a Moral Sciences Board appointed to oversee it. This was now the structure from which Marshall would later seek to detach the teaching of economics.

2 The Organisation of the Moral Sciences Tripos

The syllabus for the "Moral Sciences Tripos" as originally constituted was formed simply by bringing together a number of existing Professorial domains; but what were the "Moral Sciences"? The idea of a moral science can be dated back at least to Adam Ferguson's *Principles of Moral and Political Science* (1792), in which he describes his aim as:

> In treating of him [man] as a subject of moral science, we endeavour to understand what he ought to be; without being limited, in our conception, to the measurement of attainment or failure, exhibited in the case of any particular person or society of men. (Ferguson 1792: 2)

This then is a consideration of the human person as a being first of all distinct from other animals, possessed of mental faculties enabling that person to reason, able to discern the difference between pleasure and pain, beauty and deformity, prosperity and adversity, subject to rules of morality regarding external actions and also to legal statutes, characterised by definite virtues, and living in society with other human persons. And when the Institut national des sciences et des arts was established by the Directory in 1795, it was divided into three classes: "Physical and Mathematical Sciences"; "Moral and Political Sciences"; and "Literature and the

Fine Arts". The second class was divided into several sections: for "The Analysis of Sensations and Ideas"; "Morals"; "Social Science and Legislation"; "Political Economy"; "History"; and "Geography and Statistics" (Whatmore 2000: 112). In addition, David Palfrey draws attention to the fact that when John Stuart Mill's *System of Logic* (1843) was translated into German the "moral sciences" discussed in Book VI were translated by "Geisteswissenschaften", emphasising the mental rather than the social (political) aspect (Palfrey 2002: 124). Mill doubted whether

> The phenomena with which this science [of human nature] is conversant being the thoughts, feelings and actions of human beings, it would have attained the ideal perfection of a science if it enabled us to foretell how an individual would think, feel, or act, throughout life, with the same certainty with which astronomy enables us to predict the places and the occultations of the heavenly bodies. It needs scarcely be stated that nothing approaching this can be done. The actions of individuals could not be predicted with scientific accuracy, were it only because we cannot foresee the whole of the circumstances in which those individuals will be placed. (Mill 1973: 846–47)

No precise and universally true statement can be made regarding human action, he argued; but this was not because an individual's modes of thinking and acting do not depend on causes, rather that causal factors were varied in their combination, such that in the aggregate no two actions were quite alike. We might conclude that, by the later 1840s, the "moral sciences" were understood to include all phenomena related to human society and sociability, from the philosophical (moral philosophy) through language to the more strictly social, including an understanding of social actions and the formation of enduring human society.

Whewell's version of this sought to integrate law, history and political economy through a Christian moral philosophy, and within a fortnight of the new Tripos being approved he announced a course of 24 lectures on the history of moral philosophy from Plato to Paley, Dugald Stewart, Bentham and Mackintosh.[17] James Stephen presented his first lecture course on History three times a week in Trinity Hall during the Easter

[17] He later published *Lectures on the History of Moral Philosophy in England* (1852), which ran roughly from Hobbes to Bentham in eighteen lectures.

Term of 1850, running from Roman Gaul to the establishment of absolute monarchy under Louis XIV, although he did digress into a critique of Comte as discussed by Mill and Grote. Pryme had of course begun lecturing on political economy in March 1816, and in 1828 he had been elected Professor of Political Economy, albeit unpaid and only lecturing for one term every other year.[18]

While we might in this way enumerate activities that had a bearing on the Moral Sciences, a more significant feature was the very small number of students who actually attempted the Tripos from 1851 to 1860: there were only 66 in total. In 1860, no students at all sat for the Tripos (Palfrey 2002: 364, Table 9.1). This did not mean that no students attended the professorial lectures related to the Moral Sciences that year, since there were also undergraduates studying for the ordinary degree and seeking professorial certificates, such that from 1851 to 1860 political economy averaged 20.8 students per year, civil law 27.8—but moral philosophy 4.7. In 1858–1859, there were 62 students attending political economy lectures, 22 for civil law, and 9 for moral philosophy; the following year 46, 6 and 2, respectively (Palfrey 2002: 366–67). During the 1850s, external pressure on the University to reform both curriculum and the organisation of teaching continued, followed in the 1860s by a number of private members' bills in Parliament aimed at the removal of all religious tests. When John Grote was appointed Knightbridge Professor in 1855, he allied himself with this pressure for reform, seeking to remedy the limitations of the Moral Sciences Tripos as a one-year course that could only admit students who had already graduated with an ordinary degree. He began giving comprehensive courses of lectures, rather than the annual dozen lectures of Whewell.

John Grote had entered Trinity College in 1831, taking the Mathematics and Classics Triposes in 1835 and being elected a Fellow of Trinity College in 1837. In 1842, he was ordained, and in 1847 given a college living as Vicar of Trumpington, then a village on the outskirts of Cambridge. Here he took the opportunity of founding a dining club in his vicarage, "The Grote Club"; papers were read after dinner, and by all accounts Grote and Sidgwick were its leading lights. One of the members,

[18] See Kubo (2013); although no attention is paid here to the context in which Pryme gave his lectures, which rendered them entirely marginal to teaching at Cambridge.

J. R. Mozley, wrote a long letter to Joseph Mayor[19] after Sidgwick's death, recalling discussions between Grote, Sidgwick, Venn, Pearson and Mayor.[20] Meetings continued after Grote's death in 1866, presided over by F. D. Maurice, Grote's successor as Knightbridge Professor (Marshall 1996). For a short time in the 1860s, Grote's dining club provided an important forum for discussion in the moral sciences, bringing first Grote together with Sidgwick and then, after Grote's death, Sidgwick with Marshall.

In 1860, both Grote and Mayor wrote Senate flysheets outlining the purpose of the Moral Sciences Tripos and its need of reform. Mayor's is considerably more detailed and better organised than that of Grote, while arguing to the same ends. He did not deny, for example, that there was a whispering campaign against the Tripos as it stood: that distinction could be gained with just a small amount of cramming. Mayor denied that this was a general problem, but did concede that "It is possible also that there may be some slight foundation in fact for the stories told of distinction gained by a single night's reading" (Mayor 1860: 2–3). He attributed this to the breadth of the course, students having to cover so many different subjects that their knowledge of any one was necessarily shallow. His solution was to purge the Tripos of English Law, and add Logic and Mental Philosophy, making the Tripos more homogeneous, and he would also have preferred to see the removal of Jurisprudence and the conversion of Modern History into Political Philosophy.

This would indeed soon come to pass, but we can point up here what is happening. While originally the substance of the new Moral Sciences Tripos had been defined purely by the existence of a number of Professorial chairs not obviously entirely irrelevant to the moral sciences,

[19] In December 1863, Mayor married Grote's ward and niece Alexandrina Jessie Grote and so had to surrender his college living. He taught first at Kensington School in London, then being appointed Professor at King's College, London, first in classical literature and then, from 1879 to 1883, in moral philosophy (Gibbins 2004); more generally (Gibbins 2007).

[20] J. R. Mozley to J. B. Mayor, 21 April 1904, Holly Bank, Headingley, Leeds; Trinity College Library Add. Ms.c 104/66: "There was no doubt of Sidgwick preferring ethics to metaphysics, as he always did; the practical side in him was always very strong (I remember Alfred Marshall emphasising his admiration of this side of him, very soon after he made his acquaintance) and he distrusted metaphysics as much as Mill did – I remember his saying to me once, that he thought Kant was like a difficult mathematical book; you might hope to understand him if you gave trouble enough to the work; whereas he did not think Hegel was intelligible at all…".

Professors beginning to give regular lectures in their field only because of changes to the ordinary B.A., consideration is now being given to what properly belongs to a syllabus for the Moral Sciences. There is a shift towards grouping subjects dictated not by who might be available to lecture, but by an understanding of the Moral Sciences that was, moreover, increasingly distanced from Whewell's Christian theology; even though both Mayor and Grote were, like Whewell, ordained clergymen.

Having conceded in his flysheet that there were some grounds in criticisms made of the Moral Sciences Tripos, Mayor moved to defend it. If one took a Senior Wrangler or a Senior Classicist unacquainted with these matters, and got them to study Plato's *Republic*, or Aristotle's *Ethics*, or J. S. Mill's *Logic* or *Political Economy*, Mayor thought that even if they studied it for a year it was still conceivable they would fail to produce a good paper on it.

> For in truth such a paper as I allude to, involving the reproduction, illustration, application, and criticism of arguments, as opposed to a mere repetition of opinions, could only be floored by one who had a complete mastery of the principles of the sciences of which they treat. (Mayor 1860: 8)

Mayor therefore identified the substance of the Tripos as the study of canonical texts not in order to mechanically reproduce their content, but to gain an understanding of the arguments to which they contributed.

This was a clear view of how the Moral Sciences Tripos should be developed, and Mayor was able to articulate it in a way that Grote could not. Grote and Mayor were clearly in agreement, but Grote's own flysheet was scrappy and brief, failing to counter criticism of the Moral Sciences Tripos in a coherent manner, nor presenting arguments in its favour, as Mayor had done.[21] Grote did generally argue that the University was falling short if all it had to offer was Mathematics and two ancient languages (1860: 3); but while he followed the main lines of Mayor's

[21] Intending to read the flysheets of first Grote then Mayor on a visit to Trinity College Library in 2015, at first no copy of the Grote flysheet could be located, so I read Mayor's. Then in the afternoon a copy of Grote's was found, and so I read it having already gained an understanding of the contemporary issues from Mayor. The rather scrappy and incomplete nature of Grote's contribution was therefore very obvious. This is no disparagement of Grote, but rather a clue as to how Grote's *Examination of the Utilitarian Philosophy* (1870) came to be as coherent as it is.

arguments, he did so with much less clarity of expression. His recommendations were however clear enough: that a Pass with Honours would qualify for a B.A.; that a Moral Sciences Board be established to oversee the Tripos; and that the Laws of England be dropped in favour of Mental Philosophy. These recommendations were all approved in February 1860. Then, in 1867, the Moral Sciences Board proposed that History and Jurisprudence should be excluded, and political philosophy, previously grouped with History, be grouped with Moral Philosophy in the Moral Sciences Tripos. This now became four subjects: Moral and Political Philosophy; Mental Philosophy; Logic; and Political Economy. A further change in regulations in 1883 divided the degree into two parts. This was now the Moral Sciences Tripos of which Sidgwick was the titular head, and on which he and Marshall had been teaching since the later 1860s.

Before explaining how Sidgwick entered this story I should perhaps summarise where I have got to. At mid-century, a series of reforms created new honours courses that would enable the University of Cambridge to make the transition from seminary to modern university. In this, it was a follower: of German universities, of the University of London, of the Scottish universities, of the new English municipal colleges, and ultimately of the new American universities such as Johns Hopkins and Chicago, from where in the 1920s it adopted postgraduate study and the Ph.D. The Moral Sciences Tripos was one of these new courses, but when originally founded it was simply an additional one-year course organised around existing Professorial positions, the novelty here being that Professors would for the first time be required to deliver courses of lectures and certify students attending these lectures. Through the 1850s and early 1860s, while Grote was Knightbridge Professor, the content of the Moral Sciences Tripos became focussed on the moral sciences as such, rather than a somewhat random grouping of professorial domains. At the same time, it became a three-year honours degree course, with its own governing Board of Studies. The actual teaching was still conducted within colleges, hence the title of "College Lecturer"; this was a position held by Alfred Marshall in St. Johns, and Henry Sidgwick in Trinity.

As is plain from the way that Mayor defended the intellectual demands of the Moral Sciences Tripos in 1860, the course became defined primarily by the study of key texts. Those teaching on the Tripos therefore employed these texts to define its subject matter: Sidgwick wrote his *Methods of Ethics* (1874), then a *Principles of Political Economy* in

1883 because Fawcett's own *Manual of Political Economy* was unsuitable for honours teaching. When Alfred Marshall was appointed Fawcett's successor in 1884, he went on to publish his own *Principles of Economics* (1890), together with its catechism, *Elements of Economics of Industry* (1892). Neville Keynes published his *Formal Logic* (1884)[22]; Sidgwick his *Elements of Politics* (1891). The Moral Sciences Tripos had, by the last quarter of the nineteenth century, shifted from the somewhat accidental concatenation of subjects it had been in the 1850s to an honours degree defined in terms of central texts written by those who taught on it. The principal texts with which their names are associated were not simply an expression of their individual specialist scholarly interests; they were linked to a particular programme of study in the University of Cambridge, whose nature and prospective function can be read out of its organisation and texts. After the death of Grote in 1866, the Knightbridge Chair was held first by F. D. Maurice (1805–1872), and then by T. R. Birks (1810–1883). Marshall's reports of Maurice at the Grote Society suggest that he was by the later 1860s aged and detached; Birks seems to have made very little impression, since this was also the period when Sidgwick and Marshall were involved in promoting women's education in Cambridge. When Maurice died, Sidgwick had not yet published *Methods of Ethics*, and his relatively junior status (he was 34) meant that the post went to Birks. But in 1883 *Methods of Ethics* was already in a second edition, and it would be consistently revised and supplemented through to a posthumous sixth edition in 1901.[23]

3 Henry Sidgwick's Path to the Knightbridge Chair

Henry Sidgwick had entered Rugby School in 1852, and his mother took a house in Rugby the following year. Sidgwick was heavily influenced by one of the Rugby schoolmasters, Edward Benson, who following a career in the Church of England became Archbishop of Canterbury in 1882.

[22] See the discussion of this in Phyllis Deane (2001: 115–19).

[23] The revisions to *Methods of Ethics* were extensive, Sidgwick producing a supplement to the first edition in 1878, to the second edition in 1884, the sixth edition of 1901 including further revisions. Schneewind works with the seventh edition, taking account of the effect of previous revisions; I work with the first edition, since I presume that it is here that any filiation to the work of Grote will be more obvious.

Benson married Sidgwick's younger sister Mary in 1859; Sidgwick in turn married Nora Balfour in 1876, two years after her brother Arthur had become a Conservative Member of Parliament. A. J. Balfour had studied Moral Sciences at Trinity College, graduating in 1869. He was subsequently leader of the Party and Prime Minister 1902–1905, then as Foreign Secretary in 1917 authored the Balfour Declaration, which stated the preparedness of the British government to support the establishment of a homeland for the Jewish people in Palestine. Quite apart from Nora Balfour's own important role in their marriage, the fact that Henry Sidgwick was so personally connected to Church and State can go unrecognised in commentary fixated upon Cambridge.

In 1855, aged 17, Sidgwick entered Trinity College, Cambridge; he graduated in 1859 with firsts in both the Classics and the Mathematics Triposes. Lacking independent means, that same year he accepted a college Assistant Tutorship in Classics, becoming a member of the college at a significant turning point that would influence the path that he took. For the next few years, Sidgwick divided his interests between philosophy and theology; but also "...under Mill's influence I was also strongly led as a matter of duty to study political economy thoroughly, and give no little thought to practical questions, social and political" (Sidgwick 1906: 36). Prompted in 1862 by his reading of Renan's *Études d'histoire religieuse*, Sidgwick determined to study Hebrew and Arabic to understand Christianity as a "historical religion". This study was continued until about 1865, not least because there were two chairs for Arabic in Cambridge, and only one for Moral Philosophy. By the mid-1860s—still in his mid-20s—he seems to have reassessed his position: in 1865 he examined on the Moral Sciences Tripos for the first time, and in 1867 began lecturing on "Mental and Moral Philosophy". In 1874, he went on to add political philosophy to his teaching, and in 1879 political economy.

In 1869, Sidgwick resigned the Assistant Tutorship he had held since 1859[24] and was subsequently re-appointed to a College Lectureship in Moral Sciences. This Lectureship was a new post; hitherto all teaching in the colleges had been done by the Assistant Tutors, but they had become increasingly overburdened by the increase in demand for tuition in all subjects. In the later 1860s, colleges had begun to appoint

[24] This was in relation to the Anglican conditions placed upon him, linked to the ongoing efforts to remove religious disabilities from fellows already mentioned; I discuss the circumstances related to this in my essay (2017: 915–16).

College Lecturers, and eventually these superseded the tutors as the prime teaching appointment. And so Sidgwick's move from an Assistant Tutorship in Classics to a College Lecturer in Moral Sciences was part of a general change in the organisation of teaching—St. John's College had appointed Alfred Marshall to an equivalent post in 1868.

When in the early 1860s, Sidgwick had turned his attention to questions of philosophy and theology he was a leading member of the Grote Society—indeed, one of those attending later recollected that meetings amounted to an extended conversation between Grote and Sidgwick.[25] Mayor later recalled that the Grote Society had originated in 1861; he had been College Lecturer in Moral Sciences at St. Johns and had consulted with Grote in order to co-ordinate his lectures with him. Grote had suggested it would be a good thing to have a periodic meeting for discussion among those with an interest in philosophy, and the first meeting took place in Mayor's rooms, when Grote read an introductory paper. The next meeting was in Grote's own rooms in Trinity, after which Mayor "fell into the habit of going to dine with him at Trumpington", with discussion afterwards that "took the form of papers exchanged between G. and S".[26]

As Simon Cook has suggested, Grote sought "to fashion a philosophy conducive to both theology and science", and he was hostile to "Positivism", "which mistook phenomena for the whole of reality" (Cook 2009: 103). On his early death in 1866, Grote left behind some occasional essays and the first part of a treatise on these issues (1865). However, when John Stuart Mill had in the autumn and early winter of 1861 published a critique of utilitarianism in *Fraser's Magazine*[27] Grote had begun to draft a response, assembling a mass of notes that were then edited by Mayor and published posthumously in 1870 as *An Examination of the Utilitarian Philosophy*. Moreover, with the encouragement of a number of Oxford philosophers Mayor later put together a second part for *Exploratio Philosophica*, in the preface acknowledging the assistance of Sidgwick in reading the proofs (Mayor 1900: xii). This should remind us that the period in which Grote had originally drafted his critique of

[25] Implied by Mayor in his letter to Eleanor Sidgwick, 28 April 1904 Queensgate House, Kingston Hill (Trinity College Library Add Ms. C 1104/68).

[26] Letter of J. B. Mayor to Eleanor Sidgwick, 28 April 1904 op. cit.

[27] Republished in book form as *Utilitarianism* in 1863.

Mill on utilitarianism coincided with that period in the Grote Society when Sidgwick and Grote were reported as being so closely engaged in discussion.

Even without engaging in any detailed examination, there are clear filiations between Grote's critique of utilitarianism and Sidgwick's own *Methods of Ethics* of 1874. And if we are prepared to allow this possibility, then our approach to Sidgwick runs through argument about moral action and moral order in the early 1860s: Grote's extended evaluation of Mill's philosophy and of the manner in which the study of society and ideals for its betterment might be reconciled with a belief in a Christian God. To elaborate this point, we need therefore to return to Mill.

4 Mill's Utilitarianism

John Stuart Mill's first extended published comments on utilitarianism are "Remarks on Bentham's Philosophy", originally printed as Appendix B of Edward Lytton Bulwer's *England and the English* (1833). He began with Bentham's principle that happiness (defined as pleasure and exemption from pain) is the only end desirable in itself, and that all other things are desirable only as means to that end; and that the "production … of the greatest possible happiness, is the only fit purpose of all human thought and action, and consequently of all morality and government…" (Mill 1969a: 5). No argument for the superiority or even viability of this proposition is advanced by Bentham; and Mill points out that it can by contrast be equally argued that moral sentiments are "as much part of the original constitution of man's nature as the desire of happiness and the fear of suffering". Resolving this was not something of which Bentham was capable; for "even when he was most completely in the right, [it has] been reserved for others to *prove* him so" (1969a: 6). That Bentham devoted the greater part of his efforts to legislation rather than morals was an advantage, for the consistent consequentialism he adopted there served him better. According to Mill, the great fault of Bentham as a moral philosopher was to have

> …practically, to a very great extent, confounded the principle of Utility with the principle of specific consequences, and has habitually made up his estimate of the approbation or blame due to a particular kind of action, from a calculation solely of the consequences to which that very action, if practised generally, would itself lead. (1969a: 8)

Furthermore, from the principles of pleasure and pain as the sole springs to action Bentham derives a motive, an interest, such that our actions are governed by our interest, by a balancing of motives. Mill then points out that Bentham simply presupposes that the spring of present action is future pleasure or pain as a consequence of that action; neglecting altogether that "the pain or pleasure which determines our conduct is as frequently one which precedes the moment of action as one which follows it". The implication is that interest conveys the idea of an end for which the conduct selected is the means; but this presumes deliberation, and it is just as possible that conduct is impulsive (1969a: 12, 13).

And it is much the same with Bentham's theory of government: he envisages man in society without a government and comes to the conclusion that the best kind of government would be representative democracy.

> Whatever may be the value of this conclusion, the mode in which it is arrived at appears to me to be fallacious; for it assumes that mankind are alike in all times and all places, that they have the same wants and are exposed to the same evils, and that if the same institutions do not suit them, it is only because in the more backwards stages of improvement they have not wisdom to see what institutions are most for their good. (1969a: 16)

Bentham neglects the human qualities of habit and imagination and elevates only one part of human motivations to action, supposing men and women to be "much cooler and more thoughtful calculators than they really are" (1969a: 17).

In the 1838 memorial for Bentham that Mill published in the *London and Westminster Review* Bentham's method is singled out for praise, rather than his opinion: his way of "treating whole things by separating them into their parts ... and by breaking every question into pieces before attempting to solve it" (1969b: 83). His knowledge of human nature was limited; no one,

> probably, who, in a highly instructed age, ever attempted to give a rule to all human conduct, set out with a more limited conception either of the agencies by which human conduct *is*, or of those by which it *should* be, influenced. (1969b: 83, 93)

During the later 1850s, Mill came back to these ideas, publishing in three parts in *Fraser's Magazine* five chapters that were then published together in 1863 as *Utilitarianism*. This would represent to Grote and Sidgwick what Mill thought about human motivation and action in the early 1860s; it formed the basis for the critique that Grote drafted in 1862, and which his friend Mayor edited into *An Examination of the Utilitarian Philosophy* of 1870. As we shall see, from this perspective Jevon's political economy converges with Sidgwick's moral philosophy.

Mill starts in 1861 from the age-old problem of right action. Our reason supplies the general principles only for moral judgements, abstract doctrines that cannot be perceived empirically. Both the intuitive and the inductive school of ethics hold to the necessity of general laws; but conclude whether actions are right or wrong a priori in the first instance, and a posteriori in the second. All of these tendencies are, openly or tacitly, indebted to the precept of utility, for in one way or another action is in all moral argument linked to happiness (1969c: 206–7). Turning after this first introductory chapter to "what utilitarianism is", Mill first clears away the popular idea that utility is opposed to pleasure; for utility, properly understood, is pleasure itself:

> The Greatest Happiness Principle ... holds that actions are right in proportion as they tend to promote happiness, wrong as the tend to produce the reverse of happiness. By happiness is intended pleasure, and the absence of pain; by unhappiness, pain, and the privation of pleasure. (1969c: 210)

There is of course much more to be said, but the gist of this approach is to maintain that pleasure and freedom from pain are the sole desirable ends; and that all desirable things are desirable either for their inherent pleasure, or as means for the increase of pleasure and diminution of pain. There is in addition to this the issue of assessing the quality and the quantity of pleasures—of ranking them. This can only be achieved by subjective estimation, and this in turn introduces the capacity for pleasure and for its satisfaction—for if such capacities are low, then that person can easily be satisfied.

Linked to this is the issue of ease of attainment: the closer in space or in time a pleasure is, then the greater the temptation to opt for the lesser rather than the greater:

> Men lose their high aspirations as they lose their intellectual tastes, because they have not time or opportunity for indulging them; and they addict themselves to inferior pleasures, not because they deliberately prefer them, but because they are either the only ones to which they have access, or the only ones which they are any longer capable of enjoying. (1969c: 213)

However, this is to consider only individual agency; and this is to neglect the larger principle of the greatest happiness. Rather than deal with this directly, Mill turns to arguments about "happiness" and its consistency in one person, suggesting that the main constituents of a satisfied life are tranquillity and excitement; with a great deal of the former many can find themselves content with very little pleasure; with a great deal of the latter many can be reconciled to a great deal of pain.

When Mill then comes back to this reconciliation of the agent with the collectivity, he proposes that utilitarianism requires the individual to be "as strictly impartial as a disinterested and benevolent spectator ... as between his own happiness and that of others" (1969c: 218). "Laws and social arrangements" should constrain an alignment of the happiness of one with that of all; while "education and opinion" should use its power over human character to encourage the sense in every individual of the association of individual with collective happiness. It is however but rarely that an individual need directly considers public utility; "...in every other case, private utility, the interest or happiness of some few persons, is all he has to attend to" (1969c: 220).

The third chapter considers the existence of any sanction, any source of an obligation to conform to a moral standard. This, Mill states, is ultimately a subjective state, not an external condition. Alignment of private and public good comes from the strengthening of social ties, so that a concern for the common good itself becomes a natural part of the social state. The fourth chapter discusses arguments about proof; that a thing is desirable can only be demonstrated by people desiring it. No ultimate argument can otherwise establish such a proof. Virtue itself becomes something that is desirable; being virtuous, a means to happiness, and an end in itself.

The final chapter considers the relation of justice and utility, and Mill itemises consideration of justice under six headings: the legal rights of the individual; the moral rights of an individual; the conception of just deserts, what an individual deserves; the injustice of bad faith, of not honouring undertakings given; that justice cannot be partial, preferring one over another; and the related idea of equality, although this is mitigated by the idea that "Each person maintains that equality is the dictate of justice, except where he thinks that expediency requires inequality" (1969c: 243). Here Mill moves away from the strict terms of utilitarian argument to the varied constructions of moral rules, and the balance that has to be struck between justice and expediency. This, he suggests in conclusion, is the only real difficulty in the utilitarian theory of morals (1969c: 259).

Mill set the baseline for what utilitarianism meant in the mid-nineteenth century. From the above summary, several important points emerge. In his first evaluation of Bentham, Mill lists the three principal theses of Bentham:

1. Happiness = pleasure and is the sole end in itself;
2. Other things are desirable insofar as they contribute to the realisation of this end;
3. The production of happiness is the only fit purpose of human action and government.

He points out that Bentham merely asserts these, but in 1861 concedes that (individual) happiness is indeed the core of all moral argument. The criticisms of Bentham that Mill first raises are twofold:

1. Bentham confounds utility with specific consequences—in effect, that whatever eventuates is the product of a utilitarian calculation since
2. Bentham imputes an interest to action such that present interest is linked to future action, although present action can be either the outcome of prior circumstance or of impulse.

Only in 1861 does Mill raise the problem inherent in the Greatest Happiness principle: given that the utilitarian calculation is made by an individual, how does the Greatest Happiness result besides through simple aggregation? What is the linkage between private utility and public utility? This is addressed most coherently in the final chapter, where it is asserted that this balance between justice and expediency—the contribution or not of individual action to the greater good—is the sole real difficulty. However, he had previously identified the problem that individuals can have different capacities for happiness—and so how can one sum across individuals whose capacities differ?

By outlining Mill's arguments in some detail, here it becomes possible to judge how radically reduced Jevons' version of them was in 1862. It was this reduced version of Mill's appraisal of the utilitarian calculus that re-emerged in his *Theory of Political Economy* (1871), was developed by Edgeworth in *Mathematical Psychics* (1881), informed Wicksteed's *Common Sense of Political Economy* (1910), these ideas then being revived in the 1930s by Robbins and other at the London School of Economics. And indeed, Jevons' conception of "final utility" played an important part in Sidgwick's *Principles of Political Economy*, albeit deployed to demonstrate that different capacities to realise the means to satisfy ends led into a distributive problem. This was however the outcome of an alternative path along which Mill's arguments passed into propositions about economic action: from Grote to Sidgwick to Pigou. In conclusion, here I will examine some of Grote's objections to Mill, and suggest that, by comparing these to the arguments advanced by Sidgwick, we can form a rather broader understanding of resources for forming propositions about right action: the underlying framework of the new economics, for which "right action" provided the conceptual support for the choices made by (Jevonian) economic agents.

5 And Grote's Critique

Grote's *Examination of the Utilitarian Philosophy* was drafted, set up in type and partially printed in 1863 before Grote then decided against publication.[28] How extensive Mayor's editorial work was we can only surmise, but comparison of the two 1860 flysheets suggests that Mayor was a far more fluent expositor than Grote, and suggests that much of the coherence and impact of the *Examination* is owed to Mayor's editorial work. The book is more a series of essays than continuous argument; Sidgwick would later complain that Grote lacked system, but Grote himself made a virtue of this.

Examination of the Utilitarian Philosophy opens with the statement that

[28] Whitaker notes that Marshall's copy of the book shows signs of careful reading—(1975 Vol. I: 46 n. 29).

> The purpose of the following pages is to show that, though virtue or right action is the great source of human happiness, still the fact that it is so does not of itself constitute its virtue, or explain what we mean when we use that term. The doctrine here controverted may, roughly speaking, be called Utilitarianism. Against this doctrine, or in qualification of it, I have endeavoured to show what in my view is the manner in which we ought to regard the fact that virtue or right action is promotive of human happiness, and what other considerations or elements of moral value ought to be taken into account of in conjunction with it. (1870: 1)

And although, he went on, we might say that mankind has in the course of history passed along a path of real improvement, we are not able to determine the existence of this "improvement" merely from the fact that this is the path that has been followed; we must be able to give reasons for calling it improvement.

> That is to say, we must have the *idea* of improvement: an idea of what *ought to be*, or what it is desirable *should be*, as well as a power of observing, recording, and analyzing what *is*. (1870: 1–2)

A system of morals cannot therefore be built from observation and experience alone. Positivism would have us believe that this is indeed the path followed by other sciences, a path that moral science ought to emulate; but experience and observation is not sufficient basis for any form of moral science. Utilitarianism has adopted a position between positivism and idealism; in "happiness" it sees something that humans not only seek to gain, but which it assumes it is desirable that they should so seek. All moral science

> ...must begin with assuming that there is something imperative upon us to do, or desirable for us to do; must begin, that is, with an ideal: if it does not make this assumption, its real course is the exceedingly unphilosophical one of beginning with describing what man *does* do, and then, by degrees and unauthorizedly, altering its language and speaking of this as what he *should* do or *ought* to do. (1870: 3–4)

Comparing Mill's utilitarianism with earlier versions, Grote lists the series of objections to utilitarianism that Mill believed to be chiefly founded upon misapprehension and suggests that Mill creates a "neo-utilitarian" position that mingles older doctrines with new ones of his own; and that the objections that Mill lists relate not to his own position, but to something rather different. By answering objections to utilitarianism from a new perspective that has already incorporated the objection, Grote charges that this neo-utilitarianism was formed as a consequence of this objection, and hence admits its validity.

The second chapter addresses the issue of happiness, what it is, whether it is attainable, whether it can be described in such a way as to be an object of an action. Of course, the difficulty of determining what happiness might be is no reason to dismiss its existence; and so this line of reasoning cannot be used to rebut utilitarianism. There are instead a number of objections that can be raised, such as that

1. happiness is different for different people;
2. we know very little of how a person can bring about their own happiness;
3. or how far, for example, their happiness might be the result of their own constitution and temper;
4. we have no means of deciding whether we should try to be happy under existing circumstances, or whether we should seek to change the circumstances;
5. nor of deciding, if there are different qualities or degrees of happiness, whether we should settle for a lower, or strive for a higher (1870: 28).

As for the first, while all may agree that all action is aimed at happiness, this does not mean we can proceed to set down on paper what happiness is so that we may have "an easy or ready way of directing our action" in the best manner (1870: 29). The chief objection to utilitarianism arises then from the difficulty of determining what happiness consists in, not from its apparent difficulty of attainment; and of comparing the happiness of one person with that of another.

Turning then in the third chapter to the quality of pleasure, Grote points out that differences of quality are not measurable:

> ...the utilitarian is led astray by his language, talking as he does about pleasures as if they were separate entities, independent of the mind of the enjoyer of them: the pleasures are always mixed with something from themselves, which prevents us from speaking, with any philosophically good result, of this sort of independent comparability among them. (1870: 53–54)

The mind itself being subject to change, there is no "permanent touchstone, no currency to be the medium of the comparison" (54).

> I cannot understand a general scale of pleasures, in which so many marks will be given to drunkenness, so many to love of the fine arts, so many to something else, according to the experiences of those who have tried more than one of them. The experience and the comparison is I am aware a fact, and a fact for moral philosophy to use: but it but one fact, and its application and use but limited. (55)

Examining in the fourth chapter Mill's proof of utilitarianism, Grote argues that Mill conflates what is desired with the desirable; that what is desired must *ipso facto* be desirable. This is therefore merely a truism; the idea that the *summum bonum* is the ultimate question of morality merely an assumption, such that Mill's proof is merely circular.

> ...Mr. Mill seems to consider that he has proved that, in the same natural manner in which a man's happiness is an end to him, the aggregate happiness is an end to *each individual* of the aggregate. (70–71)

Grote returns to this issue at the opening of the fifth chapter:

> It is the individual who feels and acts; it is he who seeks for the *summum bonum*: it is his *summum bonum* or ideal welfare which is sought for: it is he also who, as a matter of fact, desires that which is pleasant, that namely which is pleasant to *him*. This, as an idea or notion, is not the same as the abstractly, or as the generally, desirable. We cannot practically speak about happiness without considering *whose* happiness it is we mean. (1870: 85)

He then reminds the reader of Mill's utilitarian formula—that actions are right in proportion as they tend to promote happiness, and wrong as they do the reverse. But, he points out, Mill fails to make clear *whose* happiness at stake. While it is the action of the agent that realises the conjunction of ends and means, it is the happiness of all that is the prime concern:

> We have got to consider therefore not only the direction of our action to the production of happiness, but the distribution of our action among the different happinesses or susceptibilities of pleasure towards which it may be directed. (1870: 88)

This issue of distribution between ourselves and others is avoided by Mill:

> In some respects, society, whether moral or political, may be considered an aggregation of similar units; but in far more important respects it is an organization of dissimilar members. The general happiness, as a fact, is the sum of the happiness of the individuals; but as an object to be aimed at, it is not this, but it is to be attained by the acting of each according to the relations in which he is placed in the society. (1870: 95)

Grote makes further important arguments against Mill, but for our purposes here we can identify three points:

1. There appears to be an inherent circularity in the utilitarian calculation, such that any consequence is presumed to be a desired outcome, "happiness";
2. how private utility is supposed to translate into public utility remains obscure;
3. there is no "common currency" by which we can measure happiness, and through which we might compare or sum individual perceptions of happiness.

Precisely, these points would later be revived by economist in arguments over the point at which workers ceased providing additional increments of effort, or consumers switched their attention from one good to another. Grote's critique of Mill anticipates all of this, but more important here is the date at which these points appeared in a published book: in 1870, before the publication of Jevons's *Theory of Political Economy*, during the period in which Marshall was teaching on the Moral Sciences Tripos, and before the publication of Sidgwick's *Methods of Ethics*. Do then these points recur in Sidgwick's *Methods of Ethics*?

6 The First Edition of Sidgwick's *Methods of Ethics*

Methods of Ethics opens with the statement that ethics can be defined as the science of conduct, seeking to determine not the actual, but the ideal: "what ought to exist, not what does exist" (Sidgwick 1874: 1).[29] He immediately raises the question of the use of "science" here, since this presumes some particular subject matter. The Moral Sciences, for example, deal with what exists: psychology as inquiry into the laws of the formation of character; and sociology as the "physiology of Society". While it is the object of these studies to explain individual and social phenomena, there is almost always a desire to improve or to regulate, applying "good" and "bad", "right" or "wrong" to the conduct or institutions described; thus passing, "sometimes half unconsciously, from the point of view of Psychology or Sociology to the point of view of Ethics or Politics" (1874: 2). While our view of what ought to be is derived from our apprehension of what is, the ideal at which we aim lies outside "all investigation of the actual". The aim of the book is therefore to focus resolutely on the ideal. There are two rational ends, Perfection and Happiness, and the book is directed to the investigation of three methods of ethics: Egoism, Intuitionism and Utilitarianism. While it will turn out that Grote's position is associated with what is here treated as Intuitionism, we might also note that the way in which utilitarianism entered into strictly economic argument conflated Egoism and Utilitarianism. At the end of Book I Ch. VI Sidgwick notes this common confusion between the two kinds of Hedonism, the Egoistic and the Universalistic; his efforts to separate these two should repay attention. It might also be noted here that Sidgwick later describes Adam Smith as "one of the most penetrating and ingenious of English moralists" (1874: 431), an endorsement of *Theory of Moral Sentiments* at a time when the work had long been neglected and treated as quite outdated.

The distributive problem of "Happiness" is identified by Sidgwick in the same way as Grote. While appearing to be a reasonable end, there is a problem, for

[29] This work was revised in detail several times, the posthumous 7th edition of 1907 being the one most commonly referred to today. Since I am interested in how close Sidgwick's arguments are to those of Grote I use the first edition only.

> ...when we ask *whose* Happiness, a controversy emerges: for to some it seems that the agent ought to seek his own happiness, and that this is what each individual's reason must necessarily prescribe to him: while other think that the view if reason is essentially universal, and that it cannot be reasonable to aim ultimately at the happiness of any one individual rather than that of any other equally deserving and susceptible of it. There are therefore two views and methods in which Happiness is regarded as the ultimate and rational end of actions: in the one it is the agent's happiness which is so regarded, in the other the happiness of all men, or all sentient beings. (1874: 59)

This issue is addressed in Book I, devoted to Egoism, empirical hedonism presuming that all pleasures and pains are commensurable,

> Or perhaps we should say that we are forced to assume all pleasures and pains to have definite quantitative relations to each other: for otherwise they cannot be conceived as possible elements of a total of which we are to seek the maximum. ......at any rate, the common opinion would seem to be, that all the pleasures that man can experience bear a finite ratio to each other in respect of pleasantness: and so that they can all be arranged in a certain scale as greater or lesser in some finite degree. (1874: 112)[30]

Consideration here of the four qualities identified by Bentham in hedonistic calculation—intensity, duration, certainty and proximity—leads to two problems: How does one person compare among sensations, and how can we compare the sensations of two or more persons?

> I do not now mean that one man's estimate of the value of any kind of pleasures differs from another's: for each sentient individual must be the final judge of the pleasantness and painfulness of his own feelings, and therefore this kind of discrepancy does not affect the validity of the judgments, and creates no difficulty until any one tries to appropriate the experience of others. But I mean that each individual's judgment of the comparative value of his own pleasures is apt to be different at different times: and that this variation is a legitimate ground for distrusting the validity of any particular comparison. (1874: 123–24)

[30]This corresponds to pp. 123–4 in the 7th edition (Hackett Publishing Company, Indianapolis 1981), but there these different ideas are split up and the impact considerably weakened by Sidgwick's revisions.

And from a strictly common-sense perspective, the hedonic calculus has a rather circumscribed application:

> The majority of human beings spend most of their time in labouring to avert starvation and severe bodily discomfort: and the brief leisure that remains to them, after supplying the bodily needs of food, sleep, &c., is spent in ways determined rather by impulse, routine, and habit, than by a deliberate estimate of probably pleasure. It would seem, then, that the common sense to which we here refer is only that of a minority of comparatively rich and leisured persons. (1874: 137)

All the same, this reveals a further problem, for should we be guided by the preferences that persons themselves state, or by those that can be inferred from their actions? Sidgwick continues on to examine the linkage made between happiness and duty, concluding that any egoistic method of the Hedonical calculus appears to suffer from major difficulties.

Book III is the longest of the four, devoted to Intuitionism, but this can here be left to one side since this bears more on the position from which Grote criticised Mill; as we can see from the above, many of the objections that Sidgwick raises against the Hedonic calculus are continuous with those of Grote. The final Book IV is devoted to Utilitarianism, and here we need to consider exactly how this is distinguished from Egoism. In particular, it is the problem of distribution (likewise raised by Grote) that requires attention. He begins with a clear association of Utilitarianism with Bentham:

> By Utilitarianism is here meant the ethical theory, first distinctly formulated by Bentham, that the conduct which, under any given circumstances, is externally or objectively right, is that which will produce the greatest amount of happiness to all whose interests are affected: or more precisely ....the conduct which will produce "the greatest possible happiness to the greatest possible number." (1874: 381)

But this Universalistic Hedonism is quite distinct from Egoistic Hedonism; that between the proposition that each ought to seek his or her own happiness and that each ought to seek the happiness of all being "so obvious and glaring, that instead of dwelling upon it we seem rather to be called upon to explain how the two ever came to be confounded..." (1874: 382).

In fact, the greater part of Book IV is devoted to reconciling Utilitarianism with Common Sense, pursuing a proof of utilitarianism and neglecting the distributional issue so well identified here. When Sidgwick returns to this issue, he acknowledges its identification by Grote explicitly, but then suggests that the argument against Bentham proposes inequality in the distribution of services, simply asserting that the reason why "each individual should distribute his beneficence in the channels marked out by commonly recognised ties and claims, are tolerably obvious" (1874: 404).

There is, then, no resolution at all here of the identification of public good with private choice that enables Bentham to maintain, simultaneously, that the individual agent acts to select means to a given end, and that the sum of all such actions is the Greatest Happiness. This would be trivially true as a simple aggregation, but Mill had already seen that public utility was more than the sum of private utility. The real difficulty in Mill was his argument that commitment to common social purposes would of itself bring about the creation of the public good; a problem that Sidgwick clearly recognised, but did not in *Methods of Ethics* resolve. Nonetheless, such a lack of resolution would provide a dynamic basic for the teaching of the moral sciences in Cambridge, undercutting the analysis of society, polity and economy in terms of any sort of Spencerian perfectibility and natural law. Nor did this involve any argument that there was an inevitably antagonistic relationship between the private and the common good, as presented in the moral philosophy of T. H. Green. This gap between individual action and public good was opened up, rather than closed down, by the need for the systematic study of government and economy and a search for policy that could reconcile individual needs and the public good.

If then Cambridge Moral Sciences can be understood in terms of responses to Millian utilitarianism, an intellectual endeavour shared in the discussions between Grote and Sidgwick during the early 1860s but only finding its way into print in 1870 and 1874 respectively, it is also possible to relate Jevons's own book of 1871 both chronologically and substantively to this line of argument. Sidgwick then went on to publish his *Principles of Political Economy* in 1883, re-synthesising Mill's political economy with a Jevonian "final utility". While soon enough eclipsed by Marshall's *Principles of Economics* in 1890, situating Sidgwick's political economy in this way does help us understand both Marshall's voluble silence on Sidgwick's *Principles*, and also some kind of understanding of quite why Marshall so implacably wished to detach his version of economics from the Moral Sciences Tripos.

And so beneath all the evasion, the misdirection and the fictionalising proclivities of Marshall in his treatment of Jevons, we can perceive a rational core: a distinction between the formal utilitarian rationalism of a Jevonian economics, and the empirically oriented economic analysis of Marshall, developed not as a rational account of economic action, but as a set of instruments and protocols for the analysis of contingent economic phenomena, "of man's actions in the ordinary business of life".

References

Anon. (1893) *The Student's Guide to the University of Cambridge*, 5th edition, rewritten, Deighton, Bell and Co., Cambridge.

Backhouse, Roger E. (2006) "Sidgwick, Marshall, and the Cambridge School of Economics", *History of Political Economy* Vol. 38 pp. 15–44.

Backhouse, Roger E., Keith Tribe (2018) *The History of Economics. A Course for Students and Teachers*, Agenda, Newcastle upon Tyne.

Clark, Alex D. D. (2008) *Mr Hopkins' Men. Cambridge Reform and British Mathematics in the 19th Century*, Springer.

Cook, Simon J. (2009) *The Intellectual Foundations of Alfred Marshall's Economic Science. A Rounded Globe of Knowledge*, Cambridge University Press, Cambridge.

Cournot, A. A. (1980) *Recherches sur les principes mathématiques de la théorie des richesses* [1838], Librarie J. Vrin, Paris.

Crisp, Roger (2015) *The Cosmos of Duty. Henry Sidgwick's Methods of Ethics*, Oxford University Press.

Deane, Phyllis (2001) *The Life and Times of J. Neville Keynes. A Beacon in the Tempest*, Edward Elgar, Cheltenham.

Ferguson, Adam (1792) *Principles of Moral and Political Science* Vol. I, A. Strahan & T. Cadell, London.

Gibbins, John R. (2004) "Mayor, Joseph Bickersteth (1828–1916)", Oxford Dictionary of National Biography.

Gibbins, John R. (2007) *John Grote, Cambridge University and the Development of Victorian Thought*, Imprint Academic.

Grote, John (1860) "To Members of the Senate", 22 February 1860, flysheet, Cambridge.

Grote, John (1865) *Exploratio Philosophica. Rough Notes on Modern Intellectual Science Part I*, Deighton, Bell, and Co., Cambridge.

Grote, John (1870) *An Examination of the Utilitarian Philosophy*, Deighton, Bell, and Co., Cambridge.

Jevons, W. Stanley (1866) "Brief Account of a General Mathematical Theory of Political Economy" [1862] *Journal of Royal Statistical Society of London* Vol. 29 Issue 2 (June) pp. 282–90.

Jevons, W. Stanley (1957) *The Theory of Political Economy*, fifth edition, Kelley and Milman, New York.

Kubo, Shin (2013) "George Pryme, Dugald Stewart and Political Economy at Cambridge", *History of Political Economy* Vol. 45 pp. 61–97.

Marshall, Alfred (1925) "Mr Jevons' Theory of Political Economy" [1872], reprinted in A. C. Pigou (ed.) *Memorials of Alfred Marshall*, Macmillan, London pp. 93–100.

Marshall, Alfred (1996) "Notes Taken During Discussions at the Grote Club Meetings, February-November 1867", introduced and edited by Tiziano Raffaelli, *Marshall Studies Bulletin* 6 pp. 49–64.

Marshall, Mary Paley (1947) *What I Remember*, Cambridge University Press, Cambridge.

Mayor, J. B. (1860) "Remarks on the Proposal to Grant the Degree of BA to Persons Who Have Obtained Honours in the Moral Sciences Course", flysheet, Cambridge.

Mayor, J. B. (1862) "The Moral Sciences" in *Student Guide to the University of Cambridge*, Deighton Bell & Co., Cambridge pp. 140–52.

Mayor, J. B. (1900) "Preface" to John Grote, *Exploratio Philosophica. Part II*, ed. Joseph Bickersteth Mayor, Cambridge University Press, Cambridge pp. v–xii.

McWilliams Tullberg, Rita (1995) "Marshall's Contribution to the Women's Higher Education Movement", in T. Raffaelli, E. Biagini, R. McWilliams Tullberg (eds.) *Alfred Marshall's Lectures to Women. Some Economic Questions Directly Connected to the Welfare of the Laborer*, Edward Elgar, Aldershot pp. 47–75.

Mill, John Stuart (1969a) "Remarks on Bentham's Philosophy" [1833], *Collected Works of John Stuart Mill* Vol. X, ed. J. M. Robson, University of Toronto Press, Toronto pp. 3–18.

Mill, John Stuart (1969b) "Bentham", *Collected Works of John Stuart Mill* Vol. X, ed. J. M. Robson, University of Toronto Press, Toronto pp. 75–115.

Mill, John Stuart (1969c) "Utilitarianism" [1862], *Collected Works of John Stuart Mill* Vol. X, ed. J. M. Robson, University of Toronto Press, Toronto pp. 203–59.

Mill, John Stuart (1973) *A System of Logic Ratiocinative and Inductive*, Collected Works of John Stuart Mill Vol.7 in 2 pts. Routledge and Kegan Paul, London.

Palfrey, David (2002) "The Moral Sciences Tripos at Cambridge University, 1848–1860", PhD dissertation, University of Cambridge.

Schneewind, J. B. (1977) *Sidgwick's Ethics and Victorian Moral Philosophy*, Oxford University Press, Oxford.

Sidgwick, Henry (1874) *The Methods of Ethics*, Macmillan, London.

Sidgwick, Henry (1906) "Autobiographical Fragment", in A. and E. M. Sidgwick (eds.) *Henry Sidgwick. A Memoir*, Macmillan, London pp. 33–8.

Skinner, Andrew S., Thomas Wilson (eds.) (1976) *Essays on Adam Smith*, Oxford University Press, London.

Tribe, K. (2017) "Henry Sidgwick, Moral Order, and Utilitarianism", *European Journal of the History of Economic Thought* Vol. 24 pp. 907–30.

Whatmore, Richard (2000) *Republicanism and the French Revolution. An Intellectual History of Jean-Baptiste Say's Political Economy*, Oxford University Press, Oxford.

Whewell, William (1852) *Lectures on the History of Moral Philosophy in England*, John W. Parker, London.

Whitaker, J. K. (ed.) (1996) *The Correspondence of Alfred Marshall, Economist,* 3 vols. Cambridge University Press, Cambridge.

Whitaker, J. K. (ed.) (1975) *The Early Economic Writings of Alfred Marshall, 1867–1890,* 2 Vols. Macmillan, London.

White, Michael V. (2015) "A Peculiar Archaeology: Searching for Mr. Giffen's Behaviour", *European Journal of the History of Economic Thought* Vol. 22 pp. 22–50.

Winstanley, D. A. (1940) *Early Victorian Cambridge*, Cambridge University Press, London.

Marshall's Influence Through the 20th Century

Destabilizing Speculation on Organized Markets: Early Perspectives in the Spirit of Marshall

Paolo Paesani and Annalisa Rosselli

1 Introduction

The reconstruction of Marshall's evolutionary approach to economics stands out among the many contributions made by Tiziano Raffaelli to the history of economic thought (Raffaelli 2003). From Marshall's early psychological writings to his unfinished book on progress, two features characterize this approach. First, the focus on the time dimension of economic decisions and their immediate and ultimate effects. Second, the idea that those decisions, and the equilibrium they lead to, reflect complex interactions between different groups of agents operating within an evolving economic and social environment (Caldari 2015). Both these features appear in Marshall's analysis of organized speculative markets, which forms the main subject of the present chapter.

P. Paesani · A. Rosselli (✉)
Department of Economics and Finance, University of Rome Tor Vergata, Rome, Italy
e-mail: annalisa.rosselli@uniroma2.it

P. Paesani
e-mail: paolo.paesani@uniroma2.it

K. Caldari et al. (eds.), *Marshall and the Marshallian Heritage*, Palgrave Studies in the History of Economic Thought,
https://doi.org/10.1007/978-3-030-53032-7_8

Marshall's ideas about speculation were mainly set out in three writings, two published during Marshall's lifetime in *Industry and Trade* (Marshall 1919: 250–268) and in *Money, Credit and Commerce* (Marshall 1923: 89–97); the other, a manuscript dated 1898, when Marshall was working on the second volume of the *Principles*,[1] was published posthumously by Dardi and Gallegati in 1992. Scattered observations in the *Principles* and Marshall's reading notes on H.C. Emery's book *Speculation in the Stock and Produce Exchanges of the United States* (Emery 1896) provide additional relevant reference.[2]

Commenting on the manuscript, Dardi and Gallegati (1992: 572) note a "shift of position from a typically nineteenth-century vision of speculation as a picturesque and sometimes objectionable, but essentially marginal phenomenon, to a modern view which places speculation at the very centre of the capitalist engine". This occurred in connection with the consolidation of organized markets for commodities and stocks at the turn of the twentieth century. That this phenomenon should attract Marshall's interest is hardly surprising, given his well-known attention to the actual working of the economy and its transformations.

As argued in detail below, three elements characterize Marshall's mature views on speculation. First, organized speculation is a form of intertemporal arbitrage, which stabilizes prices and improves allocation by conveying resources where and when they are most needed. Second, a class of professional speculators, in possession of intelligence, good forecasting skills and adequate financial means, conducts this activity. Doing so, speculators enable producers, manufacturers and savers to hedge against price risks and usually accelerate the convergence of market prices to their normal values. Third, the presence of amateur speculators is a disturbing element which makes it possible, and in some cases tempting, for professionals to profit from anticipating amateur opinion rather than price trends. When this occurs, speculation may amplify

[1] As Marshall wrote on 26 October 1899 to Bishop Westcott: "I am just now working at the good and evil of Stock Exchange fluctuations. Like everything else which I touch in my second Volume, which will be more concrete than my first, I find it grows in difficulty in my hands". In Pigou ed. (1925: 385).

[2] Emery's book was credited since its appearance as "without doubt the most thorough work on speculation written in English" (Ryan 1902: 337). Marshall perused it carefully. Marshall's reading notes and Marshall's own annotated copy of Emery's book are preserved in the Marshall Papers, Section 5 "Late Notes in Bundle" 13/2, in the Marshall Library of Economics, Cambridge, UK.

price fluctuations, pushing prices away from fundamentals with destabilizing effects. Dishonest professionals may go so far as to manipulate the amateurs' opinions by camouflaging their true intentions, spreading false information or by other illegitimate means.

While the main elements characterizing Marshall's view of speculation have already been investigated in the literature, three aspects deserve further analysis. First, whether Marshall deemed that destabilizing speculation could go so far as to overshadow normal prices completely, paving the way to Keynes's "casino finance". Second, whether the presence of amateur speculators should be accepted as inevitable or thwarted whenever possible. Third, whether, and if so to what extent, Marshall's positive view of speculation by professionals extended to all the speculative instruments and practices available at the time, from futures trading to short-selling and options.

Many recent contributions on Marshall and speculation revolve around Marshall's connection with Emery, mainly but not only in the light of their influence on Keynes (Lawlor 1994, 2006; Carabelli and Cedrini 2013). Our first aim is to expand this literature by emphasizing some aspects of context which are essential to shed light on the questions set out above. Our second aim is to discuss how those ideas connect with the debates of the time on the regulation of futures and option markets.

Regarding the first aim, Sect. 2 argues that the emergence of global organized commodity and stock markets at the turn of the twentieth century transformed the financial environment, notably in Britain and the USA. In this context, reconsideration of established ideas on speculation was called for, often against public opinion and its beliefs in the close association between speculation and gambling. This gave rise to an extensive literature, which, in the main, defended speculation by emphasizing its similarity with arbitrage and transport in space.[3] Just as transport of commodities from sites of abundant supply to places where supply is scarce improves allocation in space, transport from times of abundance to times of (expected) scarcity, using futures, improves resource allocation over time. Extension of the transport metaphor from commodities to securities hinged on similarities between the two asset classes, with *caveats* about securities being particularly exposed to the risk of instability and manipulation due to greater difficulties in identifying their normal prices.

[3] Many authors employ the transport metaphor. See, for example, Carver in Emery (1900: 118), Hadley (1904: 105–106), Lavington (1913: 39–40).

Marshall's analysis moves along these lines and in this respect exemplifies this literature.[4] Indeed, when Marshall defends constructive speculation, as he does in *Industry and Trade*, he does so discussing agricultural commodities. When he worries about the risks of manipulation by professional speculators against amateurs, as he does in the manuscript note and in *Money Credit and Commerce*, he focuses mainly on securities.

Marshall's considerations on the losses inflicted on amateur speculators by unscrupulous professionals, with echoes of his paternalistic attitude towards the lower classes and their economic well-being, intertwined with the theme of market accessibility and analysis of the advantages/disadvantages of market "democratization". As we observe in Sect. 3, opinions differed in the early literature on speculation in this connection. On the one hand, expert observers identified enhanced liquidity and diversity of opinion as the main advantages deriving from widespread market participation. On the other hand, as the number of traders increased, so did the share of amateurs and the incentive for professional speculators to reap profits by "fleecing" them, with destabilizing effects on the market. In Sect. 4, our reconstruction suggests that Marshall did not support the view that the presence of a large body of amateurs was necessary for markets to function effectively. Consequently, he was critical of instruments like options that made speculating too easy for too great a number of agents, intellectually and materially ill-equipped to do so. Section 5 concludes the chapter.

2 The Commercial Revolution and Marshall as Part of the Emerging Literature on Organized Speculative Markets

Around the 1860s, technological advances in sea and land transport (transatlantic steamships, railways) and communications (e.g. the partial completion of telegraph connection to India in 1857, the laying of the transatlantic cable in 1866) contributed to the emergence of world markets for many staple commodities, in particular cotton and wheat. With the introduction of official grading systems, used for the purpose of commodity quality assessment it became possible to standardize forward contracts, paving the way to the introduction of futures. Concomitantly,

[4]We have discussed this literature elsewhere. See Paesani and Rosselli (2019).

security markets expanded in response to the financial needs of the companies involved in this commercial revolution.[5]

Far-reaching technological changes accompanied the emergence of organized speculative markets. Between 1867 and 1882, both the London and the New York Stock Exchanges brought in the use of ticker tape and the telephone. Both innovations allowed interested parties to be immediately and constantly informed about prices even if they were not on the floor of the Exchange. The possibility to draw large profits from this new facility attracted increasing numbers of traders. In London, membership of the Stock Exchange had risen from 864 in 1850 to 4855 by 1914. In New York, the number had risen to 1100 by 1879 and remained at that level until 1914 (Michie 1986: 174). Similar changes occurred in the case of commodities. Between 1875 and 1905, organized futures exchanges appeared in the USA, Canada, Europe and Latin American, although Chicago and Liverpool—the first European market to develop futures trading—acquired and maintained early prominence globally.[6]

As the business environment became more complex, the array of variables and risk factors to take into consideration increased. This created propitious conditions for the emergence of a new class of professional speculators, endowed with wide-ranging intelligence, financial means and ability to anticipate changes in market conditions. Acting on those anticipations, professionals, "dealing in things the futures prices of which are eminently uncertain" (Marshall 1919: 252), disseminated information, relieving local traders and small investors of risks they might find difficult to assess.

Eventually, the growth of stock exchanges and organized commodity markets gave rise to a flourishing literature,[7] which distinguished speculation from gambling—two activities that public opinion often confused. One strand of this literature aimed to provide investors with practical information about trading procedures and their potential risks. Another,

[5] On this, see Michie (2007), Chs. 4 and 5.

[6] On the origins of futures trading, see Working (1953), Williams (1982), and Levy (2006) among others. On the Liverpool cotton market, see Hall (2000).

[7] On the rise of this literature, see Goss and Yamey (1976), Leathers and Raines (2008), and Berg (2011) among others.

more academic, strand focused on the positive contribution given by speculation to the efficient allocation of resources through enhancement of the allocative function of prices.

Many contributions to the second strand, including Marshall's own, sought to formulate a unified theory of speculation, equally applicable to both commodity and security markets. The gist of the argument in favour of the constructive role of speculation can be summarized as follows. Commodity price fluctuations are caused by real exogenous factors, mainly reflecting changing supply conditions. Intelligent speculators, acting pre-emptively based on correct information drawn from a global network, dampen fluctuations, conveying resources when and where they are most needed. The same argument is extended to securities, overly stressing similarities between the two asset classes. Securities, like commodities, are homogeneous, not readily perishable and standardized assets. They too are subject to price variability, although, in the case of securities, demand, reflecting expectations of future earnings, is the main driver of prices. Absence of monopoly conditions is another feature which the Stock Exchange shares with most commodity markets. Episodes of fraud and market manipulation were presented as exceptional and of little consequence in the long run.

Marshall's analysis of speculation does not distance itself from this approach. In *Industry and Trade*, Marshall focuses on commodity markets and identifies two main advantages as deriving from the activities of professional speculators: improvement in resource allocation and insurance against price risks. As for the improvement in resource allocation, being in possession of superior knowledge of prospective market conditions, professional speculation contributes "to increase the supply of things where and when they are likely to be most wanted, and to check the supply of things where and when they are likely to be in less urgent demand. This is its most conspicuous service" (Marshall 1919: 253).[8] Buying (selling) forward on the anticipation of scarcity (abundance), professional speculators influence cash prices and accelerate the convergence of prices towards their long-run equilibrium values, reflecting the

[8] See also: "[..]a speculator, who, without manipulating prices by false intelligence or otherwise, anticipates the future correctly; and who makes his gains by shrewd purchases and sales on the Stock Exchange or in Produce Markets, generally renders a public service by pushing forward production where it is wanted, and repressing it where it is not" (Marshall 1920: 359fn).

needs of the economy. Their activity requires them to gather and master a range of information relating not only to the market conditions of the commodity in which they trade, but also of all the commodities that may substitute it or for which it may be a substitute (Marshall 1920: 281). Competition among professionals enhances the process of driving prices to their equilibrium values, making it faster, more accurate and less costly. In this way, far from causing volatility, speculation contributes to reducing it. Marshall refers to reports, which show the beneficial effects of speculation in reducing the amplitude of price fluctuations (Marshall 1919: 261, fn. 2). Moreover, Marshall's reading notes on Emery's book reveal his appreciation of Emery's attempt to bear out the claimed price stabilizing effect of speculation by providing data on cotton and wheat prices prior and subsequent to the establishment of organized markets.

Marshall's second argument in defence of speculation revolves around the insurance service which professional speculators provide the ordinary entrepreneur with, insuring him "against the risk that the materials which he will need in his business will not need to be purchased at an enhanced price" (Marshall 1919: 253). For example, millers who purchase wheat spot and need insurance against price falls that can affect the prices of both wheat and flour can sell their wheat forward and thus hedge against price risks. At the same time, millers who, having made contracts to deliver flour at a specified time, need protection against wheat price rises can find it on the futures market, buying wheat forward. Millers belonging to the first set seek insurance against the fall in the price of their output. Millers belonging to the second set seek insurance against the rise in the price of their input.

> In so far as the sales of futures by the first set, and the purchases by the second, are for equal amounts and like times, the resulting risks cancel out one another: whatever excess of risk there is on the one side or the other remains to be borne by the dealers on the Exchange: and their shoulders are very strong for the work. (Marshall 1919: 260)

3 Amateurs vs. Professional Speculators and the Pitfalls of Easy Access to Markets

Marshall's recognition of the advantages of speculation does not blind him to the possibility that "dealings in organized markets are liable to abuse by unscrupulous men, aided as they often are by the folly of ill-informed speculators", as the title of a section in *Industry and Trade* reads (Marshall 1919: 262). Putting it in Marshallian terms, the difference between professional and "foolish" speculators seems to be one of power and character. As Raffaelli (1994: 122) defines it, man's character: "is displayed in the way in which he grasps at immediate advantages or, on the other hand, tries to look further". Based on this definition, amateur speculators, with their focus on short-term gains, show poor character. Professionals, on the other hand, possess the ability to foresee the long-run consequences of present actions and events and behave accordingly. This distinction echoes the contrast, dear to Victorian authors, between short-sighted individuals who cannot constrain their impulses and the morally superior agents who possess the ability to forecast the future and to abstain from immediate satisfactions, to the benefit of the whole society (Raffaelli 2003: 26–27).

Confidence in the constructive role of professional speculators does not exclude the risk that, occasionally, cliques of some of them, lured by the possibility to make a quick profit, may deviate from their standards, taking actions that contribute to destabilizing markets. On commodity markets, destabilization can take the form of a corner, where the clique gains control of the supply of a given type of commodity, subsequently "fleecing" forward sellers who must close their positions and buy from them at exorbitant prices. The presence of amateurs greatly enhances the effectiveness of these "shrewd business ventures, aimed at gains that must be balanced by losses to traders who are concerned in the same affairs" (Marshall 1919: 252).

The same problem occurs on a larger scale and more easily on the stock exchange. In general, stock prices respond to news which speculators react to. Occasionally, however, professionals may take a step further and manipulate the news and/or induce amateurs to move in the wrong direction. Selling stocks which they know will appreciate on the anticipation that amateurs will follow enables professionals to buy back those assets at a lower price, gaining both when the market is on the "wrong tack" and when "after the true state of the case is being brought home" it moves back to the right "tack" (Marshall in Dardi and Gallegati 1992: 589). These operations distort market prices with respect to fundamentals and end up with "fleeced" amateurs and professionals gaining extra profits, the fruit of deceit and market manipulation. When this occurs, speculation becomes malignant, as Marshall defines it.

> S[peculation] is wholesome when it is an attempt of persons or groups of persons to obtain for themselves value for their judgements that anything is at a higher or lower price that the true one i.e. it would have if all the circumstances of coming D[emand] & S[upply] were known generally and rightly interpreted. It is malignant when endeavours are made to move the opinion of others in the direction opposite to that which the speculators believe to be the true one. This end is bad in itself but it cannot generally be pursued with any success without means that are detestable. (note dated 16.8.1904 in Marshall papers 5/13/2)

Discussing the relevance of these operations, and their apparently growing importance, however, Marshall observes:

> The scale of operation is now larger than before; the prizes to be won are higher, and the resources at the command of the operators are more numerous and powerful. But on the other hand, competition is stronger, and the difficulty of keeping false news afloat without contradiction is greater. So and on the whole the manipulation of markets is not becoming easier. (Marshall in Dardi and Gallegati 1992: 591)

Nevertheless, the problem cannot be underestimated, and society should not stop searching for a solution to the threat to the correct working of markets represented by "international speculative combinations" which are "the source of some of the gravest practical problems with which the coming generation will have to deal" (Marshall 1920: 559).

Apart from open manipulation, professionals know how amateurs behave and can try to profit by anticipating amateurs' reactions to incoming news rather than evaluating the long-run impact on fundamentals of the facts the news concerns. Professionals come into possession of news earlier on and can correctly calculate its short- and long-run impact on prices. Amateurs come into possession of news later on, when it becomes of public domain. In this sense, they are not gamblers acting at random, but ill-informed speculators who base their action on public news, not counting that "the latest information accessible to outsiders has nearly always been acted on by well-informed persons, and has exerted the full influence, belonging to it, before it reaches the public" (Marshall 1919: 264). Short-run fluctuations in prices drive amateurs' decisions, often inducing them to make mistakes, which the more competent speculators are well aware of. "Hence it arises that by far *the larger part* of the attention even of the leading operators is given not to the distant future but to the immediate future" (Marshall in Dardi and Gallegati 1992: 589; italics added). But in *Industry and Trade* Marshall became slightly more cautious:

> It may indeed be said that shrewd, far-seeing speculators *sometimes* govern their own action, not so much by forecasts of the distant future, as by forecasts of the inaccuracy of the forecasts of that future. (Marshall 1923: 96; italics added)

Insofar as speculation focuses on the short-term response of market opinion to news rather than on fundamentals it can indeed become a permanent source of instability. It remains open to question whether Marshall went so far as to envisage that speculation could disrupt *enterprise* completely, as discussed by Keynes in Chapter 12 of the *General Theory*. On this Bateman (2006) and Dardi and Gallegati (1992) express different views. While, in Bateman's opinion, Marshall envisaged the interaction between professionals and unwitting amateurs as an ephemeral factor, closely connected with the business cycle, Dardi and Gallegati (1992) emphasize Marshall's preoccupation with that interaction, as well as his reluctance to make it public. Actually, as Dardi and Gallegati note, nowhere does Marshall express his doubts about the impact of speculation so clearly as in the 1898 manuscript, particularly when he admits that even the greatest financiers, although better equipped to foresee the future, indulge in guessing at public opinion. However, if we confine ourselves to his published works, Marshall seems to retain confidence in the market mechanism and the constructive role of speculation, especially on commodity markets, without being oblivious to its evils, due mainly to amateur speculation.

This topic is better understood in connection with the issue of market accessibility, which was widely debated in Marshall's times. Reflecting on the effects deriving from the interaction between professional and amateur speculators, expert observers, from Crump (1875) to Brace (1913), were led to question the advantages of opening organized exchanges to small operators. On the one hand, widespread participation would increase marketability and diversity of opinion, with advantages for investors in terms of enhanced liquidity and reduction in the size if not frequency of price fluctuations. On the other hand, as the number of ill-informed investors increased, so did the level of noise and the risk of incorrect price signals. Lavington (1913: 49) noted that

> [D]eliberate manipulation by powerful interests is of little importance in the London market. [...] The evil appears to arise to a far more important extent from the continuous qualitative changes in many securities, and the consequent extreme difficulty in estimating their value. As a result of this any change of price originated perhaps by professional speculators, reacts upon public opinion and produces an unreasoning speculative activity which results not in correcting, but actually in reinforcing that change.

The question then arises as to whether it would be advisable to exclude small savers and amateur speculators from trading. As his reading notes reveal, Marshall differed from Emery on the important matter of the relationship between amateur speculation and price volatility. In Emery's view, the presence of large number of buyers and sellers, even if devoid of any special knowledge or opinion on the course of prices, constituted a price stabilizing factor per se.

> The participation of the public, however, does increase numbers, and in normal times numbers themselves are a steadying influence in the market. The more buyers and sellers the less likelihood, in the long run, of wide fluctuations. Every movement of price has a more powerful body of opinion to resist. (Emery 1896: 190)

Emery contrasts this opinion with R. Ehrenberg's (1883: 206–208), who had argued that the influence of outside speculation on prices is bad because of the relative ignorance of the public of amateur speculators. Marshall sides with Ehrenberg and his idea of the harm caused by the presence of a large mass of amateur speculators. The large number is not a stabilizing factor because, far from guaranteeing diversity of opinions, it is a source of herd behaviour, as amateurs' opinions are easily swayed into the same direction, away from "true" prices.[9] The same critical attitude towards amateur speculation and its contribution to the price discovery process emerges in *Money Credit and Commerce*. On the

[9] Marshall noted in the margin of Emery's book: "Ehrenberg is right because the public is not ignorant enough. It knows what mischievous professionals want it to know and so speculates not in all directions but dominantly on that side which is against public interest" (Quoted in Dardi and Gallegati 1992: 578, fn. 13).

fact that a rising number of operations does not necessarily mean better resource allocation, Marshall comments:

> Thus stock exchanges are necessary auxiliaries of modern industry and commerce; and the services which they render to the public probably outweigh many times the evils which they cause to it. But the magnitude of the real services which they render by no means varies with the volume of operations on them, and amateur speculators are likely to lose their own fortunes, *with no gain to the public.* (Marshall 1923: 95; italics added)

Marshall is clear about the fact that stabilization of prices around normal (equilibrium) values does not depend on the number of speculators as such but rather on the presence of capable professionals, who act as a bulwark against occasional bouts of over-excitement in the market.

> Therefore, although stock exchange machinations may occasionally set for a time, an unduly high value, or an unduly low value on a particular "security," yet, in the main, the judgment of well- informed, capable men protects the general public from grave errors of judgment in their investments, so long as these are conducted with reasonable caution. (Marshall 1923: 91)

These considerations, and Marshall's concern for the losses that amateurs are bound to suffer ("the amateur speculator is nearly sure to lose in the long run", ibid.: 93), lead him to conclude that the market would work just as well if small and inexperienced investors did not have access to trading activities. On this matter, too, he differs from Emery, who defined as "chimerical" reform proposals aiming at limiting trading to the big speculators (Emery 1896: 191) who would not play their part with the same eagerness if they could not count on the handsome and easy profits deriving from the mistakes of the public. According to Marshall, on the other hand, curtailing the number of inexpert traders would improve the market mechanism by having men of character concentrate on normal prices rather than being tempted to anticipate the opinions of the amateur.

4 Short-Selling and Options: A Problematic Defence

As mentioned above, from the very outset the appearance of speculation aroused deep suspicion in public opinion, regarding it as an activity organized by the few in their own interest and to the detriment of everyone else. Because of this opposition, in the Anglo-Saxon world acceptance of all the instruments employed by organized speculation proceeded at a slow and intermittent pace. In 1860, the British Parliament repealed the Barnard's Act of 1734, which had tried to ban options, short-selling and trading on margins, making them illegal and subject to fines, and thus seriously hindering trade in futures (Banner 1998: 105–106). The prohibition had not, however, stopped the use of these instruments by professional traders. Even if the contracts were not enforceable in court, stockjobbers complied with their terms in order to preserve their reputation. The repeal of the Barnard's Act merely acknowledged that speculative trading had become "the regular and ordinary form under which the whole of that vast and beneficial business of dealing in the funds was conducted", as claimed by a member of the Palmerston government who opposed the Act (Itzkowitz 2009: 101). Acceptance of futures was completed in 1895 when British courts decreed futures trading as a legitimate commercial transaction, entitled to enjoy the protection of law.

Opposition to futures largely derived from their use in short-selling. This practice was accused of depressing prices by placing enormous quantities of "fictitious" goods on the market. In Germany, in particular, agricultural producers at the end of the nineteenth century raised this accusation against dealers, pressing lawmakers to ban futures altogether.[10] In 1911, after much turmoil, enhanced fluctuations in prices and migration of German futures trading to London and Antwerp, the law was repealed. The short-lived success of the attempt to ban futures in Germany confirmed how their abolition, far from achieving the much sought-after price stabilization, obtained the opposite result, as Marshall noted (Marshall 1919: 261).

[10] Supporters of the abolition of futures in the USA drew inspiration from the success of the German agrarian party in this respect (Emery 1898). In the early 1890s, US farmers suffering from sharp drops in agricultural commodity prices blamed their condition on speculation on organized commodity markets. The ensuing anti-futures movement, which lasted until the 1920s, provided a number of platforms to voice this opinion (Banner 2017, Ch. 3, Hochfelder 2006).

Defence of short-selling by economists, including Emery and Marshall, revolved around two arguments. Firstly, without short-selling the market would lack a mechanism to curb unreasonable rises in prices. In a market dominated by bull speculators, the possibility to sell short on the anticipation of price correction might speed up adjustment, reducing the risk of speculative bubbles. Secondly, short sales, even when prices are expected to fall, still involve a forward purchase either of goods for delivery or of a futures contract of the opposite sign. These purchases prevent prices from endlessly falling. Putting forward these arguments, economists defended the idea that short-selling contributed to reducing the size of price fluctuations (see also Brace 1913: 65). Emery maintained that "perhaps the most potent influence in preventing wide fluctuations is the much maligned short-seller. It is he who keeps prices down by his short sales, and then keeps them strong by his covering purchases" (Emery 1896: 121). Marshall, in his notes on Emery's book, approved and backed his opinion:

> As Emery says p. 121 shortsellers do good in checking rise of price due to a wave of confidence: so when the fall comes it is less than otherwise. But Emery seems to treat this as a point; it is the point. If land could have been shortsold Melbourne crisis would have been less [...][Emery] goes too far when he says 'In a real estate boom only the sanguine affect the price on the rise and only the gloomy on the fall'. But he is right in saying that 'at one end prices are more recklessly inflated and at the other more needlessly depressed than would be possible in an organised speculative market'.

In *Industry and Trade* Marshall reiterated the example of land speculation in Melbourne, which shows how short-selling can prevent bubbles. If it had been possible to sell land short "as soon as prices had gone a little beyond their reasonable level, the sellers would have enriched themselves, and conferred on Melbourne as a whole a benefit many times as large as their own gains" (Marshall 1919: 265, fn. 1).

Contemplating delivery of a good which was not in the possession of the seller at the time the contract was signed was essential to defend the idea that every short sale also implied a purchase and, more generally, to justify its use and legalization (Levy 2006). Consequently, contracts which allowed one of the parties to unilaterally avoid the obligation to deliver or which did not provide for any delivery at all were harder to defend against the accusation of being instruments in the hands of gamblers. Such was the case of options.

Options, although widely used, not only did not enjoy the protection of the courts but were explicitly banned from the "floor" and traded outside the stock exchanges. Opposition to options reflected their being perceived as risky and destabilizing. Given that sellers might run into unlimited losses if prices did not fulfil their expectations, they would post quotations far from the ruling price in order to reduce the risk of the option being exercised, unless they were confident that the markets would move in their preferred direction, possibly with the aid of manipulation. Buyers, on the other hand, could be tempted by the possibility to exercise the option to over-trade, paying at worst the small option price. Observers regarded these conditions as propitious to gambling. As Marshall observed

> There are a few cases in which dealings in options are part of legitimate trade. But there appears to be more force in the arguments for prohibiting them by law, than for prohibiting a simple buying or selling of futures; for they are relatively more serviceable to the gambler and the manipulator than to the straightforward dealer. (Marshall 1919: 257, fn. 1)

Someone like Marshall, who objected to the presence of small inexperienced investors on both theoretical and moral grounds, certainly had good reasons to contest the legitimacy of options. On this aspect too, however, his ideas were widely but not unanimously shared. The fact that the options enabled small speculators, with little capital, to enter into the market was not perceived as a problem by all. Brace (1913), for example, considered "as a question of practical morals" that options enabled unskilled traders to enjoy the pleasure of "playing the market", knowing in advance the maximum loss they might incur.[11]

Diversity of opinion on instruments that allowed people with limited means, but endowed with luck and talent, to enrich themselves quickly

[11] On the debate on market accessibility in France, see Preda (2009).

through speculation did not only depend on different theoretical conclusions but probably also reflected deeper divisions in market morality[12] and the legitimacy of a rigid class structure.

5 Conclusions

The idea that speculation exacerbates commodity and stock price volatility dates back at least from the second half of the nineteenth century in connection with the establishment of organized markets for commodities and stocks. The new commercial practices observed on those markets, including short-selling, raised controversies, with public opinion regarding those practices with suspicion as a new and dangerous form of organized gambling. In some cases, suspicion gave rise to calls for the outright abolition of futures and option markets, most notably in Germany and the USA.

Interest in the new trading practices gave rise to an extensive literature addressing different readerships. One strand of this literature, of a more academic or legal character, aimed at defining the relevant theoretical framework to understand the impact of speculation on prices and resource allocation for analytical and regulatory purposes. This framework built on a realistic representation of markets populated by agents, performing distinct functions and differing in terms of information, attitude to risk, and financial capability, with particular focus on interactions between professional and amateur speculators. A certain number of distinguished economists participated in the elaboration of this framework, including H.C. Emery and A. Marshall, on whose ideas this chapter has focused.

As argued above, Marshall's analytical arguments on the costs and benefits of speculation on organized commodity and security markets can be taken as representative of the scientific literature on the subject which emerged at the end of the nineteenth century. The essence of these arguments, originally applied to commodities and subsequently extended to securities, based on similarities between the two asset classes, was that speculation is mostly beneficial to the economy and society. Professional speculation, indeed, improves resource allocation by reducing the size

[12] Marshall remarks: "It is true that many of the largest fortunes are made by speculation rather than by truly constructive work: and much of this speculation is associated with anti-social strategy" (Marshall 1920: 598).

(if not frequency) of price fluctuations, enabling producers, manufactures and traders to hedge against price risks and increasing the liquidity (and market value) of traded assets. These benefits more than offset the costs associated with occasional market manipulation by unscrupulous speculators, especially in the case of commodities.

In his analysis of the problems caused by the presence of short-sighted and ill-informed amateur speculators, Marshall distanced himself from Emery, whose opinions he otherwise endorsed. According to Marshall, amateur speculators add noise to the market and tempt professionals away from their fundamental (and constructive) duty, i.e. to insure non-speculators against price fluctuations and ease discovery of normal prices. As the number and weight of amateur speculators increases, so does the incentive for professionals to devote their resources to anticipating short-run fluctuations in amateur opinion, which may have little if any connection with fundamentals. Based on these analytical considerations, Marshall endorsed the use of futures and short-selling by professionals while opposing options, which he saw as dangerous instruments in the service of ill-advised amateur speculation.

It was awareness of the risks deriving from the interaction between professional and amateur speculators that led Marshall to unfailingly add words of caution to his endorsement of speculation, which was never complete. As Raffaelli (2003: 137) observes, comparing Marshall's views on speculation with Keynes's own, the main difference between the two is that "Marshall believed in the reality of objective economic trends, whose fundamentals were accessible to the 'constructive' forecasts of competent industrial businessmen, an idea which Keynes openly rejected". Both Marshall and Keynes believed in the possibility that speculation, an activity based on forecasting price changes taking place in the very short period, might have disruptive effects. But Marshall did not lose faith in the possibility of separating good from evil, constructive from malignant speculation. The "remedy is not easy, and may never be perfect" as he wrote in the last chapter of the *Principles*, but Marshall did not doubt that the progress of economic science would not fail to find a solution rendering an important service to the world. Unfortunately, this time he did not prove a good prophet.

Acknowledgements Dipartimento di Economia e Finanza, Università degli Studi di Roma "Tor Vergata". We wish to thank Katia Caldari for providing us with relevant reference material and Carlo Cristiano, Marco Dardi, Ivan Moscati and other participants in the Seminar "Giornata di Studi in memoria di Tiziano Raffaelli", Pisa, 15 February 2019 for their useful comments. Usual disclaimers apply. Contact paolo.paesani@uniroma2.it.

References

Banner S. (1998) *Anglo-American Securities Regulation*, Cambridge: CUP.

Banner S. (2017) *Speculation: A History of the Fine Line Between Gambling and Investing*, New York: Oxford University Press.

Bateman B. (2006) "Speculation", in T. Raffaelli, G. Becattini, and M. Dardi (eds), *The Elgar Companion to Alfred Marshall*, Cheltenham, UK and Northampton, MA: Elgar: 470–474.

Berg A. (2011) "The Rise of Commodity Speculation: From Villainous to Venerable", in A. Prakash (ed.), *Safeguarding Food Security in Volatile Global Markets*, FAO Report, Rome: Food and Agriculture Organisation: 241–267.

Brace H.H. (1913) *The Value of Organized Speculation*, Boston and New York: Houghton Mifflin.

Caldari K. (2015) "Marshall and Complexity: A Necessary Balance Between Process and Order", *Cambridge Journal of Economics*, 39: 1071–1085.

Carabelli A.M. and Cedrini M.A. (2013) "Further Issues on the Keynes–Hume Connection Relating to the Theory of Financial Markets in the General Theory", *European Journal of the History of Economic Thought*, 20: 1071–1100.

Crump A. (1875) *The Theory of Stock Exchange Speculation*, Fourth edition, London: Longmans, Green and Co.

Dardi M. and Gallegati M. (1992) "Alfred Marshall on Speculation", *History of Political Economy*, 24: 571–594.

Ehrenberg R. (1883) *Die Fondsspekulation und die Gesetzgebung*, Berlin: J. Springer.

Emery H.C. (1896) *Speculation in the Stock and Produce Exchanges of the United States*, New York: Columbia University Press.

Emery H.C. (1898) "The Results of the German Exchange Act of 1896", *Political Science Quarterly*, 3: 286–320.

Emery H.C. (1900) "The Place of the Speculator in the Theory of Distribution", *Papers and Proceedings of the 12th Annual Meeting of the American Economic Association*, 1: 103–122.

Goss B.A. and Yamey B.S. (1976) *The Economics of Futures Trading: Readings*, London: Wiley.

Hadley A.T. (1904) *Economics*, New York and London: Putnams and Sons.

Hall N. (2000) "The Liverpool Cotton Market: Britain's First Futures Market", in *Transactions of the Historical Society of Lancashire and Cheshire*, 149: 99–118.

Hochfelder D. (2006) "Where the Common People Speculate: The Ticker, Bucket Shops and the Origins of Popular Participation in Financial Markets, 1880–1920", *Journal of American History*, 93: 335–358.

Itzkowitz D.C. (2009) "Fair Enterprise or Extravagant Speculation: Investment, Speculation, and Gambling in Victorian England", in N. Henry and C. Schmitt (eds), *Victorian Investments: New Perspectives on Finance and Culture*, Bloomington, IN: Indiana University Press: 98–119.

Lavington F. (1913) "The Social Interest in Speculation on the Stock Exchange", *Economic Journal*, 23: 36–52.

Lawlor M. (1994) "On the Historical Origin of Keynes's Financial Market Views", in N. De Marchi and M. Morgan (eds), *Higgling. Annual Supplement to Volume 26, History of Political Economy*, Durham, NC and London: Duke University Press: 184–225.

Lawlor M. (2006), *The Economics of Keynes in Historical Context: An Intellectual History of the General Theory*, London: Palgrave Macmillan.

Leathers C.G. and Raines J.P. (2008) "John Kenneth Galbraith's Contributions to the Theory and Analysis of Speculative Financial Markets", *Review of Political Economy*, 20: 551–568.

Levy J.I. (2006) "Contemplating Delivery: Futures Trading and the Problem of Commodity Exchange in the United States, 1875–1905", *American Historical Review*, 111: 307–335.

Marshall A. (1919) *Industry and Trade*, London: Macmillan.

Marshall A. (1920) *Principles of Economics*, Eighth edition, London: Macmillan.

Marshall A. (1923) *Money, Credit and Commerce*, London: Macmillan.

Michie R.C. (1986) "The London and New York Stock Exchanges, 1850–1914", *Journal of Economic History*, 46: 181–187.

Michie R.C. (2007) *The Global Security Market: A History*, Oxford: Oxford University Press.

Paesani P. and Rosselli A. (2019) *How Speculation Became Respectable: Early Theories on Financial and Commodity Markets*, paper presented at the Fifth Thomas Guggenheim Conference in the History of Economic Thought, Roma, Accademia dei Lincei, Dec. 17–18, 2019.

Pigou A.C. ed. (1925) *Memorials of Alfred Marshall*, London: Macmillan.

Preda A. (2009) "Rational Investors, Informative Prices: The Emergence of the 'Science of Financial Investments' and the Random-Walk Hypothesis", in G. Poitras (ed.), *Pioneers of Financial Economics*, Vol. 1, Cheltenham, UK and Northampton, MA: Elgar: 149–168.

Raffaelli T. (ed.). (1994) "Alfred Marshall's Early Philosophical Writings", *Research in the History of Economic Thought and Methodology, Archival Supplement*, 4: 51–159.

Raffaelli T. (2003) *Marshall's Evolutionary Economics*, London and New York: Routledge.

Ryan J.A. (1902) "The Ethics of Speculation", *International Journal of Ethics*, 12: 335–347.

Williams J.C. (1982) "The Origin of Futures Markets", *Agricultural History*, 56: 306–316.

Working H. (1953) "Futures Trading and Hedging", *American Economic Review*, 43: 314–343.

Industrial Leadership, Market Power and Long-Term Performance: Marshall's and Keynes's Appreciation of American Trusts

Carlo Cristiano and Maria Cristina Marcuzzo

1 Introduction

American trusts became a feature of American capitalism and both Alfred Marshall and John Maynard Keynes, who were in the US in the 1870s and 1930s, two turning points in US economic history, were impressed by what they saw and learnt during their visits. In this chapter, we focus on how this knowledge impacted on their respective views on industrial leadership, market power and long-term performance. We will be arguing there is certainly "a family resemblance" in their approach, which is not surprising, but certainly worth noticing. To make this point we chose to travel, as it were, backwards: starting from Keynes, whose appreciation of American trusts is revealed most clearly as he became a large investor in US assets, and tracing the ascendency of his line of thinking to his apprenticeship in economics under Marshall. We then

C. Cristiano (✉)
Università Di Pisa, Pisa, Italy
e-mail: carlo.cristiano@unipi.it

M. C. Marcuzzo
Università Di Roma, La Sapienza, Rome, Italy
e-mail: cristina.marcuzzo@uniroma1.it

K. Caldari et al. (eds.), *Marshall and the Marshallian Heritage*,
Palgrave Studies in the History of Economic Thought,
https://doi.org/10.1007/978-3-030-53032-7_9

focus on the evolution of Marshall's thoughts on monopoly, competition and industrial leadership in early work, then in the *Principles* and *Industry and Trade*. Our main conclusion is that both Keynes and Marshall, with of course their differences, shared a common appreciation of American trusts, weighting the advantages of a large industrial organization more than the loss of competitive edge.

For Marshall at least, these ideas were not obvious and took shape over a long period. Marshall visited the US before the advent of trusts, and he was impressed by the "character" of the people and their entrepreneurship. He predicted a great future for this "young" country, possibly a brighter one compared to the one he could foresee for the UK. Afterwards, he grew sceptic about trusts, but he eventually got to the conclusion that, thanks to their typically American "character", the leaders of big business in America were the new heralds of the same spirit of innovation he had observed and admired in 1875. The ideas that Keynes expressed about Franklin D. Roosevelt and the New Deal, and his choices as an investor in the US market during the 1930s, seem to reflect a similar view.

2 Keynes's Acquaintance with the United States in the 1930s

Keynes made his first trip to America in September 1917, to negotiate war finance; although he stayed in Washington a month (12 September–6 October), he did not allow himself to be impressed by American society,[1] perhaps because he had begun to realize that "by the summer of 1917 financial dominance had passed from Britain to America. Despite Keynes's – and others – efforts to reclaim it, it would remain with America for the rest of his life" (Moggridge 1992: 275).

However, in his *Economic Consequences of the Peace* Keynes had praising words about the role that the US and its President Woodrow Wilson had in the negotiations, and in a follow-up article written for a popular American magazine, Keynes depicted Wilson, as the one who "alone amongst the statesmen of Paris sought ideal aims and sincerely

[1] "[America] is a country where minorities get precious little quarter; and to my astonishment I find myself looking back to England again as a land of liberty", he wrote to Edwin Cannan (quoted in Moggridge 1992: 277).

pursued, throughout the conference, the future peace of the world as his supreme and governing purpose" (Moggridge 1992: 362).

He never visited the United States during the 1920s, despite repeated invitations (Skidelsky 1992: 20); however, he followed the evolution and performance of the American economy as testified by his investments. He did some sporadic dealings in US steel common shares between 1911 and 1913 (Keynes Papers, henceforth KP, SE/11/1/3), in 1919 (KP, SE/11/1/29), and in 1927. Moreover, between 1919 and 1924 he traded dollars as part of his speculation in currencies (KP, SE/11/1/14, 19) and while he stopped his currency speculation in 1927, he resumed it from 1932 to 1939.[2] He also speculated on futures wheat and corn in Chicago from 1924 to 1926, going mainly short, revealing his bearish expectations (Foresti and Sanfilippo 2017).

In conclusion, although Keynes did not visit America in the 1920s, he kept an eye on the American situation, but it was the eye of a speculator (in currencies and commodities) rather than of an investor; his short-term view may explain why he did not predict the 1929 Wall Street collapse and why he was not caught in it.

It was only in the second trip to America in May and June 1931 that Keynes became really acquainted with the country and its collapsing economy. He opened his Harris Foundation Lectures delivered at Chicago describing the current economic situation as "the greatest economic catastrophe [...] of the modern world" (CWK XIII: 343), envisaging no chance of a recovery in America, at least within the next months. In November of the same year, the same view was conveyed to his friend and privileged source on American matters, Walter Case,[3] that

[2] See Accominotti and Chambers (2016: 363–65): "In general, he was long the US dollar in this period, but in 1921, 1922 and 1924 he briefly adopted a short dollar position...In 1932–1939 Keynes mainly traded US dollar, French franc and Dutch guilder ...[alternating] between short and long positions in these three currencies. Having shorted the dollar in October 1932–February 1933, he closed his position on 2 March 1933, just eight days before the suspension of the US dollar's gold standard in the following months. Believing the depreciation following the suspension of gold convertibility to be overdone, he went long the dollar between April 1933 and June 1933 only to see the currency continue to depreciate. Thereafter, he consistently adopted a short dollar position, which reached its peak in December 1936."

[3] Walter Case was the president and director of Case, Pomeroy & Co., Inc. in New York and Keynes's main financial connection in the USA.

he did not see "any solid reason whatever as yet for expecting a recovery in the U.S.A. in 1932" (CWK XXI: 12).

But a few weeks later Keynes was beginning to think that the trough had been left behind (1 January 1933, CWK XXI: 142). Roosevelt was elected in November 1932 and the new administration started in March. Keynes's first favourable comment on the new course in America came on 4 July 1933, in the aftermath of the London World Economic Conference. In "President Roosevelt Is Magnificently Right" (4 July 1933, *Daily Mail*, CWK XXI: 273–77), Keynes commented enthusiastically on Roosevelt's rejection of a scheme of rigid exchange stabilization. However, the decisive point was another. Keynes's opinion of Roosevelt came soon to depend on one factor and, at least for some time, one only, namely, how much Washington was able to expand public expenditure financed by loans. In the open letter to Roosevelt published in the *New York Times* on 31 December 1933, Keynes was critical:

> The set-back American recovery experienced this past Autumn was the predictable consequence of the failure of your Administration to organize any material increase in new loan expenditure during your first six months of office. (CWK XXI: 293)

In the ensuing weeks, we find Keynes commenting appreciatively on Roosevelt's reforms (see CWK XXI: 305–12), but he always emphasized that public spending was the vital point.

The second occasion for Keynes to have a first-hand knowledge of the effects of Roosevelt's policies was during his third visit to the US, between May 15, 1934, and June 8, 1934. He stayed mainly in Chicago, New York and Washington, meeting all sort of people and collecting views on the American situation.[4] For detailed information on the economy, industry, firm or securities, he relied on published sources or personal contacts.

While believing that America could, and ought to, "Spend Its Way into Recovery", as he wrote in December 1934 (CWK XXI: 334–38), he remained sceptical about Roosevelt's determination in pursuing this policy. He was expecting the adoption of "more direct methods" of public

[4] The Appendix of Chambers and Kabiri (2016) lists all the people Keynes met during his visits to the US; among the people he met in 1931, there were mainly bankers and investment advisors; in 1934, they were mainly government officials and politicians. In both occasions, fewer were industrialists and economists.

spending—i.e. direct investments by the state and nationalizations, which he did not see coming. By November 1937, his doubts were confirmed. Roosevelt was not spending enough—he argued—and his management of three crucial sectors like housing, railways and public utilities was a failure (CWK XXI: 427–28).

3 Keynes, the Investor in the US Market and the Critic of Roosevelt's Legislations

Keynes became a full-fledged investor in the US Stock Market from mid-1932 (Cristiano et al. 2018). Trusting that the crisis of 1929–1931 was over he began to purchase, for himself, the Provincial Insurance Company, King's College and National Mutual Life Assurance Society, assets which he thought would benefit from the recovery. He continued to buy US securities despite the banking crisis in 1933, although on a smaller scale, but he soon resumed increasingly large-scale dealings in 1934, through 1935, 1936 and early 1937. By 1938, he had liquidated a large part of his US investment, which however still bulked large in his portfolio well into 1945, the war and his involvement in the Treasury having changed the circumstances. Investment trusts, together with public holding utilities,[5] had the lion share in Keynes's personal portfolio (see Table 1).

[5] A public holding utility was a corporation formed for the express purpose of controlling other corporations by the ownership of a majority of their voting capital stock. "Holding companies were established through the process of pyramiding. i.e. interposing one or more sub-holding companies between the holding companies and the operating companies. At the bottom of the pyramid would be the operating utilities, which were actually generating and distributing electricity. Control of the operating company was gained by the holding companies which through various methods were able to purchase a controlling interest in the operating companies. These holding companies in turn were bought by other holding companies until many 'levels' were added to the holding companies' structure." See Public Utility Holding Company Act of 1935: 1935–1992. Energy Information Administration, Washington, DC, 1993). Moreover, "Holding company founders generated value by managing and capitalizing their operating subsidiaries effectively and by participating in the profits by owning shares in the holding companies. Holding companies therefore only sold shares as a way of financing their operating businesses so that they could operate at the optimal scale. The primary goal of the people who built holding companies, in other words, was operating profit, and they sold securities merely as a means to this end" (Morley 2012: 13–14).

Table 1 Weight of utilities and investment trusts (%) in Keynes's portfolio

Year	*1934*	*1935*	*1936*	*1937*	*1938*	*1939*
Utilities	14.17	24.02	44.91	52.53	41.67	33.09
Investment trusts	18.71	32.31	33.67	27.89	35.50	42.97

Source Cristiano et al. (2018)

Some of the reasons of his preference for utilities[6] can perhaps be inferred by what he wrote in Chapter 12 of the *General Theory*:

> In the case of another important class of long-term investments, namely public utilities, a substantial proportion of the prospective yield is practically guaranteed by monopoly privileges coupled with the right to charge such rates as will provide a certain stipulated margin. (CWK VII: 163)

Public utility holding were targeted by Roosevelt's second wave of legislation, in particular with the Public Utility Holding Company Act of 1935, which "required holding companies to register with the SEC. The act sought to simplify the holding company structures of the utilities. [It] was intended to be a 'death sentence' for large holding company empires such as that maintained by Insull [One of the largest holding company systems in the Midwest]. Under this legislation, the controlling holding company could not be more than three times removed from any of its subsidiaries" (Markham 2002: 205).

Since his early days, Roosevelt was convinced of the necessity of introducing the "fear of competition" into the electricity sector, dismantling the monopoly power of the holding companies. It has been noted that "there is a certain irony in the fact that Roosevelt, branded a socialist by the investor-owned utility community, relied heavily on the principle of competition in designing his New Deal reforms for the electricity sector. Conversely, Roosevelt's faith in competition did not extend to the nation's collapsing agricultural and industrial sectors, where

[6]There were in particular seven utilities, whose shares (mostly preferred) Keynes held for longer periods, and six of them (American Power and Light, National Power and Light, International Hydro-Electric System, Electric Power and Light, Central States Electric and Commonwealth and Southern) were operating in the production of electric and hydro-electric power.

government-sponsored cartelization was his policy of choice" (Emmons 1953: 901).

In fact with the National Industrial Recovery Act (NIRA) of 1933 (which was soon declared unconstitutional), "industries were exempted from antitrust prosecution if they agreed to enter into collective bargaining agreements that significantly raised wages and followed industrial codes of fair competition. By 1934, more than 500 industries, which accounted for nearly 80 per cent of private, non-agricultural employment, had entered into the collective bargaining agreements called for under NIRA" (Sullivan 2004).

We have evidence that Keynes did not like Roosevelt's legislation. In his open letter to Roosevelt, 31 December 1933 (CWK XXI: 289–97), he criticized the President for his NIRA policy, which he judged ineffective and contradictory. He wrote:

> I cannot detect any material aid to recovery in N.I.R.A., though its social gains have been large. The driving force which has been put behind the vast administrative task set by this Act has seemed to represent a wrong choice in the order of urgencies. The Act is on the Statute Book; a considerable amount has been done towards implementing it; but it might be better for the present to allow experience to accumulate before trying to force through all its details. That is my first reflection—that N.I.R.A., which is essentially Reform and probably impedes Recovery, has been put across too hastily, in the false guise of being part of the technique of Recovery.[7]

Given Keynes's attitude in the 1920s, when he "applauded the on going trend toward increased reliance on public corporations, and argued that the government should not only accept the current movement toward cartels, holding companies, trade associations, pools and other forms of monopoly power, but should proactively assist and accelerate this trend in order to regulate and control it" (Crotty 1999), we would have expected him to be in favour of NIRA, which was in practice an

[7] Beaudreau (2016) argued that Keynes in his criticism showed neither understanding nor appreciation of the role of technological change in business cycles; Sheila Dow (2016) rebuked that "argument against the NIRA was that priority should be given to recovery ... which required measures to encourage investment and output, which would in turn bring about the higher wages and prices (and money supply) which were sought from reform. He argued that the reform measures of the NIRA applied in a recession might actually impede investment and output. But he did not reject the reform measures outright".

attempt to encourage collective and coordinate action by firms. In fact, during the NIRA, antitrust prosecutions were nearly entirely suspended.

In January 1934, in a broadcast, we find Keynes claiming that NIRA "tries to provide for organized planning, industry by industry, whilst avoiding the abuses of the trust or the cartel" (CWK XXI: 307). However, in June 1934, after he had met some advisers from the Planning Division of NIRA, Keynes wrote a sequel to his open letter of 31 December 1933 to Roosevelt, in which he changed his tune. He said that NIRA "embodies some important improvements in labour conditions and for securing fair trade practices", but he agreed "with the widespread opinion that much of it is objectionable because of its restrictionist philosophy (which has a proper place in agricultural adjustment today but not in American industry) and because of its excessive complexity and regimentation" (CWK XXI: 323).

As time went by, Keynes became increasingly disillusioned with Roosevelt's economic policies; in a letter he sent to Walter Stewart[8] in November 1937, among other things he mentioned disapprovingly that the "President attitude to utilities was preventing normal expansion there, however much needed" (CWK XXI: 427), which seems to indicate that he was not in favour of the Public Utility Holding Company Act. In the letter to Roosevelt of 1 February 1938, Keynes made clear which were his views on the matter of the utilities. He wrote:

> a great deal of what is alleged against the wickedness of holding companies as such is surely wide of the mark. It does not draw the right line of division between what should be kept and what discarded. It arises too much out of what is dead and gone. The real criminals have cleared out long ago. I should doubt if the controls existing today are of much *personal* value to anyone. No one has suggested a procedure by which the eggs can be unscrambled. Why not tackle the problem by insisting that the *voting power* should belong to the real owners of the equity, and leaving the existing *organizations* undisturbed, so long as the voting power is so rearranged (e.g. by bringing in preferred stockholders) that it cannot be controlled by the holders of a minority of the equity. (CWK XXI: 437)

[8] Walter W. Stewart, a former professor of economics at Amherst College and Economic Adviser to the Bank of England, had long been a partner in Case, Pomeroy and Co. and remained in touch with Keynes after Case's death.

From the above passage, it seems that Keynes was not against public utility holding companies as such; not only was he heavily invested in them, but he seems to have been approving of their organizational form.[9]

Coming to legislation to regulate investment trusts, the other preferred sector in Keynes's US investment holding,[10] although it was drafted while the Public Utility Act was been prepared and announced in the 1938 Roosevelt speech, it was enacted only in 1940. The Investment Company Act (ICA) imposed restrictions on all investment companies, defined as listed firms whose assets primarily consisted of other firms shares (see Kandel et al. 2013). Just a year before, in 1939, the weight of investment trusts in Keynes's personal portfolio had peaked at 43%, while dramatic events were looming on the horizon. In the next following months, restrictions on holdings of dollar denominated assets were enforced by UK Treasury, in which Keynes was involved in his capacity as adviser, opening up a new phase, for Keynes and the British public, in connection with the US stock market.

All the episodes mentioned in this section seem to confirm that there was a gap separating Keynes from the New Dealers. Taken together, they can also be seen as the manifestation of a more widespread difference of opinion. Keynes never found it easy to understand, let alone accept, the way the Americans managed their country. This attitude remained with him during the following years, when he was a convoy for the British Government during his several visits to the US in the 1940s. There was, however, some aspects of the American industrial organization that he seemed to have admired: utility holding companies and investment trusts. He did not invest in either of these sectors in the London Stock Exchange, indicating that his pick was due to the specificity of the American organization rather than a preference for the sectors in themselves.

The reason might have been that there were "institutional and structural differences between UK and US investment trusts, including size, capital structure, investment strategy, tax and accounting practices,

[9] On Keynes's position on the organization of the utility sector in the post-war in UK, see CWK XXII: 461–69.

[10] In the 1920s, Keynes had been involved in three investment companies organized by Osvald T. Falk in UK: the A.D Investment Trust (July 1921), the P.R. Finance Company (January 1923) and the Independent Investment Company (January 1924) (Moggridge in CWK XII: 30).

management, and costs [...] British investment trusts were invested in relatively small capitalisation issues compared to their American counterparts, which were invested in large capitalisation companies created by merger into great monopolies" (Rutterford 2009: 168).

In other words, as we have seen for the above-quoted passage from the *General Theory*, Keynes the investor believed to take full advantage of the monopoly power enjoyed by American industrial organization, and in general of the more aggressive and therefore riskier investment strategy of American trusts than their British counterpart.[11]

Keynes the economist was never a believer in free markets and competition as a means to fight unemployment of human and capital resources; he was in favour of cartels in the case of the depressed industries of coal and cotton in the 1920s, and of state-regulated boards of management of utilities (such as electricity and railways) for social considerations (CWK XXII: 461–69). His criticism of the New Deal rested on the belief that Roosevelt relied too much on an industrial policy, which he judged as contradictory and ineffective, rather than on aggregate demand management.

Patel (2016: 80) singles out Roosevelt's scarce enthusiasm for, if not overt opposition to, deficit spending as the very reason why "the New Deal was far from Keynesian". However, as Rauchway (2008: 115) has argued, Keynes also noted that "the United States needed private enterprise to help solve its problems", and in order to do so "Roosevelt needed to reenlist businessmen in the recovery effort". Galbraith (1984: 4) made a good summary of the whole story when he wrote that "Roosevelt the budget-balancer resisted Keynesian deficit strategies, but pushed for social reforms which worried Keynes".

These divergences became evident with the recession of 1937 and 1938. While Roosevelt blamed it on scarce competition and the market power of big business,[12] Keynes urged him a complete reversal of

[11] "The different management styles of British and American investment trust managers reflected a different attitude to investment. By the 1920s, Americans were happy to invest in equities and expected fund managers to seek to achieve capital gain through leverage, market timing and 'expert' stock selection. In the UK, retail investors preferred the security of fixed-interest securities and were content with a relatively low return in the form of income yield in return for safety through a conservative approach to reserves and an emphasis on a relatively passive investment strategy" (Rutterford 2009: 181).

[12] "Franklin Roosevelt created the Temporary National Economic Committee (TNEC) to study the concentration of economic power in the United States. This study was conducted by the Federal Trade Commission, the SEC, and the Department of Justice.

approach. In a passage from his letter to Roosevelt of 1 February 1938, Keynes seems to suggest that the wildest forces of American capitalism should be harnessed for the sake of recovery rather than reduced to impotence:

> You could do anything you liked with them, if you would treat them (even the big ones), not as wolves and tigers, but as domestic animals by nature, even though they have been badly brought up and not trained as you would wish [...] If you work them into the surly, obstinate, terrified mood, of which domestic animals, wrongly handled, are so capable, the nation's burdens will not get carried to market. (CWK XXI: 438)

In fact, since the first letter to Roosevelt in 1933, Keynes had been warning, that the process of reform could jeopardise "the confidence of the business world" (CWK XXI: 290) (see also Galbraith 1984: 6). However, while these remarks can account for Keynes's attacks on the New Deal reforms, they do not necessarily account for his choices as an investor. There may be at least one further reason why Keynes was not only annoyed by Roosevelt's reforms but also so keen about the US (and not the UK) utilities and investment trusts. As we try to show in the following section, this further reason is probably to be found in Alfred Marshall, and there is a long story behind it.

4 Marshall's Teaching and Vision

As reconstructed in Raffaelli (2000), the first time that Keynes dealt with the problems of business size and monopolistic power, and more specifically with the literature on American trusts, was during his apprenticeship with Marshall in 1905. As Raffaelli reported, Keynes's reading list included "J.P. Norton's and H.C. Adam's articles in the third series of the *American Economic Association*, J.B. Clark's *Control of Trusts*, J.W. Jenks's *Trust Problem*, Marshall's *Some Aspects of Competition*, A.T. Hadley's *Railroad Transportation*, T.L. Greene's *Corporation Finance*, F.H. Spearman's *Strategy of Great Railways*, E.R. Johnson's *American Railway Transportation* and C.F. Bastable's *Public Finance*

Joseph O'Mahoney, a senator from Wyoming, was the chairman of the committee. TNEC investigated monopolies and other anticompetitive restrictions, which it was thought had caused the economic contraction in 1937 and 1938" (Markham 2002: 244–45).

[…]. T. Veblen's *Theory of Business Enterprise* and R.M. Hurd's *Principles of City Land Values* are also listed" (Raffaelli 2000: 127).

These readings were carried out in the autumn of 1905, during the weeks in which Keynes was attending Marshall's lectures. They were probably part of a strategy set up by Marshall to divert Keynes, a former student of mathematics, from his initial penchant for pure theory and deductive economics: "it shows […] a much improved sense of the true relation of economic figures to reality" (quoted in Raffaelli 2000: 141), was one of Marshall's comments to a paper on railways written by Keynes as part of his homework. An important point that was made by Raffaelli (2000), and which is further developed in Cristiano (2014: 97–113), is that the apprenticeship was decisive in introducing Keynes to the idea that the "Theory of Economics […] is a method rather than a doctrine, an apparatus of the mind, a technique of thinking", as he later wrote in the introduction to the Cambridge Economics Handbooks series.

Even though the sentence in the famous letter to Strachey—"I want to manage a railway or organize a Trust" (Keynes to Lytton Strachey, 15 November 1905, first quoted in Harrod 1951: 111)—was of course only a joke, the readings on American trusts may certainly have stimulated Keynes's imagination. More important, however, would be to know what Keynes learned directly from Marshall on this topic, but on this we have barely any evidence. Marshall's unsystematic teaching prevented students from taking significant notes from his lectures, and Keynes's lectures notes make no exception. On this point, we can only guess. However, what Marshall might have said in the classroom was probably not too far removed from what Keynes later found in Marshall's *Industry and Trade*.

In 1905, Marshall had already published four editions of his *Principles* and was preparing the fifth, that appeared in 1907, while *Industry and Trade* was not yet in his plans. However, his ideas on competition had already begun to evolve, stimulated by the new phenomena that were emerging in the industrial world.

The most relevant of these innovations came from America. In *Some aspects of competition* (Marshall 1891), which is included in Keynes's reading list, Marshall put much emphasis on what was going on on the other side of the Atlantic. The paper was his presidential address to the British Economic Association, delivered in 1890, when Marshall tentatively described "[t]he success of American Trusts" as "brilliant, but perhaps not very solid" (Marshall 1891: 623). For Marshall, the main reason to be doubtful about the future of trusts was the "[d]ifficulty of combining central responsibility and individual energy" (Marshall 1891: 625). Connected with the so-called life-cycle hypothesis, this is a typically Marshallian point, which coloured Marshall's early scepticism about American trusts as well as about any other forms of joint-stock control and large business in general. But it was also an opinion that, although never abandoned, underwent some significant change along Marshall's career.

In the same speech of 1890, Marshall argued against the "false antithesis between competition and combination" (1891: 626) and foreshadowed an approach to the subject in which monopoly power is only one, and possibly not the most important, among the motivations that may lead firms to get larger. Some years later, while Keynes was making the transition from apprentice in 1905 to lecturer in 1908, the study of combination as a new form of competition had become a specific line of research, pursued in particular by David H. Macgregor.[13] On the other hand, Marshall always remained of the opinion that, in most of the cases, there is a trade-off between the size of firms and their powers of innovation. In this view, the increasing returns that scale economies can immediately offer are paid with increasing managerial costs and lower powers of innovation at a later stage. The metaphor adopted in Marshall's *Principles*, in which firms are like trees in a forest, doomed to live their place to smaller plants as soon as they had become older, conveyed the idea of an inescapable cycle of life (Marshall 1920: 315–16). Together with the concept of external economies and the Smithian idea that the division of labour (and therefore productivity) is limited by the extent of the market, the life-cycle hypothesis was one of the solutions to the problem of reconciling increasing returns with competitive conditions.

This analytical conundrum had loomed large in Marshall's mind since he read the contribution of Antoine-Augustine Cournot in 1868.[14] While Cournot's mathematical analysis led directly to the conclusion that increasing returns would inevitably result into a monopoly, what Marshall could see around in Britain was the coexistence of increasing returns and competition. To a significant extent, books IV and V of Marshall's *Principles* were a solution to this "reconciliation problem", or "Cournot problem", based mainly on British experience.

[13] On MacGregor see Cristiano (2011).

[14] For a detailed account, see Prendergast (1992).

British localised industries were a good example of how an industry could grow while its representative firms remained more or less of the same size. Moreover, their highly differentiated products prevented the size of the market for each firm to get much larger, and the result was that each firm was faced with a rapidly downward sloping demand curve that soon prevented its growth. Finally, there was the life-cycle hypothesis, which was probably rooted much more in Marshall's strong faith in the power of individuals *vis-a-vis* organization than in any solid piece of analysis or empirical evidence, but that nonetheless was never altogether abandoned by Marshall.

The first edition of *Principles* was published in 1890. It took six editions of this book before Marshall, in 1910, eventually admitted that joint-stock companies,[15] in particular, "often dwindle, but do not readily die", or "seldom die", as we now read in the definitive text of *Principles* (Marshall 1920: 316, 343). This variation, albeit significant, did not correspond to a complete change of Marshall's vision. Far from it, it was only an adaptation of the original view. In a chapter on joint-stock companies in *Industry and Trade*, Marshall once again explained that "[t]he reason why this result [i.e. the concentration in the hands of a single firm of the whole production of the world] did not follow was simply that no firm ever had a sufficiently long life of unabated energy and power of initiative for the purpose" (Marshall 1923: 316).

When the choice was between "individual or joint stock control" (Marshall 1923: 308), Marshall's preference remained with the individual. As usual, the problem with joint-stock companies was that even though they seldom die, their original power of innovation may often dwindle into routine. This is especially true "when the ownership of capital is effectively divorced from its control", and the owners of the firm have delegated management to a board of directors. "A man of restless constructive force, who finds himself on such a Board, may urge a reorganization of some part of the procedure [..]. or the scrapping of some plant that is no longer in the front rank: but he is not unlikely to appeal in vein". As "the *vis inertiae* of a great company is against him", he is "inclined to acquiesce, however unwillingly, in the general opinion, that a company, the ownership of whose capital is almost wholly in the hands

[15] Of course, joint-stock companies had a much more simplified governance than investment trusts or holding companies, but the point of the separation between management and ownership is general and applies in all these cases.

of the public, must for the greater part adhere rather closely to routine" (Marshall 1923: 318).

Marshall saw only "a possible remedy" to this problem, a solution that "has been largely adopted in America", where "[t]he shareholders may decide to give their votes in favour of those who will support the almost autocratic power of some man, or group of men, whom they know to be able, resolute, and perhaps to have a large pecuniary interest in the company" (Marshall 1923: 318). And here we come to what may be the most important difference between the US and the UK. Whereas in the UK, large concentrations of capital were producing these joint-stock companies that often "dwindle but seldom die", an even larger concentration of capital was producing in America an extremely dynamic industrial environment. In the place of the "Boards" and their routine choices, America saw the "concentration of a large volume of movable capital in the hands of powerful and enterprising owners" (Marshall 1923: 153).

Of course, America was much more than this, but this individualistic element, the existence (and prevalence) of these "enterprising owners", in the end emerged as the solution to a new reconciliation problem, the problem of reconciling big size with "initiative" and dynamism.

As the scepticism shown in Marshall (1891) seems to suggest, American industry must have represented a challenge for Marshall. It may even be said that, based as it was on the British case, Marshall's analysis of competitive equilibrium in the *Principles* found its nemesis in the "industrial leadership of the United States" as presented in *Industry and Trade*. While external economies are so relevant in the UK, internal economies of scale predominate in the US, where they can be fully exploited thanks to a huge, ever-increasing and extremely homogeneous internal market. Along with obvious geographic reasons, other elements concurred to create these conditions. A continuous flow of immigrants from several countries created a market for labour in which "diverse and mutually supplementary" skills, or "industrial aptitudes", could easily be found. At the same time, the same population was particularly "homogeneous in matters of consumption" (Marshall 1923: 141), while the rapid development of the railways system, with very low prices for ton-mile, further contributed to an ever-increasing market. This is the favourable environment in which American business leaders were operating. But why these leaders were so successful in exploiting it?

5 The American "Character"

The starting point of Marshall's analysis of the US economy in ***Industry and Trade*** is the observation that "The United States has remained young very long" (Marshall 1923: 141). For Marshall, a country is young when the spirit of enterprise and innovation prevails on the opposite forces of habits, custom, routine and tradition. This, in turn, may depend on several reasons, all of which are relevant in so far as they influence the prevailing psychology. Or, in Marshall's own words, in so far as they determine the "character" of a people, and especially of its business leaders. In this perspective, the US is a young country because:

> A powerful process of natural selection has ... called out the leaders of American industry from the many millions of lads who were born to the last generation from alert parents of many races; and who entered on life with the resolve that they would prove themselves to be abler and greater than their fellows by becoming rich: and of this effectiveness the money test is on the whole a safer test than any other which the common man can apply. (Marshall 1923: 156)

What is striking in these views is that, even though they did not emerge in Marshall (1891), they were much older than the presidential address delivered in 1890. To find their origin, we must go back to 1875, when Marshall visited the United States. As Groenewegen (1995: 202) observed, many of the seeds from which Marshall's ***Industry and Trade*** would grow much later had been sowed during the journey to America that Marshall made in the summer of 1875.[16]

Marshall arrived in New York early in June and then travelled to San Francisco and back in about four months, the expensive trip being financed with the £250 left by an uncle who had died the year before. This trip was the only one that Marshall ever made to America, and it came early in his career as well as in the industrial history of the country. It was ten years before Marshall sat on the Cambridge chair of Political Economy, fifteen years before the first edition of ***Principles***, thirty

[16] As his wife would report, Marshall "used to say 'he never spent his money so well'. It was not so much what he learnt there as that he got to know what things he wanted to learn. He was able to see the coming supremacy of the U.S., to know its causes and the direction it would take" (Mary Paley Marshall's notes to Walter Scott, quoted in Groenewegen 1995: 193; see also CWK X: 175–76).

years before Keynes's apprenticeship and forty-four years before the first edition of *Industry and Trade*. In 1875, the "multiform standardization" connected with "large masses of capital [...] in the hands of a few strong men, who retain its control in their own masterful hands" (Marshall 1923: 141), which is the most outstanding characteristic of "American industrial leadership" as described in *Industry and Trade*, was barely in sight. The factories that Marshall visited in 1875—this was his main occupation during the journey—were small firms. It was in the ensuing decade, as Marshall would later reconstruct, that "public attention was directed to the 'Trust', in the original use of the word, set up in 1882 by Mr Rockefeller and others for controlling the trade in mineral oil and its products" (Marshall 1923: 512). All the books on American trusts that Keynes read in 1905 had been written after 1875. Since the 1880s, the landscape of American industry was changing rapidly.

This notwithstanding, there is a strong element of continuity connecting the impressions that the Americans had produced in Marshall during the journey made in 1875 to the views expressed in *Industry and Trade*. Since the letters he wrote to his mother during the visit (Whitaker 1996, vol. 1: 36–84), what captured Marshall's attention most was American "character" as this is described more in detail in the two papers that Marshall wrote on America on his return to England.[17] Broadly speaking, the most important aspect of the American character is that Americans are more self-reliant and rational, and less prone to habits and customs and routines than any other people in the world, Britons being included:

> on the average an American has the habit of using his own individual judgement more consciously and deliberately, more freely and intrepidly, with regard to question of Ethics than an Englishman uses his. (in Whitaker 1975, vol. 2: 358)

> [The American] has to shape his own course in life with but little guidance from the trade, customs, and the etiquette of the society in which he lives. Thus at each step of his career he uses his own individual judgment more consciously and deliberately, more freely and intrepidly, than an Englishman does. (Marshall 1878: 65)

[17] The first of these papers, "Some features of American Industry", as reproduced in vol. 2 of Whitaker (1975), appears to be the text of a lecture that Marshall gave at Cambridge on 17 November 1875. The second one, which reproduces parts of the first, is Marshall (1878).

For Marshall in 1875 and 1878, "the chief causes" of this fact were more or less the same ones that in *Industry and Trade* explain for the youth of the US economy. The first and most important of these conditions is "*mobility*", namely "the habit of passing readily from one occupation to another and from one district to another" (Whitaker 1975, vol. 2: 358):

> The mere fact of his being bound down to a particular occupation is sufficient in general to create in the mind of an American youth a resolve that he will do something else as soon as he has the power. And the control over his actions comes to a lad at an early age in America. Again, the young American knows that in the ever changing face of American trade and industry he will easily find a field in which he may have a fair start, in which no monopoly of success can be secured by a man with ready made business connections. (Marshall 1878: 63)[18]

In the 1875 paper, the sentence "in which no monopoly of success can be secured by a man with ready made business connections" is followed by this passage:

> He dwells night and day on the stories that are told of men who with no other capital than a public school education and their own energy have accumulated wealth that have made them a place in history. Of course he desired wealth for its own sake; but his main motive is the ambition to prove himself superior in power to other men: this he can most readily do by beating them in the race for wealth, so he plays for a high stake. (Whitaker 1975, vol. 2: 360)

And as "[h]is heroes, the money kings, have hated monotony", so "he hates it" (in Whitaker 1975, vol. 2: 361). After almost half a century, some of the young Americans of 1875 had long become the new money heroes, but their "character" had not changed very much:

> There are in America a great number of men who have become very rich while still in the prime of life and full of enterprise. Some of them have little inclination towards social amusements or culture: they are conscious of being but second-rate powers in the lighter affairs of life; and are happiest when at their places of business, engaged in yet enlarging their fortunes,

[18] See also Marshall (1923: 141–46).

which they value chiefly as evidence of their organizing genius. As arts and sciences flourish best when their followers work for the approval of brethren of the craft, and not for the sake of money: so business flourishes most when the aim of the business man is not to shine in elegant society, but to be held in respect by those who are the best judges of his special form of strength. This exclusive devotion to one pursuit involves some loss to the life of the individual; but the constructive economic force which it gives to America at this phase of her development is unique. (Marshall 1923: 156)

6 Comparing Marshall's and Keynes's Views on American Capitalism

The US economy was for Marshall a kind of a natural experiment. He visited the country when big business was still in its infancy and tried to figure out what would have happened in the future. On his return from America "[h]e was able to see the coming supremacy of the U.S.", but it would be quite problematic to say that, as early as 1875, Marshall was also able "to know its causes and the direction it would take". It took some time before Marshall could understand how this "supremacy" was to come out in practice. Since the beginning, however, he saw its main driver in the "character" of the American people, of which he gave a vivid account in the two papers written in the second half of the 1870s. The application of Adam Smith's theorem, that is pivotal in the parts of *Industry and Trade* more specifically devoted to explaining the causes of American leadership as "multiform standardization", came only afterwards.

The two explanations proved to be mutually reinforcing. The extent of the US market and the nature of its demand could explain for the large exploitation of scale economies, which in turns accounted for the fact that a few leaders of industry had got so rich and so powerful. But the same elements did not account for their character, which remains the same mixture of individualism and creativity as that of the "young American" and his "heroes, the money kings", in the earlier papers.

The important lesson that could be derived from this experience was that, at least in the relatively limited span of time in which Marshall could observe the US economy after 1875, the American character had shaped the way in which big business worked rather than the other way around.

We do not know if Keynes learned this lesson in 1905, but it is very plausible that he did not. Indeed, it seems more probable that what Keynes absorbed in 1905 was the scepticism about American trusts expressed in Marshall (1891), or at least an echo of it, and that it was much later, when he read *Industry and Trade*, that Keynes could finally appreciate the value of Marshall's experience in trying to understand the evolution of American industry.[19]

Meanwhile, and afterwards, not only his investments in the US, but also his views on the scarce adaptability of UK business leaders, were not at all inconsistent with Marshall's opinions.

The arguments that Keynes used during his campaign for "rationalization" of the depressed cotton industries in the UK during the 1920s are a case in point. This was an early instance of his lack of faith in competition and *laissez-faire* as means to restore full employment of resources. But it was also a denunciation of "the apparently suicidal behaviour of the leaders of Lancashire", which "raises a question of the suitability and adaptability of business men to the modern age of mingled progress and retrogression" (CWK XIX: 585). As Marchionatti has aptly noted (1995: 442–43), "Keynes talks about the emergence of an 'acquiescence' in the behavior in the old age of an industry, causing its decay", an argument which sounds very much like the life-cycle hypothesis:

> When an industry has reached a certain age and has ceased to progress, there will always be many individuals occupying key positions, some of them redundant, some of them incompetent, some of them just overpaid, who are likely to be discomforted by any change and therefore resist it. It is acquiescence in such a situation which before now has caused great industries to dwindle and decay. (CWK XIX: 620, quoted in Marchionatti 1995: 443)

This passage is reminiscent, *au contraire*, of Marshall's remarks about the character of American entrepreneurs who do not share the inertia of their British counterparts, showing continuity of approach, in the

[19] As Keynes wrote in his obituary of Marshall, "[*Industry and Trade*] represents the fruits of Marshall's learning and ripe wisdom on a host of different matters. The book is a mine rather than a railway - like the *Principles*, a thing to quarry in and search for buried treasure. Like the *Principles*, again, it appears to be an easy book; yet it is more likely, I believe, to be useful to one who knows something already than to a beginner" (CWK X: 228–29).

passage from Marshall to Keynes, to the issue of industrial leadership and supremacy and in the comparison between US and UK.

While Keynes had certainly an appreciation of British management in a few companies, especially those connected with exploitation of natural resources in the Empire (see Marcuzzo and Sanfilippo 2020), he had greater faith in that form of industrial organization—public holding companies—which were prevalent in the US and could not be replicated—possibly for the same reasons given by Marshall—in the UK. His investment choices reflect his recognition of the superiority of the American business model and industrial supremacy, no matter how his hopes and expectations in the future of British economy remained mostly on the brighter side.

7 Conclusions

Tiziano Raffaelli has taught us that Keynes was first and foremost a pupil of Marshall, and this appears to be particularly so in the realm of industrial theory and policy. Even in the *General Theory* Keynes was reluctant to abandon the Marshallian behavioural assumptions (the "classical" postulates), although he radically opposed what he thought to be the Master main implication, i.e. reliance on market mechanism to reach full employment.

Keynes was critical of Roosevelt's industrial policies because he felt that this was not what was needed to escape the depth of the Depression, but also because he did not share the President's faith in the power of competitive markets to restore prosperity. As in the 1920s he saw in mergers and cartels a better form of organization in sectors—such as utilities—where small, atomistic firms could not exploit economies of scale and more efficient governance.

Of course, we do not know whether Marshall would have shared Keynes's views on the New Deal. But it seems altogether unlikely that he might have supported Roosevelt's "war against 'organised money'" and his "vilification of Wall Street" as described for instance in Markham (2002: 234). On the other hand, some of the arguments that Keynes used in his attempts to persuade Roosevelt from waging war on big business may sound familiar to any reader of Marshall's *Industry and Trade*. We have tried to show in this paper one lesson that Keynes might have learned from Marshall, and especially from Marshall's evolving ideas about the US economy. Marshall may have passed on to Keynes the idea that the performance of an industrial system depends much more on the "character" of its business leaders than on lowering their market power, and that it may even be better to increase their power if they are the right men in the right places. Of course, they often look like "wolves and tigers", maybe because "they have been badly brought up and not trained as you would wish" (Keynes). In fact, they certainly "have little inclination towards social amusements or culture", maybe because they "are happiest when at their places of business, engaged in yet enlarging their fortunes" (Marshall). But "the nation's burdens will not get carried to market" if we do not find the way to treat them as "domestic animals" (Keynes).

References

Accominotti O. and Chambers D. (2016), If You're So Smart: John Maynard Keynes and Currency Speculation in the Interwar Years, *The Journal of Economic History* 76(2): 342–386.

Beaudreau B.C. (2016), Keynes, the National Industrial Recovery Act and the Demise of Nascent Real Business Cycle Analysis, *Economic Thought*, open forum.

Chambers D. and Kabiri A. (2016), Keynes and Wall Street, *Business History Review* 90: 301–328.

Cristiano C. (2011), Two Marshallians: Layton and the Early MacGregor, in T. Raffaelli, T. Nishizawa, and S. Cook (eds.) *Marshall and Marshallians on Industrial Economics*, London: Routledge: 163–180.

Cristiano C. (2014), *The Political and Economic Thought of the Young Keynes: Liberalism, Markets and Empire*, London: Routledge.

Cristiano C., Sanfilippo E., and Marcuzzo M.C. (2018), Taming the Great Depression: Keynes's Personal Investment in the US Stock Market, 1931–1939, *Economia Politica* 35(1): 13–40.

Crotty J. (1999), Was Keynes a Corporatist? Keynes's Radical Views on Industrial Policy and Macro Policy in the 1920s, *Journal of Economic Issues* 33: 555–577.

Dow S. (2016), Comment on Beaudreau B. C. (2016), Keynes, the National Industrial Recovery Act and the Demise of Nascent Real Business Cycle Analysis, *Economic Thought*, open forum.

Emmons W.M. (1953), Franklin D. Roosevelt, Electric Utilities, and the Power of Competition, *Journal of Economic History* 53: 880–907.

Foresti T. and Sanfilippo, E. (2017), Keynes's Personal Investments in the Wheat Futures Markets, 1925–1935, *History of Economic Ideas* 25: 63–90.

Galbraith J.K. (1984), Keynes, Roosevelt, and the Complementary Revolutions, *Challenge* 26(6): 4–8.

Groenewegen P. (1995). *A Soaring Eagle: Alfred Marshall 1842–1924*, Aldershot: Edward Elgar.

Harrod R.F. (1951), *The Life of John Maynard Keynes*, London: Macmillan.

Kandel E., Kosenko K., Morck R., and Yafeh, Y. (2013), The Great Pyramids of America: Corporate Ownership and Regulation, 1930–1950, NBER Working Paper n. 19691.

Keynes J.M. (1971–1989), *The Collected Writings of John Maynard Keynes* (CWK), D.E. Moggridge (ed.), London: Macmillan (CWK VII, *The General Theory of Employment, Interest, and Money*; CWK X, *Essays in Biography*; CWK XII, *Economic Articles and Correspondence: Investment and Editorial*; CWK XIII, *The General Theory and After: Part 1. Preparation*; CWK XIX, *Activities 1922–1929: The Return to Gold and Industrial Policy*; CWK XXI, *Activities 1931–1939: World Crisis and Policies in Britain and America*; CWK XXII, *Activities 1931–1939, 1939–1945: Internal War Finance*).

Marchionatti R. (1995), Keynes and the Collapse of the British Cotton Industry in the 1920s: A Microeconomic Case Against Laissez-Faire, *Journal of Post Keynesian Economics* 17(3): 427–445.

Marcuzzo M.C. and Sanfilippo E. (2020), Keynes's Personal Investments in the London Stock Exchange and His Views on the Transformation of the British Economy. *Structural Change and Economic Dynamics*. https://doi.org/10.1016/j.strueco.2020.02.002.

Markham J.W. (2002), *A Financial History of the United States*, vol. II, Armok: M.E. Sharpe.

Marshall A. (1878), The Economic Conditions of America. Originally published in *Bristol Mercury and Daily Post*, 15 January 1878, reprinted as essay 8 in P. Greonewegen (ed.), *Collected Works of Alfred Marshall*, vol. 1, *Collected Essays (1872–1917)*: 61–67.

Marshall A. (1891), Some Aspects of Competition, *Journal of the Royal Statistical Society* 53(4): 612–643.

Marshall A. (1920), *Principles of Economics*, 8th edition, London: Macmillan.

Marshall A. (1923), *Industry and Trade*, 4th edition, London: Macmillan.

Moggridge D. (1992), *Maynard Keynes: An Economist's Biography*, London: Routledge.

Morley J.D. (2012), Collective Branding and the Origins of Investment Fund Regulation, Faculty Scholarship Series, Paper 4832.

Patel K.K. (2016), *The New Deal: A Global History*, Princeton and Oxford: Princeton University Press.

Prendergast R. (1992), Increasing Returns and Competitive Equilibrium—The Content and Development of Marshall's Theory, *Cambridge Journal of Economics* 16(4): 447–462.

Raffaelli T. (2000), Keynes's Apprenticeship with Marshall in 1905, *History of Economic Ideas* 8(2): 121–152.

Rauchway E. (2008), *The Great Depression and the New Deal: A Very Short Introduction*, Oxford: Oxford University Press.

Rutterford J. (2009), Learning from One Another's Mistakes: Investment Trusts in the UK and the US, 1868–1940, *Financial History Review* 16: 157–181.

Skidelsky R. (1992), *John Maynard Keynes: The Economist as Saviour, 1920–1937*, London: Macmillan.

Sullivan M. (2004), FDR's Policies Prolonged Depression by 7 Years, UCLA Economists Calculate, http://newsroom.ucla.edu/releases/FDR-s-Policies-Prolonged-Depression-5409.

Whitaker J.K. (ed.) (1975), *The Early Economic Writings of Alfred Marshall 1867–1890*, London: Macmillan.

Whitaker J.K. (ed.) (1996), *The Correspondence of Alfred Marshall Economist*, 3 vols., Cambridge: Cambridge University Press.

Between LSE and Cambridge: Accounting for Ronald Coase's Fascination with Alfred Marshall

Steven G. Medema

1 Introduction

Alfred Marshall is central to the history of economics at the University of Chicago, his *Principles of Economics* acting as a touchstone for price theory courses from Jacob Viner's offerings in the 1920s through the more recent courses taught by Gary Becker and Kevin Murphy. Chicago economists defended Marshall against both the challenges offered by the two Cambridges (e.g., Stigler 1949) and the respective ascendancies

Ning Wang, Coase's student, co-author, and dear friend has been very forthcoming in providing me with information that goes beyond what is found in the archives and Coase's published writings. I have also benefitted from the comments of Roger Backhouse, Katia Caldari, Marco Dardi, Elodie Bertrand, Geoff Harcourt, Megan Stevens, and Stephen Stigler. The assistance of the staff at the Special Collections Research Center at the University of Chicago's Regenstein Library is gratefully acknowledged.

S. G. Medema (✉)
Department of Economics, Duke University, Durham, NC, USA
e-mail: steven.medema@duke.edu

K. Caldari et al. (eds.), *Marshall and the Marshallian Heritage*, Palgrave Studies in the History of Economic Thought,
https://doi.org/10.1007/978-3-030-53032-7_10

of general equilibrium analysis and game theory. Though these non-Marshallian elements are by no means absent from post-World War II economics at Chicago, one cannot tell the story of Chicago economics or the "Chicago school" absent Marshall.

For most economists at Chicago, Marshall was simply an input, the supplier of an approach to economic analysis considered best suited for the analysis of market (and, eventually, non-market) activity and questions of government policy bearing on market outcomes. For Ronald Coase, however, Marshall was much more than this—a subject of fascination and, at times, almost a reverence and obsession. A sometimes historian of economics,[1] Coase authored five articles on Marshall between 1972 and 1990 and another, published in 1961, in which Marshall figured prominently. Much of this work was derivative of a biography of Marshall that Coase intended to write, and to the research for which he devoted a great deal of effort for some three decades, beginning in the 1960s. Coase also published several articles on Marshall during his roughly two-decade-long editorship of the *Journal of Law and Economics*,[2] an outlet that one would not typically associate with the history of economics. It is fair to say, then, that Coase was in some sense Chicago's most devoted Marshallian.

Those acquainted with Coase's background will understand the oddity of this statement. Trained in the late 1920s and early 1930s at the London School of Economics, where indifference and even antipathy toward Marshall was widespread, and a member of the LSE faculty from 1935 until his departure for the United States in 1951, Coase would not have ranked high on the list of those expected to become Marshall's first biographer, let alone one who drew on Marshall's methodological approach to castigate both modern economics generally and certain of

[1] Coase had intended to study history but was prevented from doing so by his lack of knowledge of Latin. "Ronald Coase—Biographical," https://www.nobelprize.org/nobel_prizes/economic-sciences/laureates/1991/coase-bio.html.

[2] These include Marshall's lectures on *Progress and Poverty* (Marshall 1969), three articles on the appointment of Pigou as Marshall's successor (by himself, Bob Coats, and Trevor W. Jones) and a related piece by John C. Wood on "Marshall and the Tariff Reform Campaign of 1903," as well as his own article, "Marshall on Method" and a comment on it by Hans Brems dealing with "Marshall and Mathematics."

his ("Marshallian") Chicago colleagues in particular.[3] Coase's affinity for Marshall, whom he considered both a "great economist" and a "flawed human being" (Coase 1994, viii), requires some explanation, clues toward which can be found both in his published writings and in the voluminous materials from his researches on Marshall now available in Coase's archives.[4] In the pages that follow, we will examine Coase's biographical work on Marshall and his discussions of Marshall's economics for clues as to the sources of Coase's affinity for Marshall. And as we shall see, the evidence suggests explanations that are at once personal and professional.

2 Biographer

Coase's interest in Marshall dates at least to the late 1940s, when we have record of Coase delving into Marshall's papers at the Cambridge Marshall Library.[5] The first evidence of his intention to prepare a full-blown biography of Marshall, though, is found in a letter from Bob Coats to Coase in August of 1965. Coats reported his "pure joy" upon learning of Coase's intention to write this biography, pledging to help out in any way that he could and noting that "Of course you should write the definitive Marshall after counting all the commas in the *Principles* and the hairs on his mustache!"[6] Coase himself made his intentions clear in a 1967 letter to John Whitaker, which sheds some light on Coase's motivation for writing a Marshall biography:

> My own work on Marshall should be described as biographical. The stimulus to do this kind of work (apart from an interest in Marshall) came from the discovery that there was so much wrong with Keynes' memoir. At the moment I am engaged on three separate projects in connection with Marshall:
>
> (1) Marshall's ancestry, parents and childhood.

[3] On Coase and the LSE, see, e.g., Coase (1982a), Medema (1994), Bertrand (2015b), and Thomas (2016). On Coase and Chicago, see Medema (2020), as well as Posner (1993b).

[4] The Ronald H. Coase Papers (hereafter cited as RHC Box-Folder) are housed in the Special Collections Research Center at the University of Chicago's Regenstein Library.

[5] Coase to Whitaker, October 16, 1967, RHC 105-5.

[6] Coats to Coase, August 18, 1965, RHC 105-3.

(2) The 1891–1892 lecture notes.
(3) The American visit of 1875.[7]

As it happens, only one of these three projects—that dealing with Marshall's heritage—was actually completed, and by the late 1980s Coase had entirely abandoned the idea of writing a full-blown biography.

It should be obvious that these are very disparate projects on Marshall. And, in fact, Coase had yet another Marshall project underway at the time he wrote to Whitaker—the publication of Marshall's lecture on Henry George's *Progress and Poverty*, which Coase edited and published in the *Journal of Law and Economics* along with an introductory essay by George Stigler (Marshall 1969; Stigler 1969b).[8] What was it that led Coase down these disparate Marshallian paths? Coase himself does not tell us directly, but with the benefit of hindsight it is possible to discern some clues and, perhaps, even an explanation. Let us take these items in reverse order.

2.1 The Travels

Marshall's four-month visit to the United States, undertaken in 1875, was chronicled in notes Marshall made of the trip and in an extensive set of letters to his mother.[9] The journey was made possible by a £250 legacy provided by his uncle, Charles Marshall, and was in many ways a grand adventure—£250 being a rather large sum in those days. But the trip's "real purpose," as Groenewegen (1995, 195) points out, was "visiting factories." Marshall visited a significant number of them during his American sojourn, and Groenewegen provides some insights into the various ways—often indirect—in which Marshall's time spent visiting these factories influenced his future work.

[7] Coase to Whitaker, October 16, 1967, RHC 105-5. The Keynes "memoir" to which Coase refers is Keynes (1924).

[8] The transcription of Marshall's lectures and the accompanying discussion also included, as appendices, an exchange of letters between Alfred R. Wallace and Marshall, and a report on Henry George's speech at Oxford, in which Marshall challenged George's views.

[9] Marshall's correspondence with his mother is reprinted in Whitaker (1996, vol. 1, 36–84). For a discussion of his American travels, see Groenewegen (1995, 193–203).

Coase reports that he discovered the notes and correspondence from Marshall's trip during a visit to the Marshall Library in the late 1940s.[10] The reader who has at least a nodding familiarity with Coase's background will understand immediately his interest in this slice of Marshall's life. Coase, too, traveled to the United States to visit factories. This trip took place during the 1931–1932 academic year and fulfilled the final-year requirements for his LSE B.Com. degree. Where Marshall left a trail of letters to his mother describing his travels, Coase's trail can be found in a correspondence with his good friend from LSE, Ronald Fowler.[11]

Coase's goal on this trip, which was funded by a Cassel traveling scholarship, was to develop an understanding of the rationale for what we now call vertical and horizontal integration, no theory of which was to be found in the literature at that time. Though his travels seem not to have been accompanied by the luxury and variety of experiences afforded by Marshall's substantial legacy, the fruits of Coase's factory visits and discussions with businessmen are more readily identifiable than those of Marshall: This trip generated the insights that led to his writing of "The Nature of the Firm" (1937), one of two articles highlighted by the Nobel Committee in its awarding to Coase of the Nobel Prize.[12] Coase's interest in Marshall's US visit provides an early indication of the commonality of vision for economic method that Coase saw between himself and Marshall, about which more below.

2.2 *The Lectures*

It is less obvious what it is about the student notes from Marshall's political economy lectures from 1891 to 1892, taken by A.L. Bowley,[13] that

[10] Coase to Whitaker, October 16, 1967, RHC 105-5.

[11] Copies of some of this correspondence can be found in RHC 22-8. Coase provides a commentary on this trip and his correspondence with Fowler in "The Nature of the Firm: Origin" (1988d). Coase's archives also include correspondence from this trip with Marian Hartung (his future wife) and with his parents. This author has not had occasion to consult this familial correspondence, but the fact that Coase does not refer to it in his 1988 retrospective on the origins of his work on the firm suggests that it does not shed light on the lessons for economics gleaned from his travels.

[12] Of more personal consequence is the fact that Coase met his future wife, Marian Hartung, on this trip.

[13] Groenewegen to Coase, 20 September 1990, RHC 104-11. Groenewegen (1995, 317–21) provides overview of the lecture notes.

interested Coase. He had discovered these notes among Cannan's papers at LSE, probably in 1964,[14] and Guillebaud, too, apparently had a copy in his possession.[15] Coase noted to Whitaker in 1967 that the notes "are interesting although not of major importance from the point of view of the development of his thought." As such, he did not think them of major interest to Whitaker, who was then working away at bringing to publication a selection of Marshall's previously unpublished writings. What the lectures did do, Coase said, was to "throw a good deal of light on Marshall as a teacher and expositor"[16]—a somewhat surprising comment in that, circa the late 1960s, historians of economics typically did not consider lecture notes an important resource for their researches.

Groenewegen provides some further insight into why Coase may have been attracted to these lecture notes. Despite the fact that they followed close on the heels of the publication of Marshall's *Principles*, which informed the structure of the course, the lectures, Groenewegen points out, "tended to avoid the presentation of theory," stressing instead "the moral, philosophical and applied aspects of the subject matter" and paying close attention to history (1995, 319, 320). This would have resonated with Coase—again, see Sect. 3, below—and assists us in understanding his assessment that the publication of these notes would provide "information which in various ways will be of help to others in their researches" on Marshall.[17] Though Coase had intended to publish an edited version of these notes, with accompanying "explanatory material," in the *Journal of Law and Economics* within a year or two of his writing to Whitaker, this project was never completed.[18]

2.3 Marshall's Family Background

By far the most extensive of Coase's researches on Marshall dealt with Marshall's "ancestry, parents and childhood," work that he reported to

[14] See letter from E.A.G. Robinson to Coase, March 2, 1965, RHC 104-13.

[15] A copy of these lectures can be found in RHC 110-18.

[16] Coase to Whitaker, October 16, 1967, RHC 105-5.

[17] Coase to Whitaker, October 16, 1967, RHC 105-5.

[18] Coase to Whitaker, October 16, 1967, RHC 105-5. To the best of this author's knowledge, these lectures remain unpublished.

Whitaker was "well advanced" as of 1967 and which Basil Yamey apparently was interested in publishing in *Economica*. As it happened, this research was to occupy Coase for some twenty more years, eventually yielding an article in *History of Political Economy* dealing with "Alfred Marshall's Mother and Father" (1984) and a second piece on "Alfred Marshall's Family and Ancestry," published in a volume commemorating the 100th anniversary of the first edition of Marshall's *Principles* (1990). When the latter piece was reprinted in Coase's *Essays on Economics and Economists* (1994), it was augmented by an addendum, "Did Marshall Know Where He Was Born?"—a slightly extended version of a one-page note by the same title that Coase had published in 1984.[19]

This research shows us Coase at his best, using the methods that informed his studies of the economics of public utilities, including the BBC and the British Post Office, as well as the US Federal Communications Commission.[20] These studies found Coase pouring through the archives to chase down government reports, memoranda and correspondence, legal cases, and other documentation that unmasked the history of these institutions and their operations—often to critical effect. Tracking down the details of Marshall's family history, though, proved far more challenging. Coase applied for membership in the Society of Genealogists (UK) in November 1967, hoping that he could draw on the Society's records to trace and gather information on Marshall's "ancestors and relatives" during his summer visits to London and, in July 1968, received word that he had been made an Overseas Member of the Society.[21] Over the next fifteen years or so, Coase and his research assistants scoured government and other documents in locations including London, South Africa, and Australia.[22] Interestingly, the progress of this work seems to

[19] The original note, which runs to only two paragraphs, was published in the *History of Economics Society Bulletin* (now the *Journal of the History of Economic Thought*) in 1986. See Coase (1986).

[20] Richard Posner (1993a, b) offers a less charitable view of Coase's preferred methods. This author's contention that this research "shows Coase at his best" is likely to be subject to the same criticism that Posner leveled against Coase for opining that Stigler "is seen at his best" in his studies of the history of economic thought (Coase 1991b, 472). For discussions of Coase's studies of public utilities and regulated industries, see Medema (1994) and Groenewegen and de Vries (2016).

[21] Coase to Society of Geneologists, November 13, 1967; Coase to C.M. MacKay, June 17, 1968; C.M. MacKay to Coase July 18, 1968; RHC 104-5.

[22] Coase's research on Marshall's ancestry was supported in part by Liberty Fund.

have been hindered somewhat by a research assistant in London who, apparently, was only too happy to accept Coase's funding without delivering the corresponding research—getting Coase into some difficulty with one of his grantors and leading him, after a number of years, to engage a solicitor in London to deal with the matter.[23]

We would not do well to recapitulate the many details about Marshall's family and ancestry that Coase uncovered over the course of his extensive researches. A brief summary, however, is in order.

2.3.1 A Mixed Heritage

Marshall's family background was shrouded in mystery, and even Claude Guillebaud, Marshall's nephew, could report to Coase in 1967 that "I do not know much about the Marshall side of my ancestry, and I would not know to whom to turn to find out."[24] Keynes had suggested that "the Marshalls were a clerical family of the West," his father being a "cashier" in the Bank of England (Keynes 1924, 311), and Skidelsky, presumably taking his clue from Keynes, tells us that "Marshall was yet another product of the well-connected clerical families which colonized English intellectual life" (Skidelsky 1986, 40).[25] The reality, Coase argued, was quite different.[26]

When Alfred Marshall's father, William, was married in 1840, he described himself on the marriage certificate as a "gentleman" not having an occupation. In fact, Marshall's father was a clerk—a low-level position—in the Bank of England and had been since 1830 (Coase 1984, 521). He was, by all accounts, a very severe man and strict (even by Victorian standards) disciplinarian. Guillebaud referred him "a wicked

[23] This correspondence with his London solicitor, a Mr. Michael Balin, can be found in RHC 17-9. These difficulties are also described in correspondence with the grantor, Liberty Fund. See RHC 26-12.

[24] Guillebaud to Coase, June 28, 1967, RHC 104-9. Unfortunately, Guillebaud, who died in 1971, did not live to see the fruits of Coase's labors.

[25] Coase, in a fit of sarcasm, opines that "we can almost hear the clink of the teacups on the vicarage lawns" in these assessments (Coase 1990, 9).

[26] Recent research by Megan Stevens (2020), the great-great granddaughter of Alfred Marshall's uncle, Charles Marshall (about whom more below), challenges certain of Coase's claims regarding Marshall's family and ancestry. The present paper takes no position as between Coase's claims and those made by Stevens. It bears noting, however, that if Stevens' claims are correct, they only reinforce the conclusions about Coase's motivations, discussed below.

old tyrant" (Coase 1984, 522), and Coase at various points labels him "a complete fraud,"[27] "a bigoted man" (1984, 527), and "a man of extraordinary insensitivity to the feelings of others" (1984, 524). Though he fancied himself scholarly and well qualified to oversee young Alfred's education, he was, if anything a hindrance throughout.[28]

Marshall's mother, Rebecca Oliver, was said by Mary Paley Marshall in a 1925 letter to Keynes to have been the daughter of a "chemist," a background sufficiently lowly that William Marshall's family insisted she cut off contact with her relations. The reality, though, was far worse, so to speak. Marshall's mother was, in fact, the daughter of a butcher, and most of her relations were of similar working-class stock. Because of this cover-up, Coase suggests, "lacking any direct knowledge, learning about 'the life of the working classes' became, for Marshall, a research project" (1984, 520).[29]

Though Marshall's relationship with his father was uneasy at best, he was devoted to his mother, as his extensive correspondence from America attests. Even so, the domineering influence of Marshall's father left Coase convinced that "Alfred's home life was such as would have left most people unfit for serious scientific work" (1990, 23). That Marshall "managed to survive his father's harsh regime with the fire of his genius still alight," Coase said, "must have been due to some inner strength, to something within him" (1990, 20). The question, for Coase, was where in his background that strength, and the fire of genius that it unleashed, had come from, and this was no small motivation for Coase's further digging into Marshall's family background.

His researches uncovered a variety of interesting characters, scattered about the globe, including naval officers and businessmen of varying degrees of success. Among the latter was Marshall's wealthy uncle, Charles Marshall—a figure also erroneously described by Keynes, according to Coase—about whom Coase until the late 1980s intended to write a paper.[30] Uncle Charles owned a very successful sheep station in Australia.

[27] Coase to Groenewegen, May 31, 1990, RHC 23-8.

[28] Keynes compares Marshall's father favorably with James Mill but, says Coase, "James Mill he was not" (Coase to Groenewegen, May 31, 1990, RHC 23-8).

[29] The reference in this quote is to Keynes (1924, 329).

[30] Coase to Groenewegen, February 27, 1989, RHC 23-8. But within two months of this letter, Coase had decided to fold that material into his paper on Marshall's family and ancestry. See Coase to Groenewegen, April 6, 1989, RHC 23-8, as well as Coase (1990).

He was a shrewd businessman, but part of that shrewdness involved the use of convict labor, the restrictions on the mobility of which prevented him from losing employees (as others did) following the discovery of gold in Australia in 1851 (1990, 13–20). Even the story of the most successful man in the family would need to be buried then, Coase argued, since a family concerned to maintain its social position "would not wish it to be known that Uncle Charles made the fortune from which Alfred (and other family members) benefitted in part through the employment of convict labour" (1990, 20).[31]

Though most of Marshall's family tree would give little hint of "those traits of character and intellect which enabled him to withstand his father and to play a major role in building modern economics" (Coase 1990, 21), Coase found an exception in Louisa Bentall, his grandmother on his father's side and about whom Keynes says nothing in his memoir.[32] Marshall's relations through his grandmother's line were highly successful and extremely prominent, including bankers, members of parliament, and important members of the Clapham sect. It was through this line that Alfred was, as Coase discovered, related to both Henry Thornton and E.M. Forster (21–22).[33] And it was from his grandmother, Coase contends, that Marshall inherited "those traits of character and intellect which enabled him to withstand his father and to play a major role in building modern economics" (21).

2.3.2 *Marshall's Birthplace*

The detail of Marshall's family tree was only one of the mysteries regarding Marshall's background that preoccupied Coase. A second was the place of Marshall's birth, and the related questions of whether Marshall actually knew where he was born and, if so, attempted to conceal this from those around him. Keynes, relying on information provided to

In addition to providing the legacy that funded Marshall's 1875 travel to the U.S., Uncle Charles also provided a loan that financed Marshall's studies at Cambridge.

[31] On this subject in particular, see Stevens (2020).

[32] Keynes, in fact, mentions nothing about either Louisa or her husband, William Marshall. William Marshall squandered a significant inheritance, and both Coase and Groenewegen conjecture that they were effectively omitted from the family history going forward. See Coase (1990, 22–23) and Groenewegen (1995, 33–34).

[33] Robert Thornton, Henry's great-great grandfather, was Alfred's great-great-great grandfather (Coase 1990, 21–22). E.M. Forster was Henry Thornton's great-grandson.

him by Mary Paley Marshall, reports that Marshall was born in Clapham, a "very respectable," as Coase (1984, 520) put it, suburb of London. Here again, however, the reality was very different. As Coase discovered from Marshall's birth record, he was in fact born in Bermondsey, "a much less desirable residential area, situated as it was in the midst of the tanneries, with their accompanying pungent smells, Bermondsey then being the centre of the leather industry" (1984, 520–21).[34] The American reader will appreciate Coase's note in his brief essay on Marshall's birthplace, that to say Marshall was born in Clapham rather than Bermondsey was "roughly the equivalent of saying that he was born in Westchester whereas he was really born in the South Bronx" (1986, 34).[35] It is not that Marshall never lived in Clapham, for the family moved to Clapham when Marshall was a boy of between 3 and 7 years of age. But Bermondsey, not Clapham, was his place of birth.

The part of Bermondsey in which Marshall was born was referred to as "The Leather Market" (Coase 1984, 521n.11) and, ironically, was known to Coase because of his work on "The Federal Communications Commission" (1959) and "The Problem of Social Cost" (1960). Bermondsey, you see, was used by the judges in the well-known nuisance case, *Sturges v. Bridgman* (1879)—a case which Coase encountered when he was a student at LSE and which he drew on in both of these articles—"as an example of a locality devoted to a trade or manufacture 'of a noisy or unsavoury character'" (Coase 2004, 200). Such was the quality of life in that area that the judges felt compelled to note in their decision that "'What would be a nuisance in Belgrave Square would not necessarily be so in Bermondsey'."[36] Bermondsey was not, it seems clear, the cradle of gentility.

When Coase examined the census records for 1871, the earliest ones to which he had access and the only census data that informed his 1984

[34] Specifically, Marshall was born at 66 Charlotte Row, Bermondsey.

[35] See also Coase (1994, 149).

[36] *Sturges v. Bridgman*, 11 Ch. D. (1879) at 865, quoted in Coase (1984, 521n.11). Coase went on to say that "Clapham could well have been substituted for Belgrave Square" (1984, 521n.11). In his most recent discussion of Marshall's birthplace, Coase called Bermondsey, "a very undesirable place in which to live." Coase, "Alfred Marshall and his place of birth," nd, RHC 104-8. Though this document is not dated, its contents make clear that it was written after Coase's 1994 commentary on Marshall's birthplace had been published.

article, he found that Marshall had listed his birthplace as Surrey, the county that included both Clapham and Bermondsey. This led Coase to conclude that Marshall "was willing to conceal his real place of birth, but was unwilling to tell a lie" (1984, 521). In 1881 census, however, Marshall listed as his birthplace Sydenham, in Kent, where the family had lived for a brief period between their time in Bermondsey and Clapham.[37] This updated information caused Coase to wonder if Marshall did, in fact, know where he was born or whether, instead, it was more evidence that Marshall knew full well where he was born but was attempting to conceal this information (1986, 34). A decade later, when he was able to consult the 1891 census records, Coase found that Marshall had listed his birthplace as Croydon, a place that, so far as we know, Marshall never lived (1994, 149–50). The plot, then, had thickened, but Coase was increasingly of the mind that Marshall had concealed from others, including his wife, the true location of his birth.[38]

Though Coase apparently gave up his tracking of Marshall's census records at that point, his good friend Stephen Littlechild did not, and his 2012 article in *History of Political Economy* reveals that Marshall indeed *did* know where he was born, having listed Bermondsey for himself and Clapham (correctly) for his brother on the census of 1861. Littlechild also found that the 1901 census form, this one completed while Mary Paley Marshall was away, correctly listed Bermondsey as Marshall's birthplace, while the census of 1911, completed when Mary was at home, again listed Sydenham (Littlechild 2012). It is possible, then, that *Mary* did not know where Alfred was born—that her husband had kept this concealed from her and, by extension, from those in their circle—or it could be that Mary was simply content to go along with this little white lie.[39]

[37] Coase reports that the Marshalls had moved from Bermondsey to Sydenham by 1846 and moved from there to Clapham sometime between 1846 and 1850.

[38] Coase seems to have believed that it was Mary Paley Marshall who had provided at least some of this information to the census taker, which led Stephen Stigler to suggest to Coase that Mary may have been complicit in the cover-up and that she may have "embellished the detail in a favorable direction either consciously or subconsciously" in order to protect her husband. Stephen Stigler to Coase, July 7, 1993, RHC 104-11.

[39] Making Marshall's deception regarding the Census all the more ironic is the fact that, in 1890, he provided testimony to the Parliamentary committee looking into the Census-taking process. See Groenewegen, "Marshall's evidence before the Committee appointed to inquire into the taking of the Census (1890)," *Marshall Studies Bulletin* 9 (2005). https://www.disei.unifi.it/upload/sub/pubblicazioni/msb/2005/groenewegen9.pdf.

Coase himself would lead us to believe that Marshall's concealment went to his need not to be seen as a man of working-class roots, as someone who felt the need to keep up respectable appearances in a Victorian society where these were considered important—particularly in a place like Cambridge. As with Marshall's father's description of himself as a "gentleman," and the concealment his mother's family background, the effect of disguising his true place of birth, Coase suggested, "has been to enhance Alfred's social position but to diminish his achievement" (Coase 1990, 9).[40]

2.3.3 *Explaining Coase's Preoccupation*

Why was Coase so preoccupied—one could argue, obsessed—with Marshall's family and ancestry and, along with that, the precise location of Marshall's birthplace? No error made by Keynes, save perhaps for in a central result of *The General Theory* (1936), would justify the amount of effort that Coase expended on these subjects. Here, I would argue, we must read between the lines and look to Coase's own personal history and family background.

Coase was himself born into a working-class family. He was the only child of two postal service employees, his father having been a telegraphist, both of whom had left school at age 12. In his autobiographical statement for the Nobel Committee, Coase took pains to emphasize that both of his parents were "completely literate," though "they had no interest in academic scholarship"—preferring tennis (his mother) and lawn bowls (his father). Having no parental guidance in his reading as a youth, Coase was, he said, "unable to distinguish the charlatan from the serious scholar" (Coase 1991a). Unlike Marshall's father, who was a very severe man and actively opposed Marshall's efforts to study mathematics at Cambridge, Coase reports that both of his parents were very supportive of his academic endeavors, even if they did not know quite what to make of them.[41] Even so, Coase, like Marshall, appears to have been closer to his mother than to his father.

It is interesting to compare Coase's description of his own upbringing and prospects with his statements about Marshall's. Keynes, who thought it only natural that Marshall would emerge as a renowned scholar given

[40] See also Coase (1984, 521–22).

[41] Ning Wang to the author, May 16, 2018.

his own sensibilities and the information he had been given about Marshall's family background, said that, "William Marshall was a man of 'great resolution and perception'."[42] But "This is wrong," said Coase. Marshall's father "was a man of great resolution and no perception" who had, among other things, attempted to block Marshall's effort to go to Cambridge to study mathematics.[43] In Coase's estimation, "Alfred Marshall, the scientist, owed nothing to this bigoted man" (1984, 526–27).[44] Though we have no reason to believe that Coase's father was the sort of severe man who raised Marshall, Marshall's remark that his father was "a bad educator," repeated by Coase (1984, 527), hints that Coase may have seen in Marshall someone who, like himself, was left to make his own way in gaining a proper education even if Coase did have parental support in his efforts. Ning Wang, Coase's co-author, former student and close friend, has recently written to this author that "Professor Coase would [have been] happier if his parents were able to appreciate the significance and impact of his work. He understood well, though, that given their background, that was too much to ask for."[45] One can only wonder whether Coase felt the same was true of Marshall.

There are clues, however, that Coase saw more personal commonalities between Marshall and himself than just their family backgrounds. Taken by his father to see a phrenologist at the age of 11, Coase records that he was told,

> You are in possession of much intelligence, and you know it, though you may be inclined to underrate your abilities. ... You will not float down, like a sickly fish, with the tide ... you enjoy considerable mental vigour and are not a passive instrument in the hands of others. Though you can work with others and for others, where you see it to your advantage, you

[42] Here, Keynes was simply repeating the information he had been given by Mary Paley Marshall.

[43] Marshall's father desperately wanted Marshall to study classics at Oxford, and Marshall was only able to go up to Cambridge for mathematics studies thanks to a loan from his Uncle Charles (Coase 1984, 524).

[44] Coase went on to say that "Marshall's father was completely convinced of the correctness of his own narrow views, had little regard for the feelings and wishes of others, and thought it right to control the actions of those in his power by 'an extremely severe discipline'" (1984, 527).

[45] Ning Wang to the author, May 16, 2018.

> are more inclined to think and work for yourself. A little more determination would be to your advantage, however. ... More hope, confidence and concentration required—not suited for the aggressive competitive side of business life. More active ambition would be beneficial. (1991a)

"It was also noted," Coase continued, "that I was too cautious. It was hardly to be expected that this timid little boy would one day be the recipient of a Nobel Prize" (1991a).

Whatever one might think of phrenology, the report provided to Coase was not very wide of the mark. And those with some knowledge of Marshall's personality and makeup will recognize various of the attributes ascribed to Coase. Though it is impossible to know how much of Coase's personality was derived from nature as opposed to nurture, Coase clearly believes that both forces played a role in Marshall's development:

> It is to be expected that the strict control exercised by such a father over his children would affect their attitude in later life. And no doubt Alfred Marshall's extreme sensitiveness to criticism (he suffered, Claude Guillebaud told me, the agonies of hell when he discovered that he had made a mistake), his evasiveness when there was a hint of disagreement, his dislike of controversy, and other traits were, to a large extent, the result of his upbringing. (1984, 527)[46]

But as he himself had done, Coase saw Marshall rising above the limitations imposed by the environment in which he was raised. Despite these circumstances, Coase said,

> it should also not be forgotten that, even when young, his mind ranged free, and notwithstanding strong parental pressure, he formed and acted on his own views; and, when it came to choosing his career, Alfred Marshall ignored his father and followed his star. (1984, 527)

And as in his own case, the payoff was significant:

> What is striking to me about the story I have told is the ability of Marshall to overcome very unfavorable family circumstances and to emerge, not unscathed, for some aspects of his character are not admirable, but with the power of his intellect intact and with that devotion to scholarship which

[46] See also Coase (1975, 26).

> can serve as a model to us all and which, in his case, was to produce the *Principles of Economics*. (1990, 23–24)

It would seem that we can now begin to understand Coase's obsession with Marshall's place of birth and his apparent concealment of it. We have already noted that Coase and Marshall came from similar working-class roots. The similarity extends to their birthplaces, as Willesden, where Coase was born, was at that time an industrial area, as Bermondsey was in Marshall's youth. Unlike Marshall, however, Coase seems never to have attempted to conceal these circumstances. This same forthrightness about personal circumstances apparently did not extend to Coase's father, however. As Ning Wang, has written in correspondence with this author,

> His father was serving in the army and stationed in the Middle East during the WWI and stayed there for a few years after the was over in Europe. He once showed me a photo of his father in military uniform. What made him uncomfortable as a boy at that time was when he found out that his father apparently borrowed the uniform from someone with a much higher ranking in the military. He didn't like the kind of dishonesty and pretentiousness as sometimes shown in his father's behavior.[47]

The sort of concealment practiced by Marshall and by Coase's father flew in the face of the lesson "to always be honest and truthful" that Coase had learned from his mother.[48] But there is more to it than this. Coase appears to have been most disturbed by the suggestion that coming from working-class circumstances was somehow "not enough" and so must be concealed lest it diminishes one's adult status, scholarly profile, and legacy. Coase, said Ning Wang, was struck how, "In the US, successful people often boast about their poor origins," whereas "In England, it is common for successful people to conceal their undistinguished class background."[49] In a sense, Marshall could not be made to admit for public consumption that he was like Coase. One is left to wonder whether it

[47] Ning Wang to the author, May 16, 2018.

[48] One wonders whether Coase was thinking of Marshall and his mother's influence on him when Coase wrote in his Nobel autobiography of his own mother, "My mother taught me to be honest and truthful and although it is impossible to escape some degree of self-deception, my endeavours to follow her precepts have, I believe, lent some strength to my writing" (1991a).

[49] Ning Wang to the author, May 16, 2018.

was this, as much as Marshall's more well-known personality traits, that led Coase to label Marshall a "flawed human being."

2.3.4 *Why Was There No Biography?*

It remains to answer the question of why Coase never completed the Marshall biography. One might surmise that he was in a sense "scooped" by the news of Peter Groenewegen's biography, which was published in 1995 and of which Coase became aware several years earlier. But the reality is that Coase had abandoned his own biography well before learning of Groenewegen's efforts, meaning that we must look elsewhere for clues. The pieces that make up this answer are several. Coase was, by his own admission, a notoriously slow worker. Though his publication record is vastly more extensive than is indicated by the "he only published two articles" trope by which he is often defined,[50] Coase was not one to churn out article after article. Nor did his method of working assist in this, as his research, e.g., on public utilities and on Marshall's family and ancestry illustrates. Having gone down the rabbit hole of Marshall's extended relations, not to emerge from it until after some two decades of painstaking research, Coase would have been hard pressed to complete a study of more than a fraction of Marshall's own life even if he had chosen to devote his full efforts to that project.

But for Coase, the study of the history of economics was, as he put it, a "hobby,"[51] an activity that, for him, took a back seat to his work on economic analysis. His "Marshall period" also found him publishing on topics as diverse as durable goods monopoly (1972a), public goods (1974), advertising (1977), and economic method (1982b). In 1987, Coase was asked to present three lectures on "The Nature of the Firm" at a conference celebrating the 50th anniversary of that article's publication.[52] As Coase wrote to Groenewegen in early 1989, "the effect of the conference was to rekindle interest in the firm and it led me to decide, once my present commitments were out of the way, to devote the next few years to work on the theory of the firm. One result is that I have

[50] Those, of course, are "The Nature of the Firm" (1937) and "The Problem of Social Cost" (1960).

[51] Coase to Tullberg, May 12, 1989, RHC 104-10.

[52] See Coase (1988b, c, d).

decided to wind down my research on Marshall."[53] Coase remarked in a letter to Tullberg in 1990 that he had "one other small project" on Marshall to complete—presumably his work on Marshall's birthplace—and then could hand off the research materials he had collected to others, a thought that made him "very happy."[54]

Coase's decision to abandon his work on Marshall was no doubt aided by the increased interest in the New Institutional Economics of Oliver Williamson and others, and what he (perhaps over-optimistically) saw as an opportunity to reshape economic analysis following decades during which, as he lamented in 1972, this work had been "much cited and little used" (1972b, 63). And then, with the fame and accompanying demands on his time that came with his 1991 Nobel, even his assistance to Groenewegen ground to a halt, with Coase noting that "Until you receive the Nobel Prize it is impossible to imagine the demands made on your time. ... You say that you do not wish to intrude into my leisure. At the moment I don't have any."[55]

Though Coase's work on Marshall's family background was prompted at least in part by the gaps and errors that he discovered in Keynes's memorial essay on Marshall,[56] he was well aware that he had not unlocked all of the mysteries in Marshall's background. Still tenacious about the subject as he approached his 80th birthday, Coase noted to Tullberg that "I know absolutely nothing" about Marshall's sister, Agnes, beyond having a birth certificate, calling this "yet another gap in the story I told that I hope Professor Groenewegen will fill in." Toward this end, Coase provided Groenewegen, whom he had met at the Marshall 100th anniversary conference, full access to his materials on Marshall's family and ancestry, by that point deposited in Coase's (then closed) archives at the University of Chicago, and offered to be of whatever help he could to Groenewegen in his preparation of the biography.[57]

[53] Coase to Groenewegen, February 27, 1989, RHC 23-8.

[54] Coase to Tullberg, October 22, 1990, RHC 104-11.

[55] Coase to Groenewegen, March 31, 1992, RHC 23-8.

[56] In Coase's words, "Keynes is sketchy—and wrong." Coase to Whitaker, October 16, 1967, RHC 105-5.

[57] Groenewegen to Coase, September 20, 1990; Coase to Groenwegen, October 22, 1990; RHC 104-11.

Nor was Coase convinced that he had it all right. "I'm also hoping that [Groenewegen] will correct my errors," he said. Referencing Marshall's own severe reaction to his own errors, Coase continued:

> Working as I have with research assistants all over the world and with genealogical materials with which I have little familiarity, I have always been worried that I may have misunderstood something that I was told. I don't think there are many errors but it's upsetting to think that there may be any. In this respect, if in no other, I am like Alfred.[58]

This last sentence was surely an understatement.

3 LSE Marshallian

We now come to the other, perhaps more substantive, reason for Coase's interest in Marshall. For while Coase would certainly not have been the first to attempt a biography of someone he at once considered "a flawed human being" and yet felt some personal kinship, his interest in Marshall was at least as much motivated by his view that Marshall was a "great economist" (1994, viii). Indeed, his reading of Marshall revealed an economist with views on the subject that he considered very similar to his own—views that, if more widely adopted by the profession would lead to a better brand of economic reasoning. Such a stance is, to say the least, a bit unusual coming from someone so closely associated with economics at LSE in the 1930s.

Though the typical view of economics at LSE in the 1930s is of a department pervaded with Austrian and the continental influences, Coase has insisted that a greater diversity of perspectives was in play. "Economists at LSE [in the 1930s], he said,

> were not self-consciously Austrians or Paretians or Walrasians, and certainly not Marshallians. In the United States I have heard it said that, until the late 1930s, English economics was largely confined to a study of Marshall. This was not true at LSE. Marshall was in the calendar of saints, but few

[58]Coase to Tullberg, 22 October 1990, RHC 104-11. As noted above, Coase reports that Guillebaud once told him that Marshall "suffered ... the agonies of hell when he discovered that he had made a mistake" (1984, 527). Coase (1984, 526–27) suggests that this attribute of Marshall was a result of his father's severe discipline.

> of us prayed exclusively to him. Marshall was one among many economists studied". (1982a, 34)

Coase did not cite any of the saints, including Marshall, extensively in his writings, but it is notable, and rather against LSE type, that Marshall is the only one to whom he devoted significant attention.

As Bertrand (2015a) has shown, Coase's own writings contain an odd mixture of Marshallian and LSE cost theory, sometimes relying on the one and sometimes on the other—seemingly oblivious to the potential contradiction. Subjective and objective costs, real and opportunity costs, all play a role in Coase's analysis, which led James Buchanan (1986) to chastise Coase for neglecting his LSE roots.[59] "The Problem of Social Cost" provides an excellent illustration. Coase's argument regarding the reciprocal nature of harm (1960, pp. 2–3), which could be considered the article's foundational insight, is a classic application of the LSE opportunity cost approach. Yet, the farmer-rancher parable that Coase utilizes to derive his negotiation result—the result which came to be known as the "Coase theorem"—is grounded in straightforward Marshallian real cost analysis, as was his prescription that the economic approach to externality policy involves adopting the solution that maximizes the value of output. Meanwhile, subjectivism is at the heart of Coase's critique of accounting practices and yet is nowhere in evidence in vast swaths of his writing.[60]

Coase notes that he studied Marshall's *Industry and Trade* (1919), rather than the *Principles*, in his commerce courses with Arnold Plant—the closest thing to economics instruction he had during his student years at LSE (Coase 1982a, 34)—and that this was one of the works that had shaped his views on industrial organization (1972b, 62).[61] But he emphasizes that "we did not slavishly adopt Marshall's views" and, "[i]n fact, we thought his views on cost confused and his analysis of business practices questionnable" (1982a, 34). It must be, then, that Marshall grew on

[59] Buchanan (1969) had earlier lauded Coase's contribution to the development of the LSE theory of subjective opportunity costs.

[60] See Coase (1938). Bertrand (2015a) provides further illustrations of this seeming cost schizophrenia found throughout Coase's writings. See also Medema (1994, ch. 3).

[61] *Industry and Trade* deals with the industrialization process, the organization of industry, and the effects of these on economic well-being and is both more historical and less theoretical than the *Principles*.

Coase over the years, for these 1930s attitudes do not account for Coase's later glowing commentaries on Marshall's contributions.[62]

3.1 *The Theory-Fact Interplay*

Reflecting back on that time in LSE history 50 years later, Coase said that "What was done by the economists at LSE, principally by Robbins, Hayek and Hicks, was to play a leading role in what we can now see was an international movement which brought into being, for good or ill, the modern age in economics" (1982a, 34). But when one reads Coase's numerous commentaries on modern economics,[63] there can be no question that his true sympathies lie on the "ills" side of the balance, and that an economics which reflected more of Marshall's vision and less of the influence that he (correctly or not) ascribes to LSE would have put the discipline on a better course.

It was only a few years after this commentary on his LSE years that Coase made clear what was, in reality, the great distance between his own approach and that of Robbins, and the greater commonality of his own approach with that of Marshall (Coase 1988c, 24–26). In his 1937 essay on "The Nature of the Firm," Coase (1937, 386–87) had sought to provide a definition of the firm that at once was "tractable" using Marshall's principle of substitution at the margin and which would, following Robbins's prescription from his *Essay on the Nature and Significance of Economic Science*, "'relate to formal relations which are capable of being conceived exactly'" (quoting Robbins 1932, 66). Coase was of the mind that Robbins would be favorably disposed to his analysis of the firm. In reality, however, Robbins had no interest in it. Commenting on this fifty years later, Coase says that,

> I can now see that I was wrong to expect him to respond in this way. Consider what he says in *Nature and Significance*. ... "We have all felt, with Professor Schumpeter, a sense almost of shame at the incredible banalities of much of the so-called theory of production—the tedious discussions

[62] See, for example, statements quoted in the previous section of this paper, as well as the commentary below.

[63] See, e.g., in addition to the references cited herein, Coase (1966, 1970, 1988a, 1992, 2006, 2012), as well as Bertrand (2016), Medema (1994, 1995), and Medema and Zerbe (1997).

of the various forms of peasant proprietorship, factory organization, industrial psychology, technical education, etc., which are apt to occur in even the best treatises on general theory arranged on this plan. One has only to compare the masterly sweep of Book V of Marshall's *Principles*, which deals with problems which are strictly economic in our sense, with the spineless platitudes about manures and the 'fine natures among domestic servants' of much of Book IV to realise the insidious effect of a procedure which opens the door to the intrusions of amateur technology into discussion which should be purely economic." (1988c, 24–25)[64]

Coase ascribed Robbins's attitude here to his "devot[ion] to high theory" as a result of which "I believe he felt some distaste, at any rate in the 1930s, for discussions of such mundane subjects as peasant proprietorships and industrial 'forms'." Given that the focus of Coase's 1937 analysis aligned so squarely with that which Robbins was criticizing in Marshall, he should not, he admitted, have expected that the article would attract Robbins's attention (1988c, 26).

In Coase's estimation, Marshall was at best lukewarm to the "high theory" that interested Robbins. In his article on Marshall's approach to economic method, Coase quotes the following passage from a well-known letter written by Marshall to J.N. Keynes:

> You talk of the inductive & the deductive methods: where as I contend that each involves the other, & that historians are always deducing, & that even the most deductive writers are always implicitly at least basing themselves on observed facts. ... I think the right order is first to emphasize the mutual dependence of induction & deduction, & afterwards to show in what kinds of inquiry the economist has to spend the greater part of his time in collecting arranging & narrating facts, & in what kinds he is chiefly occupied in reasoning about them & trying to evolve general processes of analysis & general theories which shall show the Many in the One & The One in the Many. (1975, 26)[65]

Coase, though, was not content to take Marshall at his word:

[64] Quoting Robbins (1932, 65).

[65] Quoting a letter from Marshall to J.N. Keynes, September 20, 1890. Reprinted as Letter 321 in Whitaker (1996, vol. 1, 338–39).

> Although Marshall claims to occupy this middle ground, and in a sense he does, if we study what Marshall says, it seems to me that *he always emphasises induction, the collection and assembly of facts and plays down what we would term "theory"*, a word which, as we have seen, he did not much like when applied to economics. (Coase 1975, 28, emphasis added)

Coase, for his part, had little use for the methodological niceties of induction and deduction. What attracted him about Marshall on this score was Marshall's interest in *collecting facts* as a starting point for his analysis—an approach which, as we noted above, also helps us to understand Coase's interest in Marshall's 1875 visit to the United States. As Coase noted in his article on Marshall's method, published on the 100th anniversary of that visit,

> Marshall himself, of course, was a great collector of economic facts not only from such sources as Government reports but also from visits to factories and from questioning businessmen and workers. His factual knowledge was apparently formidable. (1975, 28)

Among Coase's various notes for his Marshall project, we find his transcription of a fragment from Mary Paley Marshall saying, "I believe that there is no economist who knew as much about the working man and machines as he did up to the age of 40 or 50. And this gives a reality to what he says which is lacking in (e.g.) Pigou."[66] Coase no doubt appreciated this even more for what it said about Marshall than for what it said (or did not say) about Pigou.

There can be no question that Coase was attracted to this aspect of Marshall because of its resonance with his own approach to the subject. Coase's eagerness to point to Marshall's emphasis on theories that evolve out of detailed facts and observations led him to pluck from Marshall's correspondence a correction of Neville Keynes's description of von Thunen as an abstract theorist: "'You know von Thunen's *Metier* was that of an agricultural reformer'," Marshall wrote. "'His abstract economics come in by the way. He was up to his eyes in facts about rye and manure and so on'" (quoted in Coase 1975, 28–29).[67] Coase must

[66] Note by Mary Paley Marshall, nd, RHC 104-6.

[67] Quoting a letter from Marshall to J.N. Keynes, August 1889. Reprinted as Letter 268 in Whitaker (1996, vol. 1, 293–96).

have been nodding his head in agreement as he transcribed Marshall's 1899 letter to W.S. Hewins, then Director of the LSE, where Marshall noted that he had "'as little respect for pure theory (otherwise than as a branch of mathematics or the science of numbers), as for the crude collection & interpretation of facts without the aid of high analysis which sometimes claims to be a part of economic history'" (quoted in Coase 1975, 29).[68]

The reason for Marshall's insistence on fact and observation as a starting point for theorizing, Coase contends, is that Marshall's "aim was to understand the working of the real economic system, a system whose operation we could observe in the factories, the streets, and in the homes of ordinary people" (1975, 28). For Coase, the economic system studied by Marshall "always has this concrete character—it was a system which, leaving the study or the library, one could observe. And for Marshall it was important that one should get this right since it was this real system that one had to explain" (Coase 1975, 28). This disposition toward realism—including in the assumptions that underlie one's theory—was central to Coase's own approach and put him at odds with Friedman (1953) and others among his Chicago colleagues (Medema 2020).

But it was not simply Marshall's emphasis on theory grounded in facts that appealed to Coase. So too did Marshall's criticisms of many of the uses of mathematics in economics, a number of which Coase quotes in his article on Marshall's method. Marshall's objection to the extensive use of mathematics, Coase argued, was grounded in the lack of "data to support any but relatively simple constructions," the fear that "factors that could not easily be dealt with in mathematical form would be neglected" and, most of all, that "we would be tempted to engage in what he termed 'mathematical diversions' ... imaginary problems not conforming to the conditions of real life." These exercises would, for Marshall, "tend to divert our attention from the real world in which poverty causes degradation and to the study of which he thought we should devote our whole energies" (Coase 1975, 31).

These attitudes that Coase saw in Marshall reflect bright threads in Coase's own writings. Coase's published output—including the more highly theoretical pieces on natural monopoly pricing policies, durable goods monopolies, and so on—contains not a single equation, and his

[68] Marshall to W.S. Hewins, 12 October 1899. Reprinted as Letter 597 in Whitaker (1996, vol. 2, 256–59).

several criticisms of what he called "blackboard economics,"[69] beginning already in the mid-1960s, routinely disparage what he considered mathematical flights of fancy—particularly in welfare economics and policy analysis. From where Coase stood, Marshall was something of a prophet, warning of the excesses of the "high theory" turn that he saw flowing out of LSE:

> In these days, when the mathematical method rides triumphant in economics, one may ask whether Marshall's fears were well-founded. Have we been tempted to embark on "long chains of reasoning" without adequate supporting data? Do we neglect factors difficult to put into mathematical form? Do we concern ourselves not with the puzzles presented by the real economic world but with the puzzles presented by other economists' analysis? (1975, 31)

Coase's answer was certainly in the affirmative, and in Marshall, he saw a "saint" who would have agreed with his own dim views about the mathematical turn in economics—a turn that, on balance, he saw as a serious negative for the field:

> It is not, of course, possible to indict the whole economics profession—and much good work is done nowadays and some of this work is carried out with mathematical methods. Furthermore, I feel sure that Marshall would have agreed that this was so. But it would be hard to deny that the extensive use of mathematics has encouraged the tendencies that he thought its probable consequence. Marshall's thought was that the extensive use of mathematics would lead us away from what he considered to be "constructive work". I very much doubt that what has happened in recent years would have led him to change his mind. (1975, 31)

Nearly twenty years after Coase penned these words about Marshall, he was himself subjected to the charge, by Richard Posner (1993a, b) that he was hostile to the use of mathematics by economists—a charge that Coase rejected.[70] Coase's (1993) defense of his own attitudes against Posner's charge echoed his earlier comments about Marshall:

[69] See Coase (1966) and the several other references to his work in note 63, above.

[70] Posner (2011) has more recently softened his stance toward Coase's methodological approach.

> Marshall welcomed all methods providing that they assisted in constructive work—and mathematics was not excluded from this. What is I think distinctive in his position is his belief that we should not investigate "imaginary problems not conforming to the conditions of real life." He thought that we should start with the real economic system, that it was our high calling to try to explain how it worked and that we should be interested in techniques of analysis only to the extent that this helped us to achieve the main goal. (1975, 31)

3.2 The Scope of Economics

Coase also broke with his LSE roots, again siding with Marshall, over what may be the most influential piece of economic thinking to come out of LSE during the 1930s—the definition of the subject supplied by Robbins in his *Essay on the Nature and Significance of Economic Science* (1932). In "Economics and Contiguous Disciplines," Coase used Marshall's definition of economics as a whip against Gary Becker (1976) and the Chicago-driven expansion of economics beyond its traditional subject-matter boundaries. At the heart of Coase's analysis was a discussion of what economics is and should be, and he took pains to insist that "the normal binding force of a scholarly profession" is "its subject matter" (Coase 1978, 206). "What do economists study?," Coase asked. "What do they do?" His answer? "They study the economic system" (1978, 206). Coase found support for this conception of the subject in Marshall, quoting Marshall's well-known statement that "'*Political Economy*, or *Economics*, is a study of man's actions in the ordinary business of life; it inquires how he gets his income and how he uses it'" (1978, 206, quoting from Marshall 1961, vol. 2, 131).

In a later commentary, Coase both expanded on his own definition of the subject and made clear the link he saw between his view and Marshall's:

> I have a clear idea of what the subject matter of economics is (and certainly what it should be): the attempt is to understand the working of the economic system, of firms, markets, banks and the other social institutions which make up that system. Marshall in the first edition of his *Principles*

> *of Economics* defined economics somewhat differently, but essentially he looked at the subject matter of economics in the same way that I do ...[71]

Coase saw George Stigler's Knight-inspired definition of economics, featured in the 1952 edition of Stigler's *The Theory of Price*, as of a piece with Marshall's conception of the subject, noting that both have a similar subject-matter emphasis. For Stigler (1952, 1), economics was defined as "the study of the operation of economic organizations, and economic organizations are social (and rarely individual) arrangements to deal with the production and distribution of economic goods and services."[72] What these definitions "emphasize," Coase said, is that "economists study certain kinds of activity," which "accords well with the actual topics dealt with in a book on economics" and "distinguishes the economics profession" from other fields of inquiry (1978, 206, 207).

The definition of economics laid down by Robbins, which by this time had, as Coase recognized, come to dominate economic thinking,[73] was, for Coase, of a "very different kind" from his conception and that of Marshall (Coase 1978, 207). According to Robbins (1932, 15), "Economics is the science which studies human behaviour as a relationship between ends and scarce means which have alternative uses." This definition, as Coase points out, "makes economics a study of human choice" and is, he said, "clearly too wide if regarded as a description of what economists do" (Coase 1978, 207). Looking back on this discussion some years later, Coase recognized that his view, which had remained unchanged, put him at odds with the professional tide: "Given this difference in the underlying view of the nature of our subject, it is not

[71] Coase, "The Place of Economics," nd, mimeo, RHC 58-14. See also Coase (1978, 207). "The Place of Economics" may be an early draft of the introduction for the collection that was eventually published as *Essays on Economics and Economists* (1994). The volume that was eventually published, though, has a very different introduction.

[72] It is not clear whether Coase was aware of this link between Stigler's definition and Knight's conception of the subject, laid out in *The Economic Organization* (1933). Knight, like Coase, was not fond of the Robbins' definition. See Knight (1934). Curiously, the earlier editions of Stigler's text had presented a Robbins-type definition. Of course, Stigler's own work in later years moved much closer to the Robbins-Becker conception of the subject, making it ironic that Coase appealed to Stigler here.

[73] Coase, "The Place of Economics," nd, mimeo, RHC 58-14. On the history of the definition economics, see Backhouse and Medema (2009a, b), the latter of which provides an extensive discussion of the gradual acceptance of the Robbins definition.

surprising that what I say about what economists should do will be found to differ markedly from what is said by others in the economics profession."[74]

Coase's subject-matter-based view of economics led him to reject Becker's Robbins-inspired view that economics is an "approach," one that is broadly applicable to the various arena's of human behavior. In yet another break from the "Chicago school" colleagues with whom he is so closely associated, Coase was highly critical of efforts to apply economic reasoning to subjects such as law, sociology, politics, and family life. His reasons for this were several, one of them being that, once one moves beyond economic activity proper, one tends to lose the great benefit pointed to by Marshall—having the "measuring rod of money" which, for Coase, deserves a good share of the credit for economists' success in analyzing (traditionally) economic behavior (1978, 209). But there were two further reasons for Coase's pessimism about the extension of the discipline's boundaries, both tied to methodological precepts he found in Marshall. First, Coase believed that the utility maximization model, which he considered of only minimal importance to Marshall, and rational choice theory were flawed conceptions of human behavior even within the traditional economic realm and considered them of little or no use beyond it.[75] Second, and reflecting his (and Marshall's) belief in the necessity of detailed fact-gathering, Coase believed that economists lacked the institutional knowledge to make effective contributions to these other disciplines (1978, 208–9).

Coase's prediction that economists' incursions into these other disciplinary realms would be both temporary and unsuccessful was well wide

[74] Coase, "The Place of Economics," nd, RHC 58-14.

[75] See Coase to Whitaker, October 16, 1967, RHC 105-5, as well as Coase (1978, 208). Like Marshall, Coase believed that biology had the potential to offer greater insights for grounding the study of human behavior. That Coase saw this in Marshall seems clear, as one of the passages he copied from Mary Marshall's notes includes her statement that, "A[lfred] said that 1000 years hence Economics would be entirely different from the science it is today and would probably be based on Biology." "Notes of Mary Marshall," entry of 7.1.24, RHC 104-6. On Coase's own views, including the links to Marshall, see Wang (2016, 280–81). Interestingly, Becker, too, suggested that biology had great potential for informing the economic theory of human behavior. See Becker to Coase, August 25, 1976, RHC 18-1. All that said, one can see commonalities in the discussions of altruism found in Marshall and Becker. See Medema (2015).

of the mark, at least as a claim about how economists came to spend their time. Though our purpose in this paper is not to debate the accuracy of Coase's various interpretations of Marshall, one is led to wonder to what extent Marshall would actually have agreed with Coase's position on this score. Did Coase, even with all of his detailed familiarity with Marshall's *Principles*, fail to recall that Marshall had said,

> There is a large and debatable ground in which economic considerations are of considerable but not dominant importance; and each economist may reasonably decide for himself how far he will extend his labours over that ground. He will be able to speak with less and less confidence the further he gets away from his central stronghold, and the more he concerns himself with the conditions of life and with the motives of action which cannot be brought to some extent at least within the grasp of scientific method. Whenever he occupies himself largely with conditions and motives, the manifestations of which are not reducible to any definite standard, he must forgo nearly all aid and support from the observations and the thought of others at home and abroad, in this and earlier generations; he must depend mainly on his own instincts and conjectures; he must speak with all the diffidence that belongs to an individual judgment. But if when straying far into less known and less knowable regions of social study he does his work carefully, and with a full consciousness of its limitations, he will have done excellent service. (1920, 780)

Becker likely would have read this passage with approval, for Marshall, both here and elsewhere, seems to have had a less rigid definition of disciplinary boundaries than Coase—and than Coase had allowed him.[76]

3.3 Economists and Economic Policy

It is safe to say that Coase's affinity for Marshall's methodological predispositions extended to the realm of economic policy analysis. Posner (1993b, 199) has correctly pointed out that "The socialist pitfalls of high

[76] Indeed, Coase's delineation of the boundaries of economics has much in common with Pareto's. That the latter's influence on LSE thinking was not insubstantial may have something to do with this. Contrast Pareto (1906) and Pareto (1916).

theory are a constant refrain in Coase's work."[77] In abstract theoretical worlds, it is a rather simple thing to show the optimality of all manner of government actions, from the provision of goods and services to taxes or regulations to deal with market failures, and Coase thought economists were all too quick to apply the insights gleaned from the analysis of those worlds to the world around us—with grave consequences for economic efficiency. Indeed, this is arguably the main theme of "The Problem of Social Cost,"[78] and striking back at the idea that government action is an appropriate (i.e., efficiency-enhancing) solution to all manner of market failures is a theme that runs through Coase's writings.

Coase believed that sound economic policy required a detailed examination of the relative merits of alternative institutional structures for allocating resources in society—whether that be allowing (or not) the B.B.C. a monopoly position in broadcasting, allocating broadcast frequencies in the United States via administrative fiat or instead utilizing the market, or how best to deal with situations of externality, such as pollution. That said, Coase also believed that a comparison of government and private activity would often reveal the superiority of the latter and that governmental cures tended to be worse than market diseases. His extensive case studies of public utilities in Britain, and of the actions of the Federal Communications Commission in the United States, only reinforced this belief, and Coase's decision to emigrate to the United States in the early 1950s owed much to what he considered the socialistic turn in British economic affairs.

Coase found what he considered a kindred view in Marshall's entry into the debate over the British Postal Service monopoly, the subject of his first extensive engagement with Marshall in his own writings.[79]

[77] Socialist economists, such as Oskar Lange (1936, 1937) and Abba Lerner (1944), were prominent among those developing general equilibrium theory and associated approaches to welfare economics, for example.

[78] For the uninitiated, the negotiation result that we now know as the "Coase theorem" was aimed at showing that private action works as well as government in such a world. The real world of positive transaction or coordination costs, Coase emphasized, leads to imperfect markets and imperfect government, necessitating an assessment of the relative efficiencies of the various alternatives for dealing with (in this case) external effects.

[79] Coase's only published references to Marshall prior to 1961 are passing ones in an early paper on duopoly (1935, 139n.4) and "The Nature of the Firm" (1937, 386–87, 388).

Coase's article on "The British Post Office and the Messenger Companies" (1961) takes up the Post Office's defense of its monopoly against the incursions of private messenger services in the late 1800s. Marshall features here owing to his decision to respond to an "anonymous" article in *The Times* in 1891, defending the postal monopoly. Marshall's very lengthy letter prompted an equally lengthy reply from this "anonymous" Post Office defender and this, in turn, stimulated a second long letter from Marshall.[80] Coase elected to quote each of Marshall's letters in its entirety in his article.[81]

Coase conjectures, likely rightly, that Marshall's decision to inject himself into this controversy owed to his experience with the private post operated by St. John's College, a service that Marshall called "splendid" and which operated at far lower cost than its government counterpart.[82] Marshall thought the Post Office's unconditional monopoly injurious to the public welfare and advocated its abolition. The original monopoly privilege, he said, "was granted without a thorough study of its real bearings," calling its efficacy into question (Coase 1961, 54). For example, though the economies of scale benefit was asserted by the anonymous correspondent as demonstrating the importune of this monopoly, these economies, Marshall emphasized, were never actually made the subject of study, and he found claims for them questionable given that private enterprise was able to under-price the Post Office.

Marshall's letters on this subject also made much of his concern that the postal monopoly raised the specter of socialism, "the chief dangers of [which] lie ... in its sterilising influence on those mental activities which have gradually raised the world from barbarism, and have made the average English working man of today really richer than the average Englishman was not long ago" (quoted in Coase 1961, 51). Marshall allowed that "The character of Post Office business is such that we might expect a priori that there, at least, Socialism would not perceptibly tend

[80] It turns out that this anonymous corresponded was, in reality, the Post Office Solicitor, a fact that Coase believes Marshall had sniffed out.

[81] The letters were written by Marshall on March 23 and March 31, 1891 and were published on March 24 and April 6, respectively. They are reprinted as letters 351 and 353 in Whitaker (1996, vol. 2, 19–21, 22–25). Coase (1961, 50) erroneously dates the first of Marshall's letters to 1890. References given here are to Coase's 1961 quotations from the letters.

[82] See Marshall fragment in Pigou (1925, 359).

towards lethargy." "But," he continued, "experience has shown otherwise" (quoted in Coase 1961, 51). Marshall felt that the Post Office, like many government agencies, was not responsive to consumer demands for service, and private enterprise had moved into satisfy those demands (Coase 1961, 51). This competition, he argued, would stimulate the Post Office to greater efficiency. Marshall even went so far as to use his consumer surplus analysis to estimate the loss associated with the Post Office monopoly, which he placed at 6s. per person, an amount that, when totaled up, exceeded the Post Office's total net revenue (Coase 1961, 56). The effect of the Post Office monopoly, Marshall concluded, was that "we secure, as far as the influence of the Post Office reaches, most of the evils of Socialism with but few of its benefits" (quoted in Coase 1961, 51).

It is quite easy to see why Coase would have been attracted by Marshall's position here. "To Marshall," Coase said, "the significance of Post Office policy towards the messenger companies was in the light it threw on the relation between Socialism and economic progress" (1961, 61). The stinging rebukes of socialism found in Marshall's letters would certainly have resonated with Coase.[83] But there is also a methodological issue in play here. "The main thrust of Marshall's argument," Coase emphasized, "was to show that Mr. Hunter's defence of the monopoly was invalid" (1961, 61). As Coase noted, Marshall did not recommend the *unconditional abolition* of the postal monopoly; he did, however, support the abolition of its *unconditional monopoly* and "as soon as possible." But here Marshall advocated for a more nuanced approach to the problem than, in his estimation, had governed the establishment of the original monopoly. Determining how best to go about deciding in what areas the Post Office should retain their monopoly and in what areas it should be continued, he said, cannot "be discovered except by careful inquiry of people with more technical knowledge than I have" (Coase 1961, 54).[84]

[83] It may be Marshall's antipathy toward what he saw as the socialistic flavor of Henry George's *Progress and Poverty*, combined with Marshall's use of rich institutional detail in making his case against George, that led Coase to publish Marshall's lectures on George's book in the *Journal of Law and Economics* (Marshall 1969).

[84] Marshall's position in *Industry and Trade*, written nearly three decades later, was perhaps a bit less nuanced, speaking much more favorably of a postal monopoly. See Marshall (1919, 428). Given Coase's familiarity with Marshall's writings and the fact that

This is precisely the position that Coase (1959) had adopted only two years earlier in his analysis of the US Federal Communication Commission's rules for allocating broadcast frequencies—a position which he had continued to press in congressional testimony and more popular writings. Coase did not recommend the replacement of the fiat-based allocation of broadcast frequencies with a market system. What he said, instead, was that the possibility of using the market had never been considered, and that it would behoove the US government to undertake a careful analysis of the most efficient mechanism for allocating these frequencies. There can be little doubt that Coase believed that such analysis would reveal the superiority of the market here, just as Marshall had complete confidence that there were slices of the larger market in which the private messenger companies could improve on Post Office performance. But at the heart of the issue, both for Coase and for Marshall, was a failure to undertake a careful analysis of benefits and costs in the first place, instead leaping to the conclusion that governmental control was the appropriate way forward.[85]

4 Conclusion

Coase's affinity for Marshall owes, it would seem, to factors both personal and professional—to parallels between his own background circumstances and those of Marshall and perceived commonalities of vision for doing economics. But this examination of Coase's treatments of Marshall also gives us some insight into Coase as an historian of economics. Coase took the history of the subject seriously, as evidenced by his many decades of membership in the History of Economics Society. One of the insights that we can draw from the foregoing discussion is for the rather eclectic historiographic views that informed Coase's work—not just on Marshall, but on Adam Smith and others.[86] Unlike Coase's good friend, colleague,

he cut his teeth on Marshall's *Industry and Trade* as a student (and cites another part of that book in his article on the postal monopoly), it is noteworthy that Coase made no mention of this modification in Marshall's views.

[85] Coase's interest in the effects of the postal monopoly was not confined to Britain. George Priest's (1975) study of the U.S. postal monopoly was effectively commissioned by Coase and, perhaps coincidentally, was published by Coase in the *Journal of Law and Economics* as the article immediately following Coase's article on Marshall's method.

[86] See the essays reprinted in Coase's *Essays on Economics and Economists* (1994).

and fellow historian of economics, George Stigler, Coase considered biography a useful element of the history of economics. But so too the history of ideas and intellectual history. Yet as much as all of these, Coase saw the history of economics as a tool to nudge economists toward what he considered a more useful way of doing economics. That he published "Marshall on Method" in the *Journal of Law and Economics* rather than *History of Political Economy* likely was no accident, as it would have afforded him the opportunity to preach to and perhaps legitimate for a broader audience of economists the particular methodological gospel that he favored.

References

Backhouse, Roger E. and Steven G. Medema. 2009. Defining economics: The long road to the acceptance of the Robbins definition. *Economica* 76 (October): 805–820.

———. 2009. On the definition of economics. *Journal of Economic Perspectives* 23 (Winter): 221–234.

Becker, Gary S. 1976. *The Economic Approach to Human Behavior.* Chicago: University of Chicago Press.

Bertrand, Elodie. 2015a. From the firm to economic policy: The problem of Coase's cost. *History of Political Economy* 47 (3): 481–510.

———. 2015b. An underrated originality of "The Problem of Social Cost": The LSE source. *History of Economic Ideas* 23 (3): 19–43.

———. 2016. Coase's choice of methodology. *Cambridge Journal of Economics* 40 (4): 1203–1227.

Buchanan, James M. 1969. *Cost and Choice: An Inquiry in Economic Theory.* Chicago: Markham.

———. 1984. Rights, efficiency, and exchange: The irrelevance of transactions cost. In *Liberty, Market and State: Political Economy in the 1980s*. New York: New York University Press, 1986.

Coase, Ronald H. 1935. The problem of duopoly reconsidered. *Review of Economic Studies* 2 (2): 137–143.

———. 1937. The nature of the firm. *Economica* 4 (16): 386–405.

———. 1938. Business organization and the accountant (a series of 12 articles). *The Accountant* (October-December). Reprinted in *Studies in Costing*. Ed. David Solomons. Homewood, IL: Richard D. Irwin Publishers. Homewood, IL, 1952.

———. 1959. The Federal Communications Commission. *Journal of Law and Economics* 2 (1): 1–40.

———. 1960. The problem of social cost. *Journal of Law and Economics* 3 (October): 1–44.
———. 1961. The British Post Office and the messenger companies. *Journal of Law and Economics* 4 (1): 12–65.
———. 1966. The theory of public utility pricing. In *The Economics of Regulation of Public Utilities*. Evanston, IL: Northwestern University.
———. 1970. The theory of public utility pricing and its application. *Bell Journal of Economics and Management Science* 1 (1): 113–128.
———. 1972a. Durability and monopoly. *Journal of Law and Economics* 15 (1): 143–149.
———. 1972b. Industrial organization: A proposal for research. In *Policy Issues and Research Opportunities in Industrial Organization*. Ed. Victor R. Fuchs. New York: National Bureau of Economic Research.
———. 1974. The lighthouse in economics. *Journal of Law and Economics* 17 (2): 357–376.
———. 1975. Marshall on method. *Journal of Law and Economics* 18 (1): 25–31.
———. 1977. Advertising and free speech. *Journal of Legal Studies* 6 (1): 1–34.
———. 1978. Economics and contiguous disciplines. *Journal of Legal Studies* 7 (2): 201–211.
———. 1982a. Economics at LSE in the 1930s: A personal view. *Atlantic Economic Journal* 10 (1): 31–34.
———. 1982b. *How Should Economists Choose?* Washington, DC: American Enterprise Institute.
———. 1984. Alfred Marshall's mother and father. *History of Political Economy* 16 (4): 519–527.
———. 1986. Did Marshall know where he was born? *History of Economics Society Bulletin* 7 (1): 34.
———. 1988a. *The Firm, the Market, and the Law*. Chicago: University of Chicago Press.
———. 1988b. The nature of the firm: Influence. *Journal of Law, Economics, & Organization* 4 (1): 33–47.
———. 1988c. The nature of the firm: Meaning. *Journal of Law, Economics, & Organization* 4 (1): 19–32.
———. 1988d. The nature of the firm: Origin. *Journal of Law, Economics, & Organization* 4 (1): 3–17.
———. 1990. Alfred Marshall's family and ancestry. In *Alfred Marshall in Retrospect*. Ed. Rita McWilliams Tullberg. Aldershot: Edward Elgar.
———. 1991a. *Autobiography*. Nobelprize.org. 13 Dec 2012 http://www.nobelprize.org/nobel_prizes/economics/laureates/1991/coase-autobio.html.

———. 1991b. George J. Stigler. In *Remembering the University of Chicago: Teachers, Scientists and Scholars*. Ed. Edward Shils. Chicago: University of Chicago Press.
———. 1992. The institutional structure of production. *American Economic Review* 82 (4): 713–719.
———. 1993. Coase on Posner on Coase. *Journal of Institutional and Theoretical Economics* 149 (1): 96–98.
———. 1994. *Essays on Economics and Economists*. Chicago: University of Chicago Press.
———. 2004. Ronald H. Coase. In *Lives of the Laureates: Eighteen Nobel Economists*. 4th ed. Ed. William Breit and Barry T. Hirsch. Cambridge, MA: MIT Press.
———. 2006. The conduct of economics: The example of Fisher Body and General Motors. *Journal of Economics and Management Strategy* 15 (2): 255.
———. 2012. Saving economics from the economists. *Harvard Business Review* 90 (12): 36.
Friedman, Milton. 1953. The methodology of positive economics. In *Essays in Positive Economics*. Chicago: University of Chicago Press.
Groenewegen, Peter. 1995. *A Soaring Eagle: Alfred Marshall, 1842–1924*. Aldershot: Edward Elgar.
Groenewegen, John and Piet de Vries. 2016. Coase and the regulation of public utilities. In *The Elgar Companion to Ronald H. Coase*. Ed. Claude Ménard and Elodie Bertrand. Cheltenham: Edward Elgar.
Keynes, John Maynard. 1924. Alfred Marshall, 1842–1924. *Economic Journal* 34 (135): 311-372.
———. 1936. *The General Theory of Employment, Interest and Money*. London: Macmillan.
Knight, Frank H. 1933. *The Economic Organization*. Chicago: University of Chicago.
———. 1934. The nature of economic science in some recent discussions. *American Economic Review* 24 (2): 225–238.
Lange, Oskar. 1936. On the economic theory of socialism: Part I. *Review of Economic Studies* 4 (1): 53–71.
———. 1937. On the economic theory of socialism: Part II. *Review of Economic Studies* 4 (2): 123–142.
Lerner, Abba P. 1944. *The Economics of Control: Principles of Welfare Economics*. New York: Macmillan.
Littlechild, Stephen. 2012. Alfred Marshall's reported birthplace: Evidence from the censuses. *History of Political Economy* 44 (2): 331–339.
Marshall, Alfred. 1919. *Industry and Trade*. London: Macmillan.
———. 1920. *Principles of Economics*. Eighth ed. London: Macmillan.

———. 1961. *Principles of Economics*. Ninth (Variorum) ed. Ed. Claude W. Guillebaud. 2 vols. London: Macmillan.
———. 1969. Three lectures on *Progress and Poverty* by Alfred Marshall. *Journal of Law and Economics* 12 (1): 184–226.
Medema, Steven G. 1994. *Ronald H. Coase*. London: Macmillan.
———. 1995. Ronald Coase on economics and economic method. *History of Economic Review* 24 (1): 1–22.
———. 2015. The "Subtle Processes of Economic Reasoning": Marshall, Becker, and Theorizing about Economic Man and Other-Regarding Behavior. *Research in the History of Economic Thought and Methodology* 33: 43–73.
———. 2020. Embracing at arm's length: Ronald Coase's uneasy relationship with the Chicago school. *Oxford Economic Papers* 72 (4): 1072–90.
Medema, Steven G. and Richard O. Zerbe, Jr. 1997. Ronald Coase, the British tradition, and the future of economic method. In *Coasean Economics: Law and Economics and the New Institutional Economics*. Ed. Steven G. Medema. Boston: Kluwer Academic Publishers.
Pareto, Vilfredo. 1906. *Manual of Political Economy: A Critical and Variorum Edition*. Ed. Aldo Montesano, Alberto Zanni, Luigino Bruni, John S. Chipman, and Michael McLure. Oxford: Oxford University Press, 2014.
———. 1916. *The Mind and Society: A Treatise on General Sociology*. Trans. Andrew Bongiorno and Arthur Livingston. London: Jonathan Cape, 1936.
Pigou, A. C., ed. 1925. *Memorials of Alfred Marshall*. London: Macmillan. Reprinted by Augustus M. Kelley, 1966.
Posner, Richard A. 1993a. The new institutional economics meets law and economics. *Journal of Institutional and Theoretical Economics* 149 (1): 73–87.
———. 1993b. Ronald Coase and methodology. *Journal of Economic Perspectives* 7 (4): 195–210.
———. 2011. Keynes and Coase. *Journal of Law and Economics* 54 (4): S31–S40.
Priest, George L. 1975. A history of the postal monopoly in the United States. *Journal of Law and Economics* 18 (1): 33–80.
Robbins, Lionel. 1932. *An Essay on the Nature and Significance of Economic Science*. London: Macmillan.
Skidelsky, Robert. 1986. *John Maynard Keynes: Hopes Betrayed, 1883–1920*. New York: Viking Penguin.
Stevens, Megan. 2020. The wrong Marshall: Notes on the Marshall family in response to biographies of the economist, Alfred Marshall. *History of Political Economy* 52 (2): 239–273.
Stigler, George J. 1949. Monopolistic competition in retrospect. In *Five Lectures on Economic Problems*. London: London School of Economics and Political Science.
———. 1952. *The Theory of Price, Revised Edition*. New York: Macmillan.

———. 1969. Alfred Marshall's lectures on *Progress and Poverty*. *Journal of Law and Economics* 12 (1): 181–183.

Thomas, Jim. 2016. Coase and the London School of Economics in the 1920s–1940s. In *The Elgar Companion to Ronald H. Coase*. Ed. Claude Ménard and Elodie Bertrand. Cheltenham: Edward Elgar.

Wang, Ning. 2016. Emerging markets: What can we learn from Ronald Coase? In *The Elgar Companion to Ronald H. Coase*. Ed. Claude Ménard and Elodie Bertrand. Cheltenham: Edward Elgar.

Whitaker, John K., ed. 1996. *The Correspondence of Alfred Marshall, Economist*. 3 vols. Cambridge: Cambridge University Press.

"A Great Economist" and "A Careful Empiricist": Paul Samuelson's Attitude Towards Alfred Marshall

Roger E. Backhouse

1 Samuelson and the Age of Marshall

The 1930s marked the end of the Age of Marshall: Maynard Keynes turned economists away from Marshall's conception of fluctuations in economic activity; Joan Robinson and Edward Chamberlin developed new theories of imperfect (monopolistic) competition; and other economists sought an explanation of resource allocation in the general equilibrium theories of Leon Walras and Vilfredo Pareto (Backhouse et al. 2010; Backhouse and Medema 2014). A major figure in this change was Paul A. Samuelson. His *Foundations of Economic Analysis* (1947) largely displaced Marshall's *Principles of Economics* as the main source of the techniques that graduate students had to learn, and successive editions of *Economics: An Introductory Analysis* (1948) came to dominate undergraduate economics teaching. Samuelson was notorious as a critic of Marshall—a self-identified debunker of Marshall. Where Marshall

R. E. Backhouse (✉)
University of Birmingham, Birmingham, UK
e-mail: R.E.BACKHOUSE@bham.ac.uk

Erasmus University Rotterdam, Rotterdam, The Netherlands

K. Caldari et al. (eds.), *Marshall and the Marshallian Heritage*,
Palgrave Studies in the History of Economic Thought,
https://doi.org/10.1007/978-3-030-53032-7_11

had been cautious in his use of mathematics, attaching great importance to features of the world that could not be modelled formally (as Tiziano Raffaelli has conclusively shown), Samuelson was an enthusiast for mathematical economics. Although he attached great importance to data, he was at times impatient with the way Marshall sought to make his theories realistic. Especially when engaged in policy analysis, Samuelson was prepared to make arguments that were not formalised, but he kept such analysis separate from mathematical modelling in a way that Marshall did not. He found Marshall's conflating of realistic description and mathematical theory confusing.

Samuelson's importance in ending the Age of Marshall justifies examining his attitude towards Marshall in detail. Nothing in the conventional picture of Samuelson's view of Marshall is wrong—the claims made in the previous paragraph can even be supported by quotations that are sufficiently dramatic to be memorable—but this picture conceals his admiration for a great economist, albeit one who had made serious mistakes.

2 Foundations of Economic Analysis

Samuelson is notorious for having denigrated Marshall in the Introduction to *Foundations of Economic Analysis* (1947) where he wrote:

> I have come to feel that Marshall's dictum that "it seems doubtful whether any one spends his time well in reading lengthy translations of economic doctrines into mathematics that have not been made by himself" should be exactly reversed. The laborious working over of essentially simple mathematical concepts such as is characteristic of much of modern economic theory is not only unrewarding from the standpoint of advancing the science, but involves as well mental gymnastics of a peculiarly depraved type. (Samuelson 1947, p. 6)

However, despite this strong criticism, Samuelson treated Marshall with great respect as a major authority. *Foundations* contains no fewer than nineteen index entries for Marshall, and Samuelson brackets him with Cournot, Walras and Pareto as authors of "classic works" (p. 141). It is surely high praise that, half a century after the first edition had been published, Samuelson was willing to refer readers to "any good economics textbook, such as Marshall's *Principles*" (p. 21n).[1] He cited Marshall as a source on supply and demand curves, rent, utility theory, index numbers, consumers' surplus, the optimality of perfect competition, optimality conditions, the relation between marginal and average costs, and adjustment speeds (pp. 18n, 35n, 93n, 146, 197–8, 212, 242, 246, 264n). He argues that Marshall, along with Walras, was right to focus on the industry rather than the firm (p. 79).

There were criticisms, but these were mostly technical points such as might have arisen in discussing any economist whose work he took seriously. Samuelson described Marshall's discussion of the relationship of marginal and full costs as "loose," but he pointed out that even John Maurice Clark, an economist whom he admired enormously, had erred on a related point (p. 242). He wrote of "the practice of introducing certain mathematical relations as alleged 'approximations'" as a source of difficulty going back to Marshall, but not exclusive to him (p. 173). Samuelson was more critical of Marshall's analysis of consumers' surplus, arguing that if he reached "conclusions which are not completely wrong, it is nevertheless clear that he arrived at them for the wrong reasons" (p. 207). He linked this to the charge that Marshall failed to offer a satisfactory theory of the relationship between the industry and the firm. However, it is important to note that these criticisms follow criticisms of Marshall and Wicksell on the optimality of exchange under perfect competition, and of John Hicks's attempt to rehabilitate the idea of consumers's surplus. This makes it clear that in these pages (pp. 206–8) Samuelson is reviewing an entire literature that he finds deficient in various ways and, if Marshall is the focus of his criticism, that is simply because of his centrality to the field.

There are, however, two places where Samuelson picks out Marshall for particular criticism. He argues that, given Marshall's training as a mathematician, "it is strange ... that he contented himself with gratuitous, and I believe incorrect, statements that changes in the marginal utility of income were of the 'second order of smallness'" (p. 194). The use of the word "gratuitous" perhaps hints at something other than an innocent mistake, though in a footnote Samuelson concedes that there was a "small germ of truth" in Marshall's argument. This leaves a single reference where

[1] This remark is in the PhD thesis on which *Foundations* was based (Samuelson 1940, p. 27).

Samuelson is as critical of Marshall as he is in the Introduction, which relates to biology.

Marshall is well-known for his advocacy of biological rather than physical analogies, and it can be argued that evolutionary ideas were central to any understanding of his work. One of Tiziano Raffaelli's most important works is titled *Marshall's Evolutionary Economics* (2003). In view of this, it is strong criticism when Samuelson writes,

> In none of his writings does Marshall show more than a passing familiarity, such as might be expected of any intelligent layman, of the biological notions of his time. Therefore, he could not be expected to have discerned the lasting truths from the fashions of the moment. (pp. 311–2n)

Rather than drawing on biology, Marshall was drawing on doctrines promoted by Herbert Spencer, whom Samuelson presumably considered a populariser of evolutionary ideas rather than a biologist. The result of this ignorance was that Marshall misrepresented the possibilities for applying mathematical notions of equilibrium to biology. Biology, Samuelson contended, offered no new methods for discovering scientific truths, implying that Marshall was wrong to present biological methods in opposition to mechanical ones: "If the bloodstream is capable of a simple, abstract, rigorous description in terms of the usual laws of physical thermodynamics, so much the better; if not, one must be content with more complicated, unwieldy explanations" (p. 312). He then cited one of his teachers, Lawrence Henderson, who had argued that the notion of equilibrium, central to physical theory, had first been formulated in the context of a biological problem: the resistance of the human body to disease. Biological problems might be more difficult than physical ones, making it harder to apply mathematical methods, but it did not require that different methods be used. On this point, Samuelson claimed, Marshall did not know what he was talking about.[2]

[2] This discussion came in a chapter that was originally published as Samuelson (1943). Given the timing, it is possible that these remarks were stimulated by reading Viner's (1941, pp. 231–2) account of Marshall's method. Samuelson attributes to Viner a position close to his own, though he was perhaps being generous to a revered former teacher.

3 After *Foundations*

Samuelson had the habit of citing precursors, often in multiples, and often bracketed together as in "Hume-Ricardo-Marshall" model of international trade, or stating that Thornton, Marshall, Wicksell, Fisher and Keynes understood the relationship between expected inflation, real and nominal interest rates. Marshall frequently appeared in such lists. As in *Foundations*, most of these references were incidental, simply identifying Marshall as the economist associated with a particular idea. In view of this, it should not be surprising that the pages of the early volumes of his *Collected Scientific Papers*, especially volumes II and III, are littered with mentions of Marshall. As a guide, the combined index for volumes I and II contains approximately 74 entries for Marshall, a number exceeded only by Keynes, with 85 entries. For comparison, we have Hicks (60), Wicksell (55), Pigou (50) and Walras (46). This illustrates the way in which, even after the Second World War, Samuelson considered Marshall to be an economist who had to be taken seriously. Some of these citations, especially from the 1960s, treated Marshall as a historical figure, but the bulk of the citations treat him as an economist with whom it was necessary to engage.

To given an idea of the distribution of citations over time, the number of papers with at least one index entry for Marshall is listed, by decade, in Table 1. This shows that there was a definite peak in Samuelson's interest in Marshall in the 1960s, and that his interest had declined by the 1980s,

Table 1 Number of scientific papers in which Alfred Marshall is mentioned

Decade	*Number of publications*
1946–9	5
1950–9	13
1960–9	22
1970–9	11
1980–9	4
1990–9	5
2000–9	2

Source Based on a count of the number of papers in *The Collected Scientific Papers of Paul A. Samuelson* (7 volumes) (Samuelson 1966–2011) that have at least one index entry for Alfred Marshall. Two papers from 1946 are included on the ground that they were written after *Foundations*, which had a long gestation period, even though they appeared before it was published never recovering. There are several possible explanations. One is that the field had simply moved on, though, given Samuelson's practice of naming ideas, it is more likely that he was no longer writing on the fields where he saw Marshall as a precursor.

There are incidental evaluations of Marshall in Samuelson's writings in the 1950s, but these are few. Samuelson argued that "*all* the *essential* features of the Marshallian analysis" had previously been discovered by Fleeming Jenkin, whose work Marshall ought to have known, and that Marshall's analysis of bargaining between workers and employers was based on some "bizarre" assumptions (Samuelson 1951, pp. 321, 324). Shortly afterwards, Samuelson turned to Marshall's stated disdain for mathematics, putting it in a more positive light than he had in *Foundations*. He explained that because not everyone has an IQ of 300 standard deviations above the mean, many logical deductions were not immediately obvious: "That is why pencils have erasers and electronic calculators have bells and gongs." This led him to observe,

> I suppose this is what Alfred Marshall must have had in mind when he followed John Stuart Mill in speaking of the dangers involved in *long* chains of logical reasoning. Marshall treated such chains as if their truth content was subject to radioactive decay and leakage—at the end of n propositions only half the truth was left, at the end of a chain of 2n propositions, only half of half of the truth remained, and so forth in a geometric multiplier series converging to zero truth. Obviously, in making such a statement, Marshall was describing a property of that biological biped or computing machine called *homo sapiens*. (Samuelson 1952, pp. 57–8)

Though it is hard not to see an element of caricature here, he is taking Marshall's views on mathematics more seriously than he had in *Foundations*. Later in the same article, he also compared Marshall's view of mathematics, as a means whereby truth could be discovered, favourably with that of John Elliott Cairnes, who denied that it could be used to do more than communicate truths already reached by other means.

However, in private correspondence with Ian Little, he was more critical of Marshall, writing:

> His true role in history of ideas is, I am afraid we must admit, almost completely negligible. I recall my indignation some years ago to learn from the correspondence between Oliver Wendell Holmes and Pollock that Holmes, upon being urged by Pollock to read Marshall's *Principles*,

> completely brushed aside this suggestion as being rather absurd. Actually, though, if you drop the perspective of the professional economist, you seem to realize that Holmes was in good company. Marshall belongs to us economists; as he can be, and is, neglected by legislators, novelists, and philosophers. (People as different as the physicist, J. J. Thomson and Alfred North Whitehead, who knew him at Cambridge, had really quite low opinions of him as a man and as an intellect)[3]

Six years later, he made similar remarks in his AEA Presidential Address (Samuelson 1962, p. 16). However, these statements may have reflected, at least in part, a view that economists in general played a minor role in the broader history of ideas.

Significant historical evaluations of Marshall began to appear with Samuelson's Presidential Address to the American Economic Association, in which he chose to speak on the topic of "Economists and the history of ideas" (Samuelson 1962). He turned to Marshall when evaluating *A History of Economic Analysis*, by his former teacher, Joseph Schumpeter (1954). Schumpeter valued Walras higher than any other economist, and Samuelson argued that he deserved more credit for coming to this conclusion in 1935 than he would deserve when Samuelson was delivering his lecture. "Back in 1935," Samuelson wrote, "Marshall was still propped up on his throne and in large parts of the world even the zealots of the mathematical method tended to look upon Walras merely as the predecessor of the great Pareto" (Samuelson 1962, p. 4). After this critical remark, Samuelson then assessed how his reputation had risen and fallen:

> The bourse for professional reputations shows changing price fluctuations: if at one time Alfred Marshall was overpraised and quoted at an inflated price which left little consumer's surplus to the buyer, he had to pay for this by later being sold at an overdiscount.

Samuelson then spoke of the pecking order of economists in which, after contrasting Marshall's immodesty with John Stuart Mill's modesty, he assessed Marshall's place, not in the history of economics, but in the history of human thought more generally. The *hoi-polloi*, he explained, found far more in Henry George than in any academic economist, but what of "the educated man of affairs"?

[3] Samuelson, Letter to Ian M. D. Little, 2 December 1955. PASP, Box 48 (Little). Pollock was a British legal scholar and Holmes an eminent American judge.

> For years I looked for every trace I could find in books to show that someone other than an a professional economist or student had read Marshall. I realize that Marshall himself thought he was writing for the business-man; but anyone who looks at the *Principles* will realize that no businessman in good Queen Victoria's time or since would be likely to find it attractive. (Samuelson 1962, p. 16)

This was despite an "excellent" literary style. Samuelson claimed to have found only two pieces of evidence. As has been noted, Pollock urged Justice Holmes to read Marshall, and Morris Cohen attributed his eclecticism in philosophy to the eclecticism of Marshall's economics. That was all. Marshall's influence in Cambridge was little greater, as he had few students, and was not admired by his contemporaries. The Physicist J. J. Thomson had no great opinion of Cambridge economics and Alfred North Whitehead, whom Samuelson had known as a Junior Fellow at Harvard, and had previously been a colleague of Marshall's at Cambridge, did not like him: "He was a popish man who treated Mary Marshall very badly. A second class mind?" (Samuelson 1962, p. 16, attributing these remarks to Whitehead).

As Samuelson wrote shortly afterwards, he compared his attitude to Marshall with that of Joan Robinson, with whom he was then involved in an increasingly frustrating debate (frustrating to both sides) on the theory of capital.[4] They were both "debunkers" of Marshall, but whereas she considered him to be "the best of a bad neoclassical lot," Samuelson was "one of the new barbarians who deem him [Marshall] third to Walras and Wicksell" (Samuelson 1963, p. 536). Implicit in this self-identification as a debunker of Marshall was the claim that it was not because his own approach to economics was not Marshall's. The remark formed part of an obituary praising Dennis Robertson, with whom Samuelson also disagreed on fundamentals, but whom he admired.

In 1967, Samuelson contributed to a Festschrift for Edward Chamberlin, one of his Harvard teachers, who died in that year. His chapter, on the Monopolistic Competition Revolution, was primarily about Chamberlin, whom he respected without being uncritical. Samuelson conceded that Chamberlin was right to differentiate his *Theory of Monopolistic Competition* (1933) from Joan Robinson's *Economics of Imperfect*

[4]Harcourt (1972) tells the story of this debate from the Cambridge, England perspective. Backhouse (2014) tells it from the MIT perspective.

Competition (1933) which appeared in the same year. However, even though this had not been Chamberlin's own starting point, most readers would have read the book in the light of what Samuelson considered the somewhat sterile cost controversy that had developed in the late 1920s. Put differently, Chamberlin might have been a lone-wolf scholar, solving problems in his own way, but he and Robinson were part of a broader intellectual community in which there were extensive transatlantic contacts and in which it was impossible to rule out mutual influences. Samuelson was critical of participants in the debate, and of scholars who argued over who discovered the concept of marginal revenue, writing "That grown men argued seriously in 1930 about who had first used or named the curve that we now call 'marginal revenue' is a joke" (Samuelson 1967, p. 23).[5] But he was even more critical of Marshall. He began a section headed, "Exorcizing the Marshallian incubus" with what is probably his strongest ever criticism of Marshall.

> The ambiguities of Alfred Marshall paralyzed the best brains in the Anglo-Saxon branch of our profession for three decades. By 1930 the profession had just about reattained the understanding of the pure theory of monopoly that Cournot had achieved in 1838; and it had yet to reattain the understanding of the theory of competitive general equilibrium that Walras had achieved by 1878 or 1896. (Samuelson 1967, p. 22)

The basis for this judgement was the belief that the only economist to take the theory significantly further than Mill, Cournot, Dupuit, and Mangoldt (all known to Marshall) was Marshall's contemporary, Francis Edgeworth, and that it was not until the work of Heinrich Stackelberg (1934), John von Neumann and Oskar Morgenstern (1944) that economists reattained the depth of his analysis. Samuelson claimed that Marshall had confused two generations of scholars by aiming for a "spurious verisimilitude" (Samuelson 1967, p. 24). Following Viner's (1941, p. 231) earlier analysis of Marshall as having felt guilty about indulging in the pleasures of mathematics, Samuelson engaged in psychological speculation about Marshall: he "was a victim of what the modern Freudians call self-hate. He was a good chess player who was ashamed of playing chess, a good analytical economist who was ashamed of analysis" (Samuelson 1967, p. 25).

[5] Page references to Samuelson (1967) are to the reprint in Samuelson (1966–2011), Vol. 3.

4 A Great Economist Who Could Have Been Even Greater

Samuelson did present himself as a debunker of Marshall, but focusing exclusively on this conceals is the extent to which Samuelson admired Marshall. When introducing the theory of supply and demand to his undergraduate readers he described him as "the great English economist" (Samuelson 1948, p. 475, n. 1) or "Cambridge University's great economist" (Samuelson 1980, p. 362). Samuelson's analysis of momentary, short-run and long-run equilibrium might not do justice to the complexity of Marshall's treatment of time, but he was linking Marshall's name to what was, for his student readers, probably the most important tool they needed to learn. In a letter to David Laidler, discussing Marshall's monetary economics, Samuelson wrote the evaluation on which the title of this chapter is based:

> Marshall did not fail to get an A because he omitted dealing with erosion of metallic money supply. This is a grave error in a reader of Mill, in a great economist (A[lfred]. M[arshall]. *was* a great economist even though your picture is too flattering), and in a careful empiricist. (Samuelson, Letter to David Laidler, 3 December 1993. PASP, Box 48 (Laidler), emphasis in original)

Given Samuelson's commitment to empiricism and to applying economics, this evaluation is higher praise than it might seem if he is incorrectly seen as just an economic theorist.

Later in life, Samuelson came to emphasise the fluctuations in Marshall's reputation. In a memorial to Joan Robinson, he offered an explanation.

> Alfred Marshall, it will be recalled, was at the peak of his fame when he died in 1924. Two-thirds of a century later, after the Anglo-Saxon world had come to digest the contributions of Leon Walras, Knut Wicksell, and Irving Fisher, it is realized that Alfred Marshall's reputation—deservedly great—was overrated in the 1900-30 period. If the world excessively overvalued Marshall, Oxbridge outrageously treasured his writings. A. C. Pigou, as successor to Marshall's Cambridge chair, protected his memory like a watchdog (and, in consequence, Pigou's own great originality was never properly recognized). (Samuelson 1989, p. 126)

Marshall had been overrated because economists were insufficiently familiar with Walras, Wicksell and Fisher, and also because Pigou had been excessively defensive of his teacher, minimising his own originality. In assessing this quotation it is important to note that Samuelson always had an immense regard for Pigou; perhaps he could see Pigou as a genuine generalist like himself. Overrating Marshall was the mirror image of undervaluing Pigou.

The same focus on fluctuations in Marshall's reputation can be found in Samuelson's reflections on the fiftieth anniversary of *Foundations*.

> In 1935 Alfred Marshall still ruled the roost in fame. What goes up too far comes down too low. Like Gustav Cassel's, his textbook filled a real need; but like Isaac Newton, he had an inhibiting influence on two generations of followers. (Samuelson 1997, p. 9)

These remarks are critical but it is hard not to read implicit praise into the comparison with Newton. Samuelson went on to argue that Marshall's potential was even greater than his achievement.

> Marshall never lived up to his potential, for reasons of health and temperament. Before 1890 he knew the defects in his own constructs (consumers surplus, partial equilibrium, ...) but never did he follow up with the needed improvements. As Whitehead said to me, "Marshall was more Popish than saintly. We liked Mary Paley Marshall better." (Samuelson 1997, p. 9)

Given the context—a retrospective on *Foundations*—it might not be going too far to infer that it was Samuelson who provided the improvements that Marshall failed to provide. "Popishness" could help explain Marshall's inhibiting influence on his successors, and the younger generations' preference for Mary Marshall was consistent with Samuelson's remark, made in an essay focused on anti-Semitism, about "The great Alfred Marshall [being] a notorious femmophobe" (Samuelson 2002, p. 50).

Samuelson's last published assessment of Marshall came in an interview with Kotaro Suzumura, in which he naturally focused on welfare economics.

> I think Marshall was a great economist, but he was a potentially much greater economist than he actually was. It was not that he was lazy, but his health was not good, and he worked in miniature. Early on, in 1874,

> when Marshall deduced that alternative multiple equilibria of supply and demand could occur, he noted that this rebutted any notion that laissez faire markets could be relied on to achieve maximal interpersonal well being. (Suzumura 2005, p. 329)

Marshall derived his most important welfare conclusion very early in his career (sixteen years before the publication of his *Principles of Economics*) but failed to develop these ideas as far as a trained mathematician should have been able to do. He had been a great economist but could have been even greater.

References

Backhouse, R. E. (2014) MIT and the Other Cambridge. *History of Political Economy* (Annual Supplement, *The History of MIT Economics*, ed. E. R. Weintraub), pp. 252–271.

Backhouse, R. E., B. W. Bateman, and S. G. Medema (2010) The Reception of Marshall in the United States. In *The Impact of Alfred Marshall's Ideas* (Eds, T. Raffaelli, G. Becattini, K. Caldari, and M. Dardi), Edward Elgar, Cheltenham, pp. 59–80.

Backhouse, R. E. and S. G. Medema (2014) Walras in the Age of Marshall: An Analysis of English-Language Journals, 1890–1939. In *Economics and Other Branches—In the Shade of the Oak Tree: Essays in Honour of Pascal Bridel* (Eds, F. Allison and R. Baranzini), Pickering and Chatto, London.

Chamberlin, E. H. (1933) *The Theory of Monopolistic Competition*. Harvard University Press, Cambridge, MA.

Harcourt, G. C. (1972) *Some Cambridge Controversies in the Theory of Capital*. Cambridge University Press, Cambridge.

von Neumann, J. and O. Morgenstern (1944) *Theory of Games and Economic Behaviour*. Princeton University Press, Princeton, NJ.

Raffaelli, T. (2003) *Marshall's Evolutionary Economics*. Routledge, London.

Robinson, J. (1933) *Economics of Imperfect Competition*. Macmillan, London.

Samuelson, P. A. (1940) *Foundations of Analytical Economics: The Observational Significance of Economic Theory*. PhD dissertation, Harvard University.

Samuelson, P. A. (1943) Dynamics, Statics, and the Stationary State. *The Review of Economics and Statistics*, 25(1), 58–68.

Samuelson, P. A. (1947) *Foundations of Economic Analysis*. Harvard University Press, Cambridge, MA.

Samuelson, P. A. (1948) *Economics: An Introductory Analysis*. McGraw Hill, New York.

Samuelson, P. A. (1951) Economic Theory and Wages. In *The Impact of the Union* (Ed, D. M. Wright), Harcourt Brace, New York, pp. 192–197.
Samuelson, P. A. (1952) Economic Theory and Mathematics—An Appraisal. *American Economic Review*, 42(2), 56–66.
Samuelson, P. A. (1962) Economists and the History of Ideas. *American Economic Review*, 52(1), 1–18.
Samuelson, P. A. (1963) D. H. Robertson (1890–1963). *Quarterly Journal of Economics*, 77(4), 517–536.
Samuelson, P. A. (1966–2011) *The Collected Scientific Papers of Paul A. Samuelson*, 7 volumes (Vols. 1–2, ed. J. Stiglitz, 1966; Vol. 3, ed. R. Merton, 1972; Vol. 4, eds. K. Nagatani and K. Crowley, 1977; Vol. 5, ed. K. Crowley, 1986; Vols 6–7, ed. J. Murray, 2011), MIT Press, Cambridge, MA.
Samuelson, P. A. (1967) The Monopolistic Competition Revolution. In *Monopolistic Competition Theory, Studies in Impact: Essays in Honor of Edward H. Chamberlin* (Ed, R. E. Kuenne), Wiley, New York, pp. 105–138.
Samuelson, P. A. (1980) *Economics: An Introductory Analysis*. McGraw Hill, New York.
Samuelson, P. A. (1989) Remembering Joan. In *Joan Robinson and Modern Economic Theory* (Ed, G. R. Feiwel), New York University Press, New York, pp. 121–143.
Samuelson, P. A. (1997) How Foundations Came to Be. In *Paul A. Samuelson's "Foundations of Economic Analysis", Vademecum zu einem Klassiker der Gegenwart* (Eds, J. Niehans, P. A. Samuelson, and C. C. von Weizsacker), Verlag Wirtschaft und Finanzen, Dusseldorf, pp. 27–52.
Samuelson, P. A. (2002) Pastiches from an Earlier Politically Incorrect Academic Age. In *Editing Economics: Essays in Honour of Mark Perlman* (Eds, H. Lim, U. S. Park, and G. C. Harcourt), Routledge, London, pp. 47–55.
Schumpeter, J. A. (1954) *A History of Economic Analysis*. Oxford University Press, New York.
Stackelberg, H. (1934) *Marktform und Gleichgewicht*. Julius Springer, Vienna.
Suzumura, K. (2005) An Interview with Paul Samuelson: Welfare Economics, "Old" and "New", and Social Choice Theory. *Social Choice and Welfare*, 25(2–3), 327–356.
Viner, J. (1941) Marshall's Economics, in Relation to the Man and to His Times. *American Economic Review*, 31(2), 223–235.

Index

K. Caldari et al. (eds.), *Marshall and the Marshallian Heritage*, Palgrave Studies in the History of Economic Thought, https://doi.org/10.1007/978-3-030-53032-7

The manufacturer's authorised representative in the EU is Springer Nature Customer Service Centre GmbH, Europaplatz 3, 69115 Heidelberg, Germany. If you have any concerns regarding our products, please contact ProductSafety@springernature.com

Printed and bound by CPI Group (UK) Ltd, Croydon, CR0 4YY
30/09/2026
02225494-0006